GEORGE WASHINGTON'S CHINAWARE

GEORGE WASHINGTON'S CHINAWARE

WRITTEN BY SUSAN GRAY DETWEILER WITH
PROLOGUE AND EPILOGUE BY CHRISTINE MEADOWS
A BARRA FOUNDATION/MOUNT VERNON LADIES' ASSOCIATION BOOK

Harry N. Abrams, Inc., Publishers, New York

To Bob McNeil, whose encouragement
has been the catalyst for this book and for many
other studies in American cultural history

Edited by Louise Heskett and Joanne Greenspun
Designed by Bob McKee
Photographs by Will Brown unless otherwise credited on page 230

Library of Congress Cataloging in Publication Data

Detweiler, Susan Gray.
George Washington's chinaware.
Bibliography: p.
Includes index.
1. Porcelain—Catalogs.   2. Washington, George,
1732–1799—Art collections—Catalogs.   3. Washington,
Martha, 1731–1802—Art collections—Catalogs.
I. Title.
NK3740.W37D4   738.2′074′0155291   81-14993
ISBN 0–8109–1779–3   AACR2

Printed and bound in Japan

Frontispiece: Chinese porcelain mug sent to Mount Vernon
from London in 1766 (see page 26)

CONTENTS

CONTENTS

CONTENTS

PREFACE

George Washington's ceramic choices—whether Chinese porcelains and English queensware for Mount Vernon or French porcelain for his official presidential table—attest to individual and national taste in a pivotal period of American cultural history. From the first recorded shipment of "fine oblong china dishes" in 1757 to the last inventory after the death of Martha Washington in 1802, records and artifacts associated with the Washingtons also contribute substantially to the history of eighteenth-century ceramics.

Washington's interest in household furnishings is evident in the early orders of his bachelor years for "neat and fashionable" stoneware for Mount Vernon and in his later concern about proper French porcelain ornaments for the presidential tables in New York and Philadelphia. Born into the Tidewater Virginia gentry whose men found architecture, interiors, and the dining table appropriate pursuits in the art of "genteel" living, he deliberated and corresponded about those matters as early as age twenty-five and as late as 1798, the year before his death. Although the extent of her conversational influence cannot be judged, Martha Dandridge Custis Washington seems to have left the business of purchasing furnishings—as was customary in that society—to both of her husbands. The only orders she is known to have sent to London occurred between her marriages, and her few requests for blue-and-white china for Mount Vernon were not made until the last decade of her life.

During the Revolution, Washington became increasingly conscious of his precedent-setting role as leader and world representative of the new American people. He realized that his duties also extended to social matters in his roles as commander in chief and later as president. In spite of his protestations that he preferred "republican simplicity," it is clear that a taste for fashionably furnished interiors was encouraged by his position and eventually by his contacts with the mercantile "aristocracy" of Philadelphia and New York. Those friendships with shipping merchants who sent trade vessels to both China and France and his associations with the foreign diplomatic corps influenced selections of ceramic tableware and ornaments for Mount Vernon and for the presidential table. Thus, Washington—as the most prominent consumer in the new nation—participated in the postwar dissolution of an English monopoly on American taste and trade and the turn to China and France as new sources for porcelain tableware.

For several reasons ceramics have been separated from the other decorative or applied arts as the focus of this study. Washington purchased and corresponded about furniture, silver, and glassware as well as about porcelain and earthenware, but ceramic tableware served a particularly important social function for him and for his fashionable contemporaries. Representing the status and taste of a family in addition to satisfying a practical need, elegantly equipped tea and dinner tables in eighteenth-century England and France, and therefore in prosperous American households, were the center of social intercourse. "The art of the table," a term found in French and English cookbooks of the period, described the disposition of dishes in elaborate, symmetrical compositions sometimes resembling plans for formal gardens. During Washington's lifetime, silver serving pieces and silver or confectionary ornaments—initially used for such table compositions during the seventeenth and early eighteenth centuries—were replaced by comparable porcelain elements at the French court, where European standards of taste and fashion were established.

Ceramic tableware remained one of the most sought-after objects of fashion throughout the eighteenth century. From the early connoisseur's demand for Chinese porcelains to the increasing importation of Chinese wares by the Dutch, British, and other East India companies—and the creation of royal and private factories on the Continent and in England—trade in ceramics of all kinds became a factor in the economies of several European nations and in the commerce between the American colonies and England. Consequently, the demand for tableware and ornaments was stimulated and manipulated by the invention of new bodies, forms, and decorations. George Washington often expressed his desire for the "new" and "fashionable" when ordering a succession of wares. "Queen's Ware" replaced saltglazed stoneware at Mount Vernon in 1769, shortly after Josiah Wedgwood began his marketing campaign in 1767. Later, when political conditions and American mercantile taste inspired a demand for French table services, Washington was among the first Americans to acquire such a service.

Since the complex industrial process needed for successful competition with manufacturers of foreign tablewares was not established in the United States until the early years of the present century, importation of refined stonewares, earthenwares, and porcelains has—with a few minor exceptions—always been necessary. In the mid-eighteenth century, a chair or a silver porringer could be produced by one local craftsman, but the production of an affordable tea or table service of 45 to 300 pieces required the specialized division of labor associated with the later industrial revolution. Preparation of clays, modeling, throwing, turning, cutting of blocks, casting of molds, firing of kilns, glazing, painting, and gilding were coordinated individual activities which might be required to produce one sauceboat or a three-piece mantel garniture.

Importation meant international shipping and interurban movement after arrival at American ports. Such movement generated correspondence, advertisements for cargoes, and invoices which would generally be unnecessary in a local sale by a neighborhood craftsman. From 1757 through 1772, Washington sent orders for Chinese and English porcelains and earthenwares to Bristol and London. His careful accounts reveal the names of suppliers, a general description of the wares, and prices to be charged against sales of his exported tobacco. In addition, there is substantial correspondence about these orders and, later, about the acquisition and movement of other imported porcelains.

Ceramic artifacts, which survive particularly well in an archeological context, confirm and illuminate the written record of eighteenth-century wares owned by Washington and his contemporaries. Excavations in Virginia by archeologists associated with Colonial Williamsburg and the Smithsonian Institution have unearthed redwares, creamwares, stonewares, and porcelains which parallel the entries in Washington's invoices. The few sherds found at Mount Vernon have been used occasionally in this study to illustrate and identify those entries, but future systematic excavations there could add considerably to the knowledge about wares used by the Washingtons.

In contrast to a desk or sideboard, the multiple units of a table service suggest the survival of at least a few pieces which reveal something about the appearance of the whole. Washington's porcelain services, especially those of the postwar period, were preserved when possible by the Law, Peter, Lewis, and Custis–Lee families. Occasionally given away as mementoes by Martha Washington and her descendants, pieces from the services designated in her will and those bought by the family at the sales following her death have nevertheless survived in remarkable numbers as objects of aesthetic and historical interest.

George Washington was a careful household manager who counted, inventoried, itemized, and corresponded about furnishings and other domestic matters. His orders to merchants in Bristol and London and the reciprocal invoices from 1757 to 1772; his personal, military, and presidential accounts; and his letters about the acquisition and transportation of "fashionable" and "neat" furnishings in Virginia, New York, Philadelphia, England, and Paris offer a nearly complete account of his ceramic choices for the dining tables over which he presided. They also offer significant documentation for social, trade, and market practices in a period which encompassed the expansion of American commercial history from colonial dependence on England to the early ventures in independent trade with China and continental Europe. The numerous references to ceramics found in Washington's account books, inventories, invoices, and correspondence have been arranged chronologically in an annotated appendix toward the end of this volume. They contain information about terminology, prices, and sources and about the economic and social functions of ceramics in an especially influential eighteenth-century family.

Recognition of the importance of his papers to posterity encouraged Washington and his heirs to preserve his correspondence and account books. Thus, a detailed record of domestic acquisitions, including numerous references to ceramics, is contained in the archives of his public and private life. By the terms of George Washington's will, all of his papers as well as Mount Vernon itself were bequeathed to his nephew, Judge Bushrod Washington, upon the death of Martha Washington. Judge Washington, in turn, divided his inheritance between his nephews—John Augustine Washington II, who received Mount Vernon, and George Corbin Washington, who inherited the bulk of the papers which he sold to the United States government in the first half of the nineteenth century. The papers are now available in a microfilm edition indexed and published by the Library of Congress as part of the Presidents' Papers Series. Other important letters, invoices, and account books are found at Mount Vernon, the Morristown National Historic Park, Winterthur, the Historical Society of Pennsylvania, and in a few private collections. Letters written by Washington were published in thirty-nine volumes, edited by John Fitzpatrick, from 1931 to 1944; and Washington's diaries have recently been annotated and reissued by the

Mount Vernon Ladies' Association and the University of Virginia. A new edition of the Washington Papers, including letters received by him, will soon be published by the same two institutions.

John Augustine Washington III sold Mount Vernon to the Mount Vernon Ladies' Association of the Union in 1858. At a time preceding most historic preservation efforts in the United States, Washington's scattered memorabilia began to be returned to his estate by family and collectors less than sixty years after his death. The retrieval of papers and furnishings by the Association, as described by Christine Meadows in the Epilogue, has been the primary objective in the restoration of the Washington household.

Descendants of John Parke Custis, Martha Washington's only child to leave progeny, have preserved stories about many of the objects owned by the Washingtons. In some instances, provenance for a piece was recorded not long after the death of Mrs. Washington in 1802, and these notes have also been preserved. Britannia Wellington Peter Kennon (1815–1911), youngest of Martha Parke Custis Peter's eight children, was especially thorough in recording her knowledge about the many Washington pieces retained by the Peter family. Edmund Law Rogers, grandson of Mrs. Washington's eldest granddaughter, Eliza Parke Custis Law, also wrote about his "collection of souvenirs of Mount Vernon." George Washington Parke Custis (1781–1857), who was raised by the Washingtons and who received two porcelain services and a bowl by the terms of his grandmother's will, wrote extensively about Mount Vernon. Although Custis preserved many of the Mount Vernon furnishings at his home, Arlington House, and left them with the house to his daughter, Mrs. Robert E. Lee, most were scattered during the Civil War. Fortunately, these objects had been seen at the Custis–Lee house and their histories recorded in 1858 by Benson J. Lossing.

Visitors' descriptions and journals and the papers of Washington's associates—especially those of Tobias Lear, his principal secretary, and Gouverneur Morris, businessman and diplomat—add contemporary corroboration to the material found in the Washington Papers. The Lear letters and a presidential account book kept by him are owned privately, although they were edited and published in 1906 and 1933. The Gouverneur Morris papers are in the Library of Congress and are available on microfilm; his diary, kept in France from 1789 through 1793, has been published twice, and the unexpurgated edition of 1939 contains several important references to his purchases in Paris for President Washington.

This study began with a search for references to the Washingtons' ceramics in all available source material, followed by consideration of the historical context, and proceeded to a final correlation of the documents with existing or comparable stoneware, earthenware, and porcelain objects. I hope that the results will be informative and will eventually elicit additional facts about the persons and events associated with George Washington's acquisition of ceramics for his private and official residences as well as about the variety of ceramics available to Americans from 1755 to 1799. At the very least, the references, historical material, and existing objects are clues to the actual taste, personality, and circumstances of George Washington himself.

Susan Gray Detweiler
February 1982

PROLOGUE:
THE
HOUSEHOLD

Toward the end of his life, George Washington Parke Custis, Martha Washington's grandson, published his recollections of Mount Vernon and its principal inhabitants. Custis's memories of the place went back to his childhood, when he and his sister Eleanor Parke, the two younger children of Mrs. Washington's only son, John Parke Custis, were taken there to live shortly after the death of their father in 1781.[1] By 1783, when General Washington retired to private life, the grandchildren were an established part of the household administered by their grandmother. For twenty years they lived within a congenial circle of Virginia relatives and neighbors. As pampered members of the presidential household for eight years, they were uniquely privileged to observe and to participate in the life of the nation's "First Family." Custis, more than his sister, perhaps, was profoundly affected by these rich, youthful experiences. Much of his artistic and literary output in later life reflected his hero worship of Washington. "Wherever Washington established a home," he wrote, "whether temporary or fixed, whether amid the log huts of Morristown or the Valley Forge, the presidential mansion in New York or Philadelphia, or his own beloved Mount Vernon—everywhere order, method, punctuality, and economy reigned. His household, whether civil or military, was always upon a liberal scale, and was conducted with due regard to economy and usefulness."[2]

The household in Custis's day centered about the mansion, a large two-and-one-half-story Georgian manor house with flanking kitchen and office dependencies attached on the west front by covered walkways. On the east side, front-ing the Potomac River, a two-story piazza extended the width of the house. A cupola surmounting the roof—topped by a weathervane in the shape of a dove of peace—had been Washington's last embellishment to the house that had evolved from a simple story-and-a-half cottage, built by his father Augustine Washington in the 1730s. Washington raised the house a full story in 1758 in anticipation of his marriage to Martha Dandridge Custis, the widow of Daniel Parke Custis and mother of two small children. In 1773, finding it necessary to expand his home, Washington undertook a south-wing addition that would provide a master bedroom on the second floor and beneath it a private study for himself. He also planned a second wing at the north end of the house as a two-story formal dining room. The Revolution interrupted his personal supervision of these important additions. In his absence, his cousin and wartime manager Lund Washington carried the building program forward by informing the general in weekly reports of the workmen's progress. Washington's first inspection of his house at its finished dimension was postponed until October 1781, when he stopped briefly at Mount Vernon on his way to and from Yorktown.

In 1783, the Washingtons resumed the domestic routines that had characterized the prewar household, but they were now celebrities and their home had become a mecca for many. Washington compared it "to a well resorted tavern as scarcely any strangers who are going from north to south or from south to north, do not spend a day or two at it. . . ."[3] The reception and accommodation of these guests taxed his financial resources, and he complained of the expense of maintaining these well-intentioned admirers. "My expenses," he wrote in 1787, "not from any extravagance, or an inclination on my part to live splendidly, but for the absolute support of my family and the visitors who are constantly here, are exceedingly high."[4] His defense against these incursions was a personal routine rigorously adhered to and a domestic economy that he hoped to keep within tolerable bounds. A letter of 1786 from Washington to his old friend George William Fairfax, then living in England, alludes to the unusual demands on his household. "My manner of living is plain," he insisted, "and I do not mean to be put out of it. A glass of wine and a bit of mutton are always ready, and such as will be content to partake of them are always welcome. Those who expect more will be disappointed."[5]

Fairfax, a former neighbor and companion of the happy years between Washington's marriage in 1759 and Fairfax's departure for England in 1773 to claim ancestral estates, knew Mount Vernon well. He could appreciate his correspondent's social burdens and his need to economize, but he also knew from personal experience that Mount Vernon's host had always provided amply for his guests, and he must have felt certain these friendly traditions would persist. Even before the war Mount Vernon was rarely without guests, but they were less likely to be total strangers of the kind who made their way to Washington's home in the post-Revolutionary and post-presidential periods. Relatives and friends typified the prewar visitor, and most strangers came by introduction of family acquaintances. Washington kept a record in his diary of their arrivals and departures, dinner guests were mentioned by name, and it was noted when a departing guest accepted the use of Washington's carriage. Fame carried heavy social burdens. In the month of September 1786, thirty-eight house guests of one or more days' duration and an additional fifteen dinner guests enjoyed the hospitality of the manor. During July 1798, eighty-five people dined at Mount Vernon with fourteen house guests added to the total. This unusually large number was occasioned in part by a large Fourth of July celebration in Alexandria and the arrival within that week of James McHenry, secretary of war, who came to deliver personally Washing-

ton's commission as lieutenant general and commander in chief of the army then forming in expectation of war with France. Washington entertained for his distinguished visitor, who remained in the company of the retired president for several days.[6]

Experience and skillful management were needed to run the household and to keep the disruption of large numbers of guests to a minimum. Mrs. Washington assumed the task on a daily basis, and though an occasional housekeeper was hired to relieve her of the tedium, it was, on the whole, her personal supervision that motivated the staff. Mrs. Washington's knowledge of the domestic arts was learned at the home of her parents in New Kent County, Virginia. She was the eldest of eight children and doubtless shared some responsibility for the care of younger siblings in a household which was only moderately affluent. When she married Daniel Parke Custis at the age of eighteen, she became the mistress of a home that reflected her husband's position as a member of a prosperous and influential Virginia family. At Mount Vernon, she was remembered by her guests as a cheerful and pleasant hostess who remained unaffected by the pomp that surrounded so much of her life as the wife of a successful general and the first president of the United States. Content in her domestic role, she wrote in 1789 that her "grandchildren and domestic connections made up a great portion of the felicity which I looked for in this world."[7]

Martha ran her large and busy household with about a dozen servants who came with her at the time of her marriage and later intermarried with the slave population at Mount Vernon. In 1759, her household staff numbered eleven: one full-time and one part-time waiter; two women in the kitchen who served as cook and scullion; two women who did the washing and ironing; and one seamstress who worked on the sewing and mending. Mrs. Washington and her two children had personal servants and her husband a body servant.[8] Twenty-seven years later, she continued to manage with the same number; however, by 1786 men had taken on the cooking. On the shoulders of the temperamental Hercules and his assistant Nathan fell the responsibility of preparing the food; Frank and Austin were full-time waiters; three women were now required to do the sewing; two housemaids and two washers completed the list. General Washington's valet was a man named Will.[9]

Washington Custis remembered his grandmother's "admirable management of her servants and household, going through every department before or immediately after breakfast. . . . her young female servants were gathered in her apartment to sew under her own supervision and they became beautiful seamstresses. . . . bad bread was a thing entirely unknown at Mount Vernon; that too was mixed every night under the eye of the mistress. Immediately after breakfast Mrs. Washington gave orders for dinner appointing certain provisions, a pr of ducks, a goose or a turkey to be laid by, to be put down in case of the arrival of company; a very necessary provision in that hospitable mansion. A ham was boiled daily. The cook who rejoiced in the name of Hercules, was . . . something of a tyrant, as well as a capital cook. . . ."[10]

Regrettably, no description of a dinner prepared during Hercules's reign over the Mount Vernon kitchen survives, but there is no reason to think that it would have been markedly different from those abundant and varied dinners reported at a later period by Mount Vernon guests. The gardener was kept busy supplying the needs of the general's table, for the master expected "everything that a Garden ought to produce, in the most ample manner,"[11] and Mrs. Washington, who had a particular fondness for fresh vegetables, thought they were "the best part of our living in the country."[12] In season, fresh fish were in abundant supply in the waters off Mount Vernon. Salted down, they could be enjoyed at other times as well. If fish lacked appeal, beef, ham, or fowl were tempting alternatives. The Washingtons' guests, like other eighteenth-century diners, selected according to their preference from a variety of dishes offered in courses. Joshua Brookes, who dined with the Washingtons in 1799, left an excellent description of a Mount Vernon dinner. He was served "leg [of] boil[ed] pork, top [at head of table]; goose, bot [at foot of table]; roast beef, round cold boil[ed] beef, mutton chops, hommony, cabbage, potatoes, pickles, fried tripe, onions, etc. Table cloth wiped, mince pies, tarts, cheese; cloth of[f], port, madeira, two kinds [of] nuts, apples, raisins. Three servants. . . ."[13]

Amariah Frost, a guest in 1797, enjoyed much the same variety of meats, vegetables, and sweetmeats. "The dinner was very good, a small roasted pigg, boiled leg of lamb, reasted fowles, beef, peas, lettice, cucumbers, artichokes, etc., puddings, tarts, etc., etc. We were desired to call for what drink we chose. . . ."[14] On this occasion, toasts were given and Frost goes on to describe a polite exchange of salutes among the diners. General Washington had a glass of wine with the lady seated next to him, and his example was followed round the table.[15]

The group with whom Frost dined was a small one as Mount Vernon dinners went. Ten or more was usual and Julian Niemcewicz, the poet and friend of Thaddeus Kosciusko, was present in 1798 when "the table in the great hall was set out with a Sèvres porcelain service with places for 20. . . ."[16] This would have been the china purchased by Washington in 1790 from Count de Moustier, the French minister, and used throughout the presidency. The great hall to which Niemcewicz referred was the large dining room, where almost thirty people could be accommodated at trestle tables, which were more functional than a conventional dining table.

Dinner, the principal meal of the day, was served at three o'clock, and Washington, who expected punctuality, is said to have allowed a five-minute grace period for differences in watches before sitting down to dinner. Punctuality at meals was something Washington tried to cultivate in Washington Custis. "Make it an invariable rule," he wrote the lad, "to be in place (unless extraordinary circumstances prevent it) at the usual breakfasting, dining and tea hours. It is not only disagreeable, but it is also very inconvenient, for servants to be running here, and there, and they know not where, to summon you to them, when their duties, and attendance, on the company who are seated, renders it improper. . . ."[17] Amariah Frost reported that Washington directed his guests where to sit. It was customary for Washington to sit at Mrs. Washington's right, and family and guests in assigned order around the table. Guests were not

1. The piazza at Mount Vernon, watercolor by Benjamin Henry Latrobe (1764–1820), 1796. President Washington gazes across the Potomac through a telescope while Nelly Custis, dressed in the latest Parisian fashion, poses languidly against a column. Mrs. Washington in a conservative cap and dress presides over the tea table next to an unidentified guest. The child is thought to be Benjamin Lincoln Lear, son of Tobias Lear, Washington's personal secretary. (Collection of James W. Tucker)

necessarily offered preferred seating next to the host and hostess.[18]

The usual hour for breakfast at Mount Vernon was seven o'clock. Manasseh Cutler, a Massachusetts congressman, who visited Martha Washington in 1802, was impressed with his breakfast, which was large by present-day standards. He was served ham, with "cold corn-beef, cold fowl, red herring and cold mutton, the dishes ornamented with sprigs of parsley and other vegetables from the garden. At the head of the table was the tea and coffee equipage where she seated herself, and sent the tea and coffee to the Company. . . ."[19] Henry Wansey, an English merchant, joined the First Lady for breakfast in Philadelphia in 1796 and was surprised by the simplicity of his "sliced tongue, dry toast, bread and butter" breakfast.[20] Only one servant attended Mrs. Washington on that occasion.

Tea, that most popular of eighteenth-century beverages, was served at Mount Vernon about six or seven o'clock. In good weather, Mrs. Washington presided at her tea table on the piazza, as depicted in a charming watercolor by Benjamin Latrobe, sketched when he was a guest of the Washingtons in July 1796. Routinely, tea was the last meal of the day, but an occasional cold supper was offered at nine. As this was Washington's habitual hour to retire, supper was not a regular part of the Washingtons' day.

George and Martha Washington were instinctively hospitable. They were considerate hosts, and special guests were treated like members of the family. They took pleasure in their friends, and though Washington might privately bemoan the constant stream of strangers at dinner and wish for "a few social friends at a cheerful board,"[21] he bore this, as he did all things, with equanimity. At Mount Vernon, a guest's room was his home, "the servants of the house are yours," wrote George Grieve, "and whilst every inducement is held out to bring you into the general society of the drawing-room, or at table, it rests with yourself to be served or not with everything in your own chamber."[22] At the prospect of having his friend David Humphreys spend the winter of 1787 at Mount Vernon, Washington stipulated only that his guest should "do as you please: I will do the same; and that no ceremony may be used or any restraint be imposed on any one."[23]

Washington's habits were extremely regular, and there were frequent comments about this element in his character. He rose early, sometimes at four, and personally prepared the fire in his study where he dressed. He read and wrote before breakfast and at seven joined Mrs. Washington and the others for breakfast, which for him consisted of hoe cakes and honey. Afterward, he set out to ride circuit on his plantations, checking crops, work in progress, and in general overseeing his estate before joining his guests for dinner. More work followed before tea, after which he retired—this ritual seldom varied.

The Mount Vernon household gave George Washington immense satisfaction. He left it for public service only because he believed that he had no honorable option but to accept a commitment more compelling than his personal wishes. His preference for the life of a Virginia farmer was recognized by his contemporaries and eulogized by Henry Lee, who, following the familiar "First in War" tribute, cited Washington as "Second to None in the Humble and Endearing Scenes of Private Life."

Christine Meadows, curator
The Mount Vernon Ladies'
Association of the Union

I

MOUNT VERNON,

1754 TO 1758

2. English saltglazed stoneware serving dish, ca. 1755. The same press-molded "basket and star-diaper" pattern is seen on fragments found at Mount Vernon. (City Museum and Art Gallery, Stoke-on-Trent)

"Inclosed is an Invoice of Sundries which I entreat you to buy and send me by the first Ship in the Spring either to the head of Potomack or Rappahannock; the cost of these things will amount to more than the Tob.° &.ᶜᵗ for which Reason I shall take the earliest oppertunity of remitting you a Bill of Exchange. I have left many of the Articles with blank prices leaving it discretionary in you to fix them with this only desire, that you will choose agreable to the present taste, and send things good of their kind. . . ." [From George Washington— while on Braddock's expedition—to Richard Washington in London, December 6, 1755 (W 1: 253)]

During the Christmas season of 1754, George Washington leased Mount Vernon from his half-brother Lawrence's widow, Anne Fairfax Washington Lee, and, with characteristic energy, began creating the future nation's foremost household. Already "universally esteemed"[1] in Virginia at the age of twenty-two for his campaign on the frontier, he had resigned as colonel of the Virginia Regiment in November after a humiliating dispute over his potential rank in the British regulars. His temporary severance from military ambitions and the availability of Mount Vernon conveniently coincided at a time when Washington decided to leave his mother's home, Ferry Farm, in order to become a planter and entrepreneur in the image of his father Augus-

tine and his older half-brother Lawrence, who had died in 1752.

George, left fatherless at age eleven in 1743, had been a frequent guest at Mount Vernon, Lawrence's home, and at Belvoir, the impressive estate occupied by Col. William Fairfax, whose daughter, Anne, had married Lawrence Washington in 1743. Colonel Fairfax, his son George William, and Lawrence Washington exerted an inestimable amount of influence on young George's career decisions and his social aspirations. Both George William Fairfax and Lawrence Washington had been educated in England and both lived as members of the English gentry on large estates in Tidewater Virginia. Their friendship with young George Washington probably encouraged a refinement of taste and aesthetic sensibilities already apparent as early as 1748 when he described the elegant clothing he preferred in a journal he kept on a surveying expedition.[2] These characteristics had been fostered by his associations at Mount Vernon and Belvoir on the Potomac, but were not encouraged by his mother, whose home was a plain, eight-room house on 260 acres. After the death of Augustine Washington in 1743, an inventory of the furnishings at Ferry Farm revealed that the family lived quite comfortably but not extravagantly.[3]

George Washington's surveying skills afforded him an early opportunity to escape his mother's restrictions and to

3. Lawrence Washington (1718–1752), by an unknown artist. Lawrence was George Washington's half-brother and owner of Mount Vernon until his death in 1752. George, fourteen years younger than Lawrence, was a frequent visitor to his brother's household and to that of the influential Fairfaxes at neighboring Belvoir. (The Mount Vernon Ladies' Association collections)

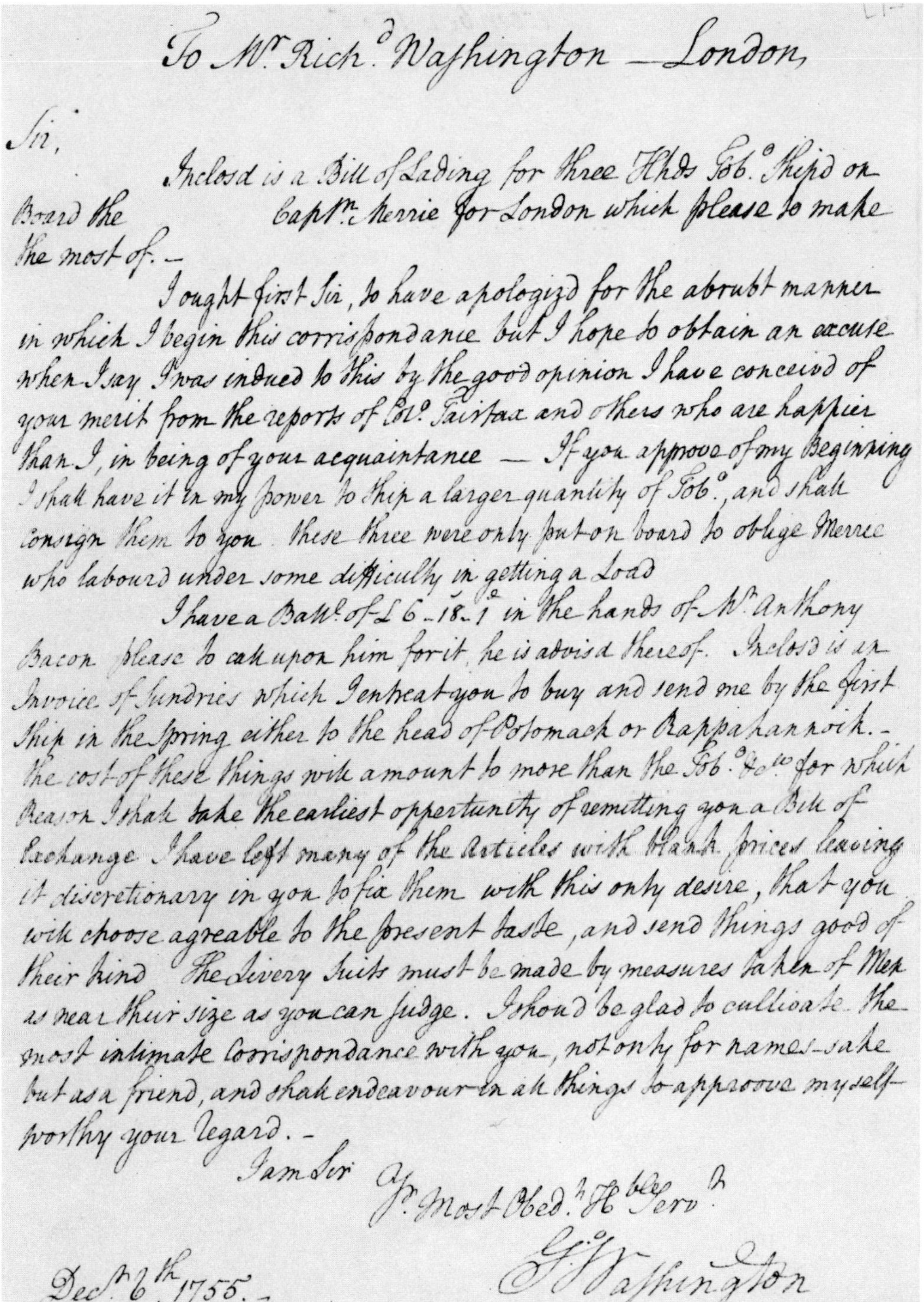

To Mr. Richd. Washington — London,

Sir,

Inclosd is a Bill of Lading for three Hhds Tobo. shipd on Board the Captn. Merrie for London which please to make the most of. —

I ought first Sir, to have apologizd for the abrupt manner in which I begin this corrispondance but I hope to obtain an excuse when I say I was indued to this by the good opinion I have conceivd of your merit from the reports of Colo. Fairfax and others who are happier than I, in being of your acquaintance — If you approve of my Beginning I shall have it in my power to ship a larger quantity of Tobo., and shall consign them to you. these three were only put on board to oblige Merrie who labourd under some difficulty in getting a Load

I have a Ballo. of £6–18–1 in the hands of Mr. Anthony Bacon. please to call upon him for it, he is advisd thereof. Inclosd is an Invoice of Sundries which I entreat you to buy and send me by the first Ship in the Spring either to the head of Potomack or Rappahannock. — the cost of these things will amount to more than the Tobo. Do. to for which Reason I shall take the earliest oppertunity of remitting you a Bill of Exchange I have left many of the Articles with blank prices leaving it discretionary in you to fix them with this only desire, that you will choose agreable to the present taste, and send things good of their kind The Livery Suits must be made by measures taken of Men as near their size as you can judge. I should be glad to cultivate the most intimate corrispondance with you, not only for names-sake but as a friend, and shall endeavour in all things to approove myself worthy your regard. —

I am Sir

Yr. most Obedt. & Hbble Servt.

G: Washington

Decr. 6th 1755. —

4. Washington's copy of a letter introducing himself to Richard Washington, a merchant in London, December 6, 1755. At the age of twenty-three, Colonel Washington was establishing his household at Mount Vernon. He required livery for his servants, "horse furniture" with the Washington crest, and "1 fashionable gold Lac'd Hatt," according to the accompanying invoice. (Courtesy, The Library of Congress)

strengthen his ties with the Fairfax family. In 1748, he and his friend, George William Fairfax, were part of an expedition to lay out tracts of land near the south branch of the Potomac River for George William's cousin, the eccentric proprietor, Lord Fairfax. Even the return of the Fairfaxes to England in 1773 failed to diminish that friendship or to dim memories of elegant Belvoir, where Washington declared he had spent "the happiest moments of my life."[4] Washington's Ledger A, the cash book covering the years 1749 through 1772, reveals the mutual benefit of the relationship in repeated references to the exchange of goods, services, and even servants. His diaries noted frequent visits to Belvoir, return visits by the Fairfaxes to Mount Vernon, and several expeditions with "Fairfax."

In 1755, when George Washington began to furnish Mount Vernon, he turned to neighboring Belvoir—to George William, his wife Sally Cary, and to Belvoir's master, Col. William Fairfax—for advice in matters of fashion and housekeeping. Belvoir, built between 1734 and 1736 by the colonel, was an established landmark in Tidewater Virginia, while down the river, George Mason's spectacular Gunston Hall, with its lavishly carved interiors, was under construction from 1755 to 1759.[5] An inventory of mahogany dining-room and parlor furniture and other furnishings such as a "Sconce Glass gilt in Burnished Gold" and "crimson Morine Drapery Window Curtains" which were sold at Belvoir in 1774 offers a partial picture of the aristocratic establishment George Washington admired and frequently visited.[6]

CONSIGNMENT AND CREDIT

Within a year of leasing Mount Vernon, Washington was ready to order tableware for his household beyond the few items such as salts, a mustard pot, and a pepperbox, which had been purchased locally.[7] At the suggestion of Col. William Fairfax, on December 6, 1755, he sent to Richard Washington in London an "Invoice of Sundries" along with three hogsheads of tobacco from his first growing season at Mount Vernon and an authorization for the collection of

£6.18.1. from Anthony Bacon.[8] The credit with Bacon remained from an earlier order for gilt buckles, "rich gold Embroidered Loops," and gold lace which Washington had placed through John Carlyle, a Scottish merchant and ship owner in the nearby town of Alexandria.[9] Washington realized that the articles ordered would cost more than the value of the tobacco and the money from Bacon, but he promised to send a "Bill of Exchange" to cover the difference. In return, he asked deferentially that his supposed kinsman, Richard Washington, fix the prices and that he "choose agreable to the present taste, and send things good of their kind."[10]

The correspondence between the Virginia and London Washingtons reflected the story of the tobacco trade and of the importance of credit to the southern colonial economy. The consignment system and the bill of exchange enabled the planter to trade tobacco—picked up at his own wharf or at a nearby warehouse by English ships—for manufactured goods, foodstuffs, and luxuries.[11] Credit, often a great deal of it, was established initially on the basis of trust and references. In Washington's case, Colonel Fairfax was his sponsor for dealings with Richard Washington in England. The merchant in London, Bristol, or Liverpool was used by the planter as a commission merchant or factor to receive and sell the tobacco and as an agent in the purchase of articles in English shops. Although in Virginia and Maryland there were British factors who purchased tobacco outright from planters, Washington preferred to ship his tobacco from the Hunting Creek warehouses in Alexandria to Bristol and London for consignment.

An obvious disadvantage to any planter was his necessary dependence on the overseas merchant to set prices for tobacco and for the goods ordered in return. Another problem on both sides was the confusion caused by long-distance selling, shopping, and transport. Washington's correspondence about tableware and other goods from December 1755 through April 1758 recounts several instances of delay, breakage, and uncertainty. The first order sent to Richard Washington in December 1755 requested a variety of items including servants' livery, "horse furniture,"

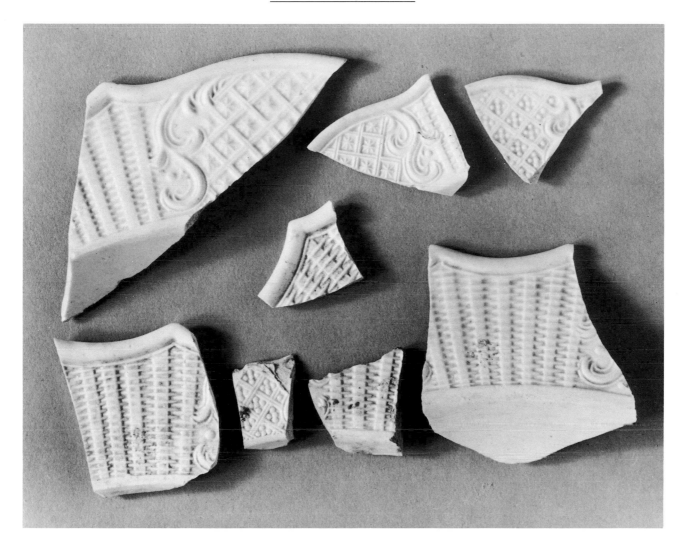

and a "fashionable gold Lac'd Hatt." These goods were shipped from London on the *Endeavor* in April 1756, but Washington's subsequent orders, including one for porcelain tea- and tablewares, were not filled as promptly by the merchant whom Washington thought was a kinsman.

At first, Colonel Washington blamed the confusion and delay in receiving goods from London on his prolonged absence from Mount Vernon and his consequent lack of attention to business and private affairs. During an extended military expedition in 1756, he found it necessary to ask "the favour of Colo. Carlyle on Potomack and Fielding

5. Fragments of saltglazed stoneware meat dishes and plates found at Mount Vernon. All are portions of the basket and star-diaper border pattern. "White stone" plates, dishes, tart pans, mugs, teapots, butter dishes, mustard pots, and tureens were shipped to George Washington by Thomas Knox from Bristol in 1757 and 1758, and stoneware sweetmeat plates were shipped by Richard Farrer from London in 1761. (The Mount Vernon Ladies' Association collections)

6. Saltglazed stoneware tureen and three platters. These pieces are comparable to the "finest white stone Dishes 6 sizes" sent by Thomas Knox of Bristol to Mount Vernon in 1757 and the "6 White stone soop Dishes" or tureens sent in 1758. (City Museum and Art Gallery, Stoke-on-Trent)

Lewis, Esqr., on Rappahannock" to ship his tobacco and "draw for Sundry things which I am in want of."[12] A missing order for two sets of china, which were eventually sent from London in August 1757, may have been among the requests submitted by Carlyle, a prominent Alexandria merchant, and Fielding Lewis, Washington's brother-in-law, because there is no mention of the porcelain in the existing orders for furniture, interior decorations, and tools for Mount Vernon. Unfortunately, missing letters among the early orders to England in the Washington Papers contribute to historical uncertainty about these first important acquisitions of porcelain. In any case, Washington began to suspect that his supposed kinsman either had not received certain of the orders due to hostilities between England and France which resulted in misrouting of vessels or that he was inexplicably slow about selling the tobacco and procuring the items requested.[13] Finally, showing doubt about the London merchant's capabilities, Washington wrote on December 26, 1757: "I have been under concern for sometime past at your long Silence; and have been put to many Shifts, and some Expence for want of my Goods: I have wrote you several times and address'd Copies, to which be refer'd. . . . I hope you will take the first opportunity of sending me (if you have not already done it) all the Goods which, from time to time I have wrote for. . . ."[14] In the meantime "despairing of oppertunities of consigning" to Richard Washington, he sent fourteen hogsheads of "the best Mountn. Sweetscented" tobacco to Thomas Knox in Bristol.[15]

Washington had previously sent tobacco and orders for sundry articles to Thomas Knox on January 18, 1757, but that letter and the accompanying shopping list—referred to in a letter of December 26, 1757—do not survive. The invoice from Knox of goods shipped on the *Recovery* on September 28, 1757, does reveal, however, that Washington had ordered dinner- and teawares of "finest white stone," which arrived before January 8, 1758. On the latter date, Washington angrily wrote to Knox of the Bristol shipment, "the Crate of Stone ware dont contain a third of the Pieces I am charg'd with, and only two things broke, and every thing very high Charg'd."[16] Despite his obvious annoyance,

more tobacco was sent to Knox and, in the same letter of complaint, stoneware tureens, china bowls, and plates were ordered to supplement the tableware in the recently arrived crate.[17]

SALTGLAZED STONEWARE

Although the porcelain dinner- and teawares may have been ordered from London by Washington in 1756, saltglazed stoneware constituted Washington's first documented receipt of ceramics other than locally obtained condiment containers.[18] The porcelains were shipped, according to the invoice, in August 1757, a month before the stoneware left Bristol; however, they did not arrive at Mount Vernon until March 1758. Not one of the stoneware pieces from these early orders has survived the hardship of daily use or changes of fashion, but archeological and documentary evidence provides some information about form and pattern.

Popular press-molded border patterns for stoneware plates and other pieces in 1757 would have been one or more of the following: dot star diaper and basket panels divided by vertical scrollwork; six barley or rice-dotted panels on what came to be called "Queen's" shape in creamware; a raised milled rim on a plain, octagonal border; or a complex raised floral composition.[19] Numerous sherds of all these patterns have been found in Virginia, but only plate and platter border fragments of the diaper and basket design have been found at Mount Vernon. It is probable, therefore, that at least the plates and platters or "dishes" of the large white stoneware service shipped by Thomas Knox from Bristol in September 1757 and the supplementary pieces shipped a year later bore the raised dot-star-diaper and basket decoration which had evolved in English factories from Meissen's "Oldbrandenstein" and "Mixed Pattern" plate borders.[20]

Brown, gray, and yellow saltglazed stonewares, made in England since medieval times, were usually imitative of Germanic products, but the white, thinly potted tablewares of Staffordshire were an English invention which proved to be a great commercial success.[21] The body of white clay and calcined flint, a combination introduced in England about

7. Eight pieces from the Chinese porcelain tea set believed to be the "Compleat Sett fine Image china" shipped from London to Mount Vernon in 1757. Elegant Chinese ladies and amusing children were popular subjects for mid-eighteenth-century porcelains intended for the West. *Famille-rose* enamels were used for the cheerful scenes in reserves framed by underglaze-blue flowers and scrollwork. (The Mount Vernon Ladies' Association collections)

8. Chinese porcelain teapot from the service sent to Mount Vernon in 1757. The round body, twiglike or bird-beak spout, and scroll handle are copied from European teapots of the same period. Height: 6½ inches. (The Mount Vernon Ladies' Association collections)

9. The underglaze-blue borders and the gold ground pattern of this Chinese porcelain "Image" or "Mandarin" pattern mug—which descended through the Peter family—match the same decorative elements on the mug in fig. 11, but the family scene is an entirely different composition painted by a different hand. Mark: ⚡ in overglaze-puce. Height: 5¼ inches. (The Mount Vernon Ladies' Association collections)

10. Probably one of four one-quart Chinese porcelain mugs sent to Mount Vernon from London in 1766. An underglaze-blue framework of dragons and other Chinese motifs encloses a domestic scene painted in *famille-rose* enamels. The seated woman and dancing children are arranged in the kind of composition termed "Image" on the invoice from Washington's agent in London. Height: 5¼ inches. (Peter family collection)

11. Another view of the same mug showing handle with thumb rest and remnants of gold vermiculate ground pattern around reserves of puce-colored landscape and floral motifs in the manner of the Meissen factory. The underglaze-blue cell or honeycomb border developed from Chinese ground patterns of the Yung Chêng period (1723–1735).

1720, could be pressed into metal or alabaster dies or, as slip, poured into plaster molds.[22] The molding process resulted in crisp relief decoration resembling the ornamentation of metalwork from which many of the patterns and forms originated.[23] The English, American, and Continental market for attractive, "flint white" tablewares, which were inexpensive and strong enough to withstand heat and daily use, was substantial. That market and the Staffordshire potting industry were succinctly described in a 1762 petition to Parliament for the opening of a road to provide access for transport of goods and materials.

In Burslem, and its neighbourhood, are near 150 separate Potteries, for making various kinds of Stone and Earthen Ware; which together find constant Employment and Support for near 7000 People. The Ware of these Potteries is exported in vast Quantities from London, Bristol, Liverpool, Hull and other Sea Ports, to our several Colonies in America and the West Indies as well as to almost every Port in Europe. Great quantities of Flint Stones are used in making some of the Ware, which are brought by Sea from different parts of the Coast to Liverpool and Hull; and the clay for making the White Ware, is brought from Devonshire or Cornwall....[24]

12. Punch bowl and wine bottles on a convivial table in South Carolina, drawn by George Roupell, ca. 1760. Stemmed glasses were used for punch as well as for wine. (Courtesy, The Henry Francis du Pont Winterthur Museum)

13. Chinese porcelain punch bowl made early in the reign of Emperor Ch'ien Lung (1736–1795). Complex compositions of pheasants, hummingbirds, bluebirds, and peacocks with chrysanthemums and peonies are skillfully painted around the exterior in *famille-rose* colors. Other enameled decorations include the outer rim frieze of flowers and Chinese "cloud" motifs with ground patterns of curls, interlocking crosses, and flowers and the inner rim frieze of alternating pink and blue bands of trellis ground patterns with scroll-frame reserves. The decoration of this punch bowl —which is the oldest and finest piece of Chinese porcelain known to have been owned by the Washingtons—does not show the European influence of later wares intended for the West. The bowl was acquired by the Mount Vernon Ladies' Association from the Peter family. Thomas Peter bought "4 Cracked Bowls" at the sale following the death of Mrs. Washington. Height: 6½ inches; diameter: 15½ inches. (The Mount Vernon Ladies' Association collections)

14. Interior of punch bowl. Peonies and chrysanthemums are arranged ▶ in a Chinese porcelain lantern or vase meant to be suspended from its fanciful dragon handle.

By 1770, white, saltglazed stoneware was replaced by newly fashionable but equally inexpensive creamware, a leadglazed earthenware which had the advantage of taking decoration before glazing.[25] In the inflationary twentieth century, it is interesting to note that six dozen white stone plates cost Washington £1.4. in 1757 and that six dozen creamware plates also cost him £1.4. in 1770.

George Washington's large table service of white stoneware for his bachelor household at Mount Vernon consisted of nine forms in the two shipments from Bristol. Breakage must have been anticipated because Washington received 108 plates, some of which were for soup. There were six sizes—two each—of serving platters and bowls, or "dishes," and four sizes—twelve each—of "Patti pans," which were low, straight-sided, or star-shaped tart dishes. Two dozen mugs for beer and cider were sent in two sizes, as were "Slop Basons" for tea dregs. Six teapots, twelve butter dishes, twelve mustard pots, and six "soop Dishes," probably tureens, were also included. All the forms, except perhaps the teapots and mugs, were available in England in the diaper and basketwork pattern.[26]

The service was still in use after Washington's marriage in early 1759 to Martha Dandridge Custis. In September 1760, he ordered a dozen white stone butter plates, which, in the return invoice, were called sweetmeat plates. These were small, multipurpose plates of about six to eight inches. "White stone hand Basons" were added at that time; milk pans in 1763; and basins, bottles, and chamber pots for bedroom use in 1764. A dozen utilitarian white stone "butter pots" and more chamber pots arrived in 1765. The table service was probably used by the Washingtons until 1770, when a comparable creamware service also including 108 plates was shipped to Mount Vernon.

The inexpensive stoneware service first ordered during Washington's bachelor years at Mount Vernon was obviously intended for daily breakfast and dinner use because smaller sets of Chinese porcelain dinner- and teaware had been ordered at virtually the same time. No cups or saucers were listed in the invoices from Thomas Knox, so Washington must have planned to use the porcelain tea service, which

finally arrived in March 1758, for evening tea.[27] The saltglazed teapots and slop bowls could be used for breakfast tea, perhaps with cups or mugs purchased locally or in Philadelphia. In May 1758, Washington wrote to Philadelphia merchant David Franks and asked him to "provide" six china cups and saucers. There is no subsequent record of such a shipment to Mount Vernon, but nearly a year later, on his return from Williamsburg in April, Washington noted in his ledger a reimbursement of £ 0.9.1. to his younger brother and farm manager, John Augustine, who had paid a Mr. Seymour for "6 China Cups & Saucers."[28]

FIRST ORDERS FOR PORCELAINS

In spite of absence, confusion, and delay, Washington managed to acquire a considerable amount of tableware during his first years at Mount Vernon. An analysis of the invoices sent to and from Richard Washington in London and those listing the saltglazed wares from Thomas Knox in Bristol affords a picture of tablewares considered fashionable by Tidewater Virginia planters. If saltglazed stoneware—relatively cheap and available in large services—was ordered for daily use by Virginia planters, Chinese porcelain was thought more appropriate for entertaining at dinner and tea. The invoices also suggest the kinds of ceramics Washington would have seen in his neighbors' dining rooms at Belvoir and Gunston Hall, and in John Carlyle's new house in Alexandria. Fashion was especially important to the colonial gentry and to those who would emulate them. Washington's lifelong interest in quality and fashion was revealed in the letters of December 1755, when he directed his London agent, Richard Washington, to "choose agreable to the present taste, and send things good of their kind," and he repeated in January 1758, "pray let them be neat and fashionable or send none. . . ."[29]

By January 1758, the porcelain dinnerware ordered at an unknown earlier date[30] still had not arrived, but the saltglazed stoneware had been delivered with losses due to damage. Foreseeing additional breakage, Washington wrote again to Richard Washington on January 8 to order another dozen porcelain platters and soup plates, and two dozen additional dinner plates. He complained, "I have had an opportunity of seeing the great damage china is apt to come to in its transportation to this Country. . . ." In March the goods from London finally arrived—the china unbroken—and after writing a scathing remark about the indolent Captain Dick who had delayed delivery, Washington noted tersely that the additions ordered on January 8 would not be necessary. In April the cancellation of the extra china was repeated with the apology, " . . . You will perhaps think me a crazy fellow to be ordering and counter ordering Goods almost in a breath." Instead of extra china and "horse furniture," he now wanted a blue velvet suit and several pairs of shoes. This request for elegant clothing undoubtedly had been inspired by his visit in March to "Mrs Custis" and the anticipation of their January 1759 wedding.[31]

The porcelains which finally arrived in March 1758 were actually the first ceramics ordered by Washington, although the shipment was received two months after the stoneware service. The August 20, 1757, invoice from London which accompanied the large shipment of tools, furniture, and tableware listed a "fine . . . china" dinner service consisting of a tureen, eleven oblong platters, and three dozen plates as well as a "Compleat sett fine Image china."[32] The dinner and tea sets of porcelain are assumed to have been Chinese, since Oriental services were more readily available for export to the colonies in 1758 than those of the relatively new English porcelain factories and since both Washingtons used the term "china," which in the mid eighteenth century usually referred to the porcelain products of Ching-tê Chên.

The dinner service is unknown, but the "Compleat sett fine Image china," which cost £3.10.—less than half as much as the dinner service in the same shipment—can be identified with a tea service of about 1755. The service is decorated with complex, underglaze-blue scrolls and flowers around reserves of Chinese figures in the opaque enamels called *famille-rose* by Albert Jacquemart in his influential *Histoire de la Porcelaine* in 1862. Nine pieces of the service have been returned to Mount Vernon from several family sources.

Previous interpretations of the term "Image china" on the 1757 invoice have concluded that Washington received porcelain figures instead of a tea service. He used the term "images" for table ornaments in later years, but the early invoice described a pattern of painted figures on useful wares, not statuary for table or mantel. An invoice dated November 1766 also used the term "Image" to describe four quart-size mugs. Two mugs of that size with *famille-rose* Chinese figures and complex blue borders are now at Mount Vernon. "Image" as a term for figural designs on porcelain was used later in the eighteenth century by the Caughley and Worcester factories in England for copies of Chinese porcelains.[33]

Elegant Chinese ladies and children in elaborate buildings or gardens were popular motifs on export porcelain after 1750.[34] Reflecting the constant exchange of influence between the European factories and the decorators at Ching-tê Chên and Canton, the decorative scheme of reserve panels surrounded by rococo floral and foliate scrollwork probably evolved from Meissen and other European prototypes. Pseudo-Chinese figural designs were in turn used at Worcester and other English and Continental factories in the 1760s. Often a man or "Mandarin" was depicted with other figures in the landscape and architectural settings. The origins of the popular nineteenth-century export ware called "Rose Mandarin" are found in these mid-eighteenth-century examples designed for the West.[35]

Vessel forms in Washington's tea service are comparable to the forms found in other services of 1758 or earlier. The shape of the milk jug, an inverted helmet with molded lobes rising from the base, derived from French silver-gilt and faience models. The form was used for export wares as early as the beginning of the eighteenth century and was included in tea and coffee sets exported to England and the Continent from about 1750 through the early years of the nineteenth century.[36] The lug handles of the sugar bowl also repeat silver or pewter prototypes.[37] The model for the globular teapot with its baroque, curved spout, conical knob, and scroll handle could have been an English pot of the same period.[38] In addition to the teapot, sugar bowl, and milk jug, other components of a typical mid-century tea service

15. Chinese porcelain punch bowl, ca. 1760, decorated in the "Mandarin" or "Image" style popular in the West from the middle of the eighteenth century. Chinese figures play games and converse in an imaginary garden setting with an intriguing perspective of receding wall openings. The inner rim bears a frieze of gilt spearheads, or *ju-i* motifs resembling the French *fleur-de-lis*, but probably derived instead from the Chinese ceremonial scepter. The bowl has been lent to the Mount Vernon Ladies' Association by the heirs of George Washington Parke Custis. Diameter: 15 inches. (The Mount Vernon Ladies' Association collections)

16. Reserves framed by strapwork between the two major figure scenes on one side of Washington's "Mandarin" punch bowl. Obviously derived from European—especially Meissen—prototypes, the small scenes are surrounded by a gilt ground pattern of plumelike scrolls which the European factories had originally borrowed from the Chinese.

17. Chinese porcelain punch bowl, Ch'ien Lung, ca. 1750. Both the outer border of fish-roe diaper and the inner border of fish scales bounded by a rococo shell or feather edge with gilt foliate pendants are adapted from European models which had incorporated Chinese ground patterns as decorative motifs. The pink enamels used here for the borders and flowers were characteristic of *famille-rose* decoration. Called *yang-ts'ai* (foreign colors) by the Chinese, the palette—which also included green, yellow, blue, and violet enamels—was in full use by 1736, the first year of Emperor Ch'ien Lung's reign. Washington's bowl was catalogued as item no. 88 in a sale held in Philadelphia in 1890 by the heirs of his nephew Lawrence Lewis, who married Martha Washington's granddaughter, Eleanor (Nelly) Parke Custis, on February 22, 1799. Diameter: 16 inches. (The Mount Vernon Ladies' Association collections)

for the West were included in the Washington set. The slop basin served to rinse cups and hold the dregs from cups and teapot, while the round tray or dish was used under the teapot or to hold spoons or to serve food.

In January 1758, Washington asked Thomas Knox for "½ Doz'n fashiol. China Bowls from a large to a Midlg. Size"; however, the Bristol merchant sent twelve, ranging in volume from one quart to more than a half gallon. All must have been porcelain if the relative prices of china and stoneware listed in the Knox invoices are used as indicators. By 1750, tea services had evolved to suit western social habits, and the punch bowl also was manufactured to accommodate a popular English concoction.[39] Punch was not usually served at meals; therefore, it was not important that the punch bowl match sets of tableware. In fact, the bowl as the focus of the convivial table and as a room ornament was usually decorated more elaborately than other porcelains and earthenwares. Stemmed glasses were used with the independent punch bowl, which contained mixtures of rum, brandy, sugar, citrus juices, milk, or tea.[40]

The list of objects inventoried in Mount Vernon's "Sweet Meat Closset" after Mrs. Washington's death in 1802 included "8 China Bowls" valued at forty-four dollars. Four Chinese export porcelain bowls displaying decorations appropriate to 1758 have been returned to Mount Vernon. In all probability, Martha Custis Washington brought some or all of her "8 China Bowls" to Mount Vernon shortly after her marriage in 1759, so that any extant punch bowls sent by Knox cannot now be identified.[41] Later purchases of the form included two inexpensive "China" punch bowls, probably blue and white, ordered in June 1766 and sent from London in November of that year. Several punch bowls were ordered in "Queen's China" in August 1770, but no later documents for bowls appear in the Washington Papers other than a reference to an unidentified antique bowl given to him in 1793.

II

EARLY

MARRIED YEARS

AT

MOUNT VERNON,

1759 TO 1773

"Gentln. The Inclos'd is the Minis-
ters Certificate of my Marriage with
Mrs. Martha Custis, properly as I am
told, Authenticated, You will therefore
for the future please to address all your
Letters which relate to the Affairs of the
late Danl. Parke Custis Esqr. to me, as
by Marriage I am entitled to a third
part of that Estate, and Invested like-
wise with the care of the other two thirds
by a Decree of our Genl. Court. . . . On
the other side is an Invoice of some
Goods which I beg of you to send me by
the first Ship bound either to Potomack
or Rappahannock, as I am in immedi-
ate want of them. Let them be Insur'd,
and in case of Accident reshipp'd witht. Delay; direct for me at
Mount Vernon Potomack River Virginia; the former is the name
of my Seat the other of the River on which 'tis Situated." [From
George Washington at Williamsburg to Robert Cary and Com-
pany in London, May 1, 1759 (W 2:319–20)]

18. English saltglazed stoneware chamber pot, incised flowers and leaves filled with oxide of cobalt before firing, ca. 1760. In March 1761, Richard Farrer supplied a dozen "blew & white stone Chamber Pots" to be shipped to Mount Vernon. They may have been similar to this chamber pot, which was excavated in a mid-eighteenth-century context in Philadelphia. (Independence National Historical Park Collection)

The marriage of Colonel Washington to Mrs. Daniel Parke Custis at "White House," her plantation on the Pamunkey River in Virginia, in January 1759 created an important family alliance and raised George Washington's financial affairs to a position of real affluence. Daniel Parke Custis had died without leaving a will, but Virginia law decreed that after marriage Washington would receive his wife's third of the Custis property as well as control of the remaining two-thirds inherited by young John Parke and Martha Parke, the Custis children.[42]

Consequently, management of the Custis tobacco accounts in London was assumed by Washington, who also had access to books, tools, and other items in the estate inventories. The initials "GW" appear in the columns on those inventories opposite such entries as "hasps" and "Hatchets" which he removed before the per-

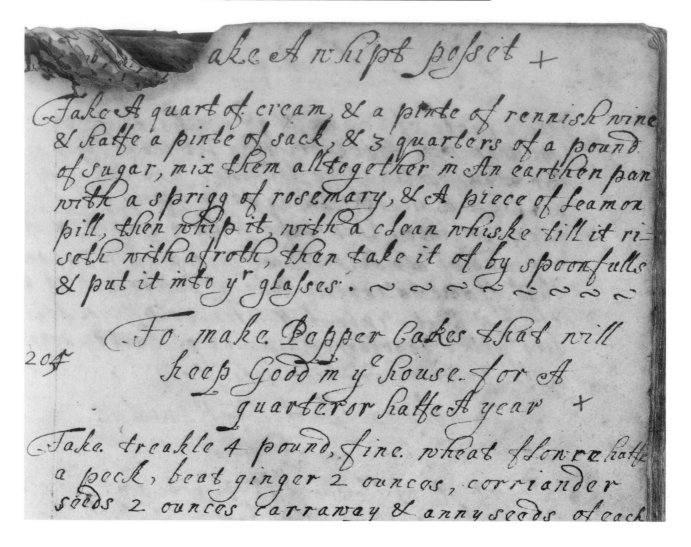

ake A whipt posset +

Take A quart of cream, & a pinte of rennish wine & halfe a pinte of sack, & 3 quarters of a pound of sugar, mix them alltogether in An earthen pan with a sprigg of rosemary, & A piece of leamon pill, then whip it, with a clean whiske till it riseth with a froth, then take it of by spoonfulls & put it into yr glasses. ~ ~ ~ ~ ~ ~

20 To make Pepper Cakes that will keep Good in yr house. for A quarter or halfe A year +

Take treakle 4 pound, fine wheat flowre halfe a peck, beat ginger 2 ounces, corriander seeds 2 ounces carraway & anny seeds of each

19. "To Make A whipt posset," from a cookbook written by Mrs. John Custis. One recipe is dated April 30, 1706, the year Francis Parke married John Custis. Her daughter-in-law, Martha Dandridge Custis, brought the collection of about two hundred recipes, including "To Boyle a Carpe," and "To make an hartychooke Pie," to Mount Vernon after her marriage in January 1759 to Colonel Washington. (Manuscript Department, The Historical Society of Pennsylvania)

sonal property was sold.[43] Lands in the vast estate were estimated at 17,438 acres, and as of November 26, 1757, the estate had a credit of £3,697 with Robert Cary and Company, the London mercantile firm which sold Custis tobacco and shipped supplies and furnishings to the Custis households in Virginia.[44]

After a few months in Williamsburg, where Washington joined the Virginia Assembly as a burgess, the newlyweds set out for Mount Vernon. Martha Dandridge Custis Washington brought her household items in baggage wagons from the Custis plantation in New Kent County and from Six Chimneys, the Custis townhouse in Williamsburg. The Custis papers at the Virginia Historical Society include an "Account of Sundrys taken and used by Mrs Custis out of the Inventories" of the Daniel Parke Custis estate.[45] Tableware, furniture, and horses from White House and Six Chimneys and "Goods Mrs. Custis had out of those Shipped by Cary & Company" were listed in the "Account." It is probable that most, if not all, of the ceramics were carried to Mount Vernon in April 1759, or later when the Custis properties were sold; there was only a small amount of china and glassware listed in the personal-property sale document, and those few things were appraised but not sold.[46]

None of the ceramic entries in the Custis inventories is described in detail sufficient for absolute identification, but there are existing artifacts which are likely to have been among those transferred from the two Custis establishments to Mount Vernon. Two Chinese porcelain tureen stands and covers in the so-called "tobacco-leaf" pattern have been preserved by a Custis descendant with a nineteenth-century note stating that they belonged to Mrs. Daniel Parke Custis. "Eight china bowls" from the Williamsburg house may have included one or more of those at Mount Vernon today. A "set gilt China" valued at four pounds in the 1757 account is assumed to have been a tea service. Its cost was about half that of the dinnerware listed as plates and dishes.[47]

EARLY CH'IEN LUNG TEAWARES AND TOBACCO-LEAF TUREENS

Three extant pieces from a polychrome-and-gilt Chinese porcelain tea set of about 1740 were probably among the Custis furnishings brought to Mount Vernon in April 1759. A shallow dish at the Smithsonian's National Museum of American History, and a matching cup and saucer at the Historical Society of Pennsylvania in Philadelphia, have recently been found to share a provenance traced to Eleanor (Nelly) Parke Custis Lewis, the youngest of Martha Washington's three granddaughters. On Washington's birthday in 1799, Nelly Custis married Lawrence Lewis, a nephew of her famous guardian, at Mount Vernon. The shallow dish was sold to the United States government with the Lewis Collection in 1878, while the cup and saucer were given to the Historical Society in the nineteenth century by Ann Willing Jackson, whose father, Maj. William Jackson —an aide to President Washington—had received them from Mrs. Lewis.[48] The romantic but plausible story that the tea set was used at the Washingtons' wedding at "White

House" on the Pamunkey River is recorded in an old note attached to the cup and saucer in Philadelphia.

The decoration and the body of the bowl and cup and saucer are consistent with a date of about 1740. Porcelains of eggshell delicacy bearing polychrome figures presented without background were developed for Chinese taste, not specifically for the western market, where more elaborate ornamentation was usually preferred. These restrained compositions, based upon Chinese legends, were executed in *famille-rose* colors during the early years of the reign of Emperor Ch'ien Lung (1736–1795). Many were made for the Chinese court, but they were also admired in the West and copied in England by the Worcester factory in the 1750s.[49] The scene on the Custis bowl and cup is probably taken from a Chinese literary source such as the *Romance of the Three Kingdoms*.[50]

Tureen covers and stands of two sizes from a Custis dinner service in the "tobacco-leaf" pattern of *famille-rose* enamels are preserved by the Peter family, descendants of Martha Custis Washington. The platters are lozenge-shape with scalloped rims, and the matching tureen covers display fully modeled floral finials and finely painted leaves and flowers in a style dating to 1757 or earlier.

Varieties of the so-called "tobacco-leaf" pattern, appropriately chosen for a Virginia planter by his agent in London, first appeared on Chinese porcelain made for the European market early in the Ch'ien Lung period.[51] The opaque, *famille-rose* enamels were used in a gaudy combination not seen on wares made to Chinese taste in the same period.[52] The pattern, which persisted on export porcelain into the nineteenth century, probably was derived from certain Japanese "Nabeshima" porcelains which used decorations of large-scale, overlapping leaves and flowers rendered in a conventionalized manner.[53] There is no reason to believe that the name "tobacco-leaf" was used by the Chinese for these designs, but it has become a convenient label for classification of several related patterns. Another "tobacco-leaf" variation occurs on a punch bowl which was given to the Mount Vernon Ladies' Association in 1946 by a member of the Peter family. As mentioned previously, porcelain punch

20. Daniel Parke Custis (1711–1757), painted ca. 1750 by John
Wollaston (fl. 1736–1767). Custis used Robert Cary and Company in
London as his agent in the sale of tobacco and the procurement of supplies
and furnishings. Upon his marriage in 1759 to Mrs. Custis, George
Washington assumed management of the Custis accounts and began using
Cary as his own "Virginia merchant." (Washington–Custis–Lee Collec-
tion, Washington and Lee University)

21. Mrs. Daniel Parke Custis, later Martha Washington, painted by John Wollaston (fl. 1736–1767), ca. 1750. (Washington–Custis–Lee Collection, Washington and Lee University)

◄ *22.* Chinese eggshell porcelain saucer-dish, ca. 1740. Legendary characters are presented without background in the restrained manner preferred by the Chinese. The gilt, cross-hatch border with reserves of plumelike scrolls is also of Chinese rather than European origin. The dish could be used under the teapot in a tea service or to hold lumps of sugar. The latter function is portrayed by another saucer-dish visible in a portrait of Susanna Truax, dated 1730, in the Garbisch collection at the National Gallery of Art. Diameter: 8¼ inches. (Lewis Collection, The National Museum of American History, Smithsonian Institution)

23. Chinese porcelain teabowl and saucer, ca. 1740. Decorated to match ► the saucer-dish in the Smithsonian's Lewis Collection, this cup and saucer also shares a Lewis provenance. Ann Willing Jackson gave the pieces to the Historical Society of Pennsylvania sometime after 1852 with the accompanying note: "This cup and saucer were presented to my father the late Major William Jackson by the late Mrs. Eleanor P. Lewis, granddaughter of Mrs. Washington . . . as one of a set used at the wedding of her grandmother Mrs. Martha Custis to General Washington." Height of cup: 1½ inches; diameter of saucer: 4 inches. (The Historical Society of Pennsylvania)

24. Chinese porcelain tureen cover, ca. 1755. One of several so-called "tobacco-leaf" designs using large, overlapping leaves and flowers painted in *famille-rose* enamels to cover the entire surface of an object. This kind of decoration—produced only for export—is not characteristically Chinese, but is comparable to contemporary Japanese designs. The flowers are skillfully painted, but the gilding is carelessly applied. Wares from China were often "clobbered," or given additional enameling or gilding, in Europe. Only two tureen covers and stands are known to remain from the service which "belonged to Mrs. Daniel Parke Custis (née Dandridge afterwards Mrs. Washington)," according to an old label. Length: 6½ inches. (Peter family collection)

25. Chinese porcelain punch bowl, ca. 1760. A restrained "tobacco-leaf" pattern features a shaded pink peony and a Chinese rosette of fish-egg and cracked-ice ground patterns on alternating brown, blue, and yellow lobes. The bowl descended through the Peter family and—like that in fig. 13—may be one of four purchased by Thomas Peter in 1802. Diameter: 11¼ inches. (The Mount Vernon Ladies' Association collections)

bowls were ordered by Washington in 1758 and 1766, and Martha Custis Washington probably brought her eight punch bowls to Mount Vernon after her marriage in 1759.

In addition to the elegant Chinese gilt tea set and the "tobacco-leaf" tureens, Martha Custis removed objects from the inventories of her first husband's estate. Some entries in the inventories reveal a taste for ceramics beyond those intended exclusively for tea- and dinner-table use. "Fruit peices" and "flower peices" valued at a relatively expensive five pounds per set were itemized with other articles of china in the Custises' Williamsburg house. These may have been ornamental porcelain objects of English manufacture from the Bow, Chelsea, Derby, or Longton Hall factories. Chelsea, at a slightly later time, made large circular tureens topped by life-size bunches of flowers or fruit.[54]

ROBERT CARY AND COMPANY AND RICHARD FARRER, "CHINAMAN"

Ornamental porcelains to replace or supplement the fruit and flower pieces were among the first objects ordered by the Washingtons from Robert Cary and Company, the London agent to whom Daniel Parke Custis had sent his tobacco and from whom both Custis and his widow had ordered clothing, furniture, tools, glassware, toys, and even nonperishable foods. The orders and the corresponding invoices from Cary in the Custis and Washington Papers offer an exceptionally detailed account of mid-eighteenth-century material culture in both Virginia and England and of the consignment-purchase system in the royal colony. Robert Cary (1730–1777), Virginia merchant, of London and Hampstead, managed a consignment business established during the lifetime of his grandfather, James Cary of London, salter and Virginia merchant, who died in 1694.[55]

Dissatisfied with the tobacco prices obtained in Bristol by Thomas Knox and in London by Anthony Bacon and frustrated by the delays in the agency of Richard Washington, George Washington must have been pleased to find another firm ready to sell his tobacco with that of the Custis estate and to supply necessities and luxuries from the best shops in London. On May 1, 1759, the new husband wrote to "Rob.t Cary Esq.r & Comp.a Merchts London" to assert his position and legal rights following his marriage. The traffic of tobacco and goods thus established between George Washington and Robert Cary continued until at least February 17, 1773, when the last invoice preserved in the Washington Papers was sent from London. This invoice arrived nearly ten years after the Virginia planter had finally begun to heed the early warnings sent by his uncle, Joseph Ball, in London, that a planter must not "send his Tobacco to England to be sold here, and goods sent him; if he does, he will soon get in the merchant's debt, and never get out again. . . ."[56] By 1763 Washington had converted much of his acreage to diversified crops which he could market personally.

A request attached to the May 1, 1759, letter of introduction to Cary asked for curtains, fabric, furniture, and glassware, and "4 Fashionable China Branches, & Stands, for Candles." The orders were filled and sent the following August. They were accompanied by a lengthy invoice listing goods under the name of the London shopkeeper or craftsman who supplied them. Cary had procured china and glassware from Richard Farrer—or Farrar—for Daniel Parke Custis, and he continued to patronize the well-known London "Chinaman" on behalf of George Washington for the next thirteen years.

The term "Chinaman" was used in the eighteenth century to describe merchants who specialized in imported Chinese porcelains. There were over a hundred such "Chinamen" in London between 1711 and 1774, and the peak period for wares imported from the East was 1761 through 1770, according to customs records.[57] Although these retailers were also the main support of the English porcelain factories, the heavy duties imposed on imported tableware toward the end of the century caused the failure of many.

English ceramics historians remember "Chinaman" Richard Farrer (1692/93–1775) as the father-in-law and mentor of Miles Mason, the successful manufacturer of "patent stone china." Farrer lived in Great House, Chigwell Row, Essex, but conducted his retail glass and china business in London from 131 Fenchurch Street, a location convenient to sales at the main warehouse of the East India Company on Leadenhall Street.[58] According to most sources, he entered partnership with Richard Garrett in 1772. The invoices in Washington's accounts, however, are headed "Farrer and Garrett" as early as January 1770. Garrett ran the business after Farrer's death in 1775 until 1784, when Miles Mason assumed management.

A survey of the invoices sent to Washington by Robert Cary from 1759 to 1772 reveals that Farrer supplied an extraordinary range of wares, from churns, milk pans, and chamber pots to teawares, silver salvers, and, in March 1761, a "Glass Pyramid in 8 arms" as well as the elegant porcelain candlesticks in the first shipment. The wares sent to Virginia were of Chinese, English, and German manufacture. They were sent in response to specific requests from the master of Mount Vernon, but the requests were not always precisely satisfied. Discrepancies can be found between the orders and the responses from London, both of which are reproduced in the Appendix. Comparison of the reciprocal documents often produces information about contemporary terminology and taste as well as providing clues to the identification of form, decoration, and manufacture of ceramics offered by an eighteenth-century London retailer.

"BRANCHES AND CANDLESTICKS WITH FLOWERS"

In response to Washington's May 1759 request for fashionable porcelain branches and stands for candles, Farrer supplied two pairs of "Branches and Candlesticks with flowers" at different prices for each pair. Four allegorical figures representing the seasons and music which had not been ordered but which helped to fulfill the "fashionable" aspect of Washington's wishes were included. The figures were priced separately, so they must have been independent of the candlesticks. Perhaps they were meant to stand in front of them or to be attached in some way.[59]

The candlesticks and two of the figures have disappeared, but archeological and documentary evidence in Virginia points to the probability that they were English porcelain. The inventories of the Governor's Palace and other dwellings in Williamsburg document the existence of English ornamental porcelains in eighteenth-century Virginia. One such inventory taken after the death in 1770 of Norborne Berkeley, Lord Botetourt, the Royal Governor, listed "22 Chelsea China figures" and two pairs of "English china candlesticks." His predecessor, Governor Francis Fauquier, who died in 1768, had forty pieces of "Ornamental china."[60] English porcelains dating to the mid-eighteenth century have also been excavated at several sites in Virginia.[61]

Richard Farrer may have had such articles in stock at his fashionable London showroom. If the ornaments were of Chelsea manufacture, he could have purchased them at the spring factory sales of 1756 or 1759. No catalogue for the 1759 sale held at Burnsall's "Great Auction-Room in Charles Street, Berkly-square" is known, but advertisements offered

"some beautiful large Groups, and single Figures for Brackets, with many other Articles for Table, Tea, & Coffee services. . . ."[62] Three years earlier, on March 29, 1756, a Mr. Ford sold "Last Year's Curious Production of the Chelsea Porcelain Manufactory" in his auction room at St. James, Haymarket. The catalogue for the 1756 sale is known, and it lists several candlestick and figure designs including "A most beautiful group of figures representing the 4 seasons" and "two beautiful figures playing on the flute and guitar."[63]

Two mid-eighteenth-century porcelain figures holding baskets of flowers and, therefore, probably representing spring or summer, have been purchased by the Mount Vernon Ladies' Association from the family of Stephen Decatur. The Decatur family are collateral descendants of Tobias Lear, Washington's close friend and secretary during the presidential years. The porcelain figures returned to Mount Vernon with a history of having been given to the children of Lear's sister by the Washingtons in the 1790s.

The only mark—if it is a mark—on the figures is a raised oval ring on the base of the female figure. Although the male figure in particular and the bases of both figures resemble a pair of Chelsea figures bearing the brown anchor mark used as early as 1758, they also resemble a pair of Derby figures in the Schreiber Collection at the Victoria and Albert Museum in London.[64] In addition, the turquoise green seen on the bodice of the female figure is considered to be peculiar to Derby decorations of about 1756.[65] The lack of the dry patches typically found on the bottoms of Derby figures, however, adds one more element of confusion to the attribution of Washington's figures, which must be labeled Derby or Chelsea for lack of definitive laboratory evidence.

PIPKINS, CHAMBER POTS, AND MILK PANS

The ornamental candlesticks and figures and the dessert glassware of the 1759 order represent Colonel Washington's new requirements after his marriage to the wealthy widow Custis. They also illustrate the upper end of the range of wares available in Richard Farrer's Fenchurch Street store.

26. Two English soft-paste porcelain figures, ca. 1755–1759. Baskets of flowers identify these figures on rococo bases as allegorical "seasons." They are unmarked, and the manufacturer has not been identified. In fact, they display characteristics ascribed to several factories. The Chelsea, Derby, Bow, and Longton Hall establishments all were manufacturing figures —often based on German models—in the 1750s. In May 1759, "Chinaman" Richard Farrer sent "1 pair Seasons & 1 pair Music's figures" from London to the newly married Washingtons at Mount Vernon. These figures, which are believed to correspond to those on the invoice, returned to Mount Vernon with a history of having been given to the niece of President Washington's secretary, Tobias Lear. Height: 4¼ inches. (The Mount Vernon Ladies' Association collections)

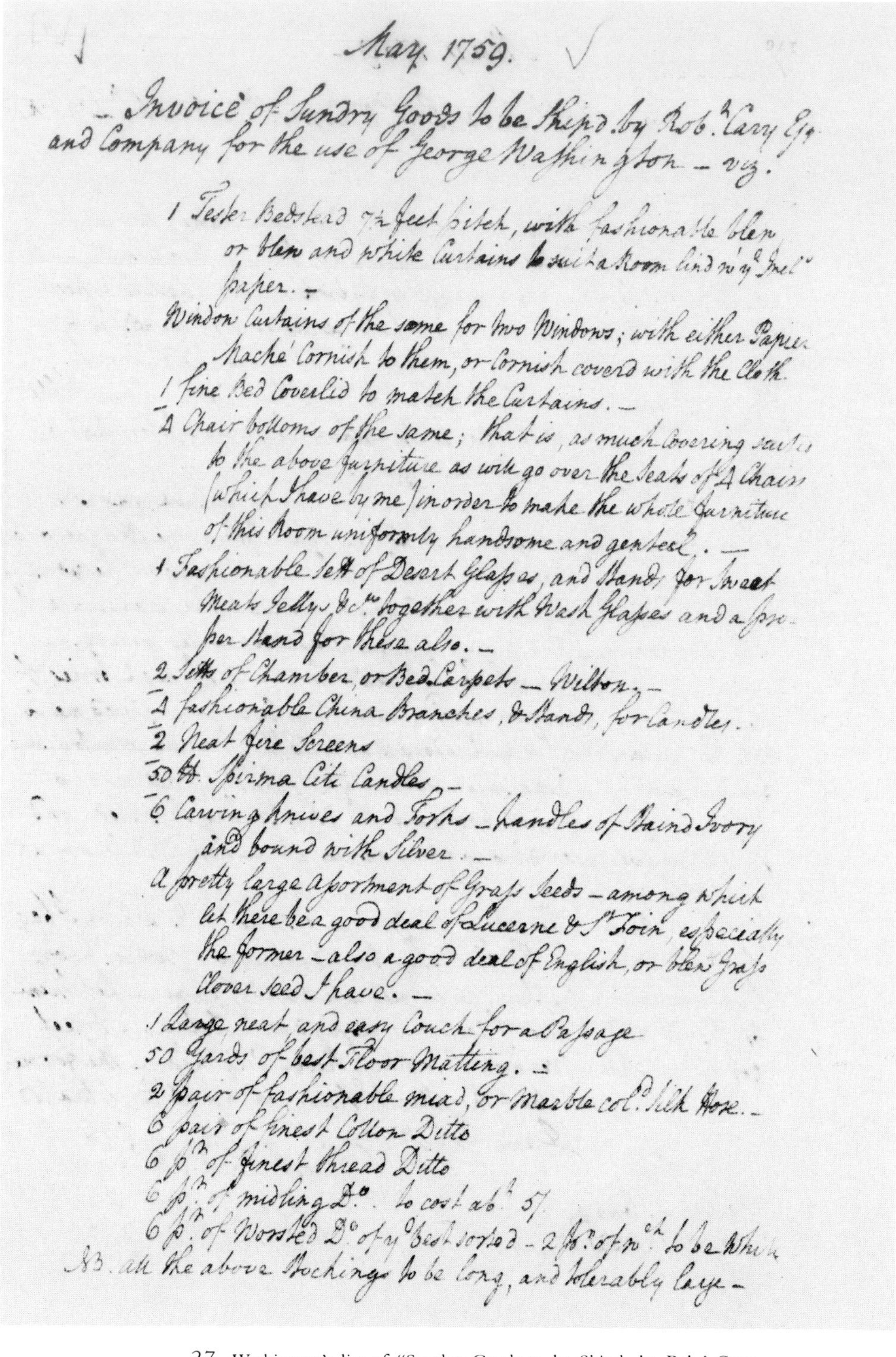

May 1759.

— Invoice of Sundry Goods to be Shipd. by Rob.t Cary Esq,
and Company for the use of George Washington — vz.

1 Tester Bedstead 7½ feet pitch, with fashionable blew
    or blew and white Curtains to suit a Room lind wt yᵉ Inclosd
    paper. —

Window Curtains of the same for two Windows; with either Paper
    Maché Cornish to them, or Cornish coverd with the Cloth.

1 fine Bed Coverlid to match the Curtains. —

4 Chair bottoms of the same; that is, as much covering suited
    to the above furniture as will go over the Seats of 4 Chairs
    (which I have by me) in order to make the whole furniture
    of this Room uniformly handsome and genteel. —

1 Fashionable Sett of Desert Glasses, and Stands for Sweet
    Meats Jellys &ca together with Wash Glasses and a pro-
    per Stand for these also. —

2 Setts of Chamber, or Bed Carpets — Wilton. —

2 fashionable China Branches, & Stands, for Candles.

2 Neat fire Screens

50 ℔. Spirma Ceti Candles. —

6 Carving knives and forks — handles of stained Ivory
    and bound with Silver. —

A pretty large assortment of Grass Seeds — among which
    let there be a good deal of Lucerne & St Foin, especially
    the former — also a good deal of English, or blew Grass
    Clover Seed I have. —

1 Large neat and easy Couch for a Passage

50 Yards of best Floor Matting. —

2 pair of fashionable mixd, or Marble colᵈ Silk Hose. —

6 pair of finest Cotton Ditto

6 pr. of finest thread Ditto

6 pr. of midling Dᵒ. to cost abt 5/

6 pr. of Worsted Dᵒ of yᵉ best sorted — 2 pr. of wᶜʰ to be White

N.B. all the above Stockings to be long, and tolerably large —

27. Washington's list of "Sundry Goods to be Shipd. by Rob.ᵗ Cary
Esq." sent to London May 1, 1759, three months after his wedding and
shortly after his return to Mount Vernon with Mrs. Washington. Among
the furnishings and clothing requested were sweetmeat glasses and porcelain candle-branches. (Courtesy, The Library of Congress)

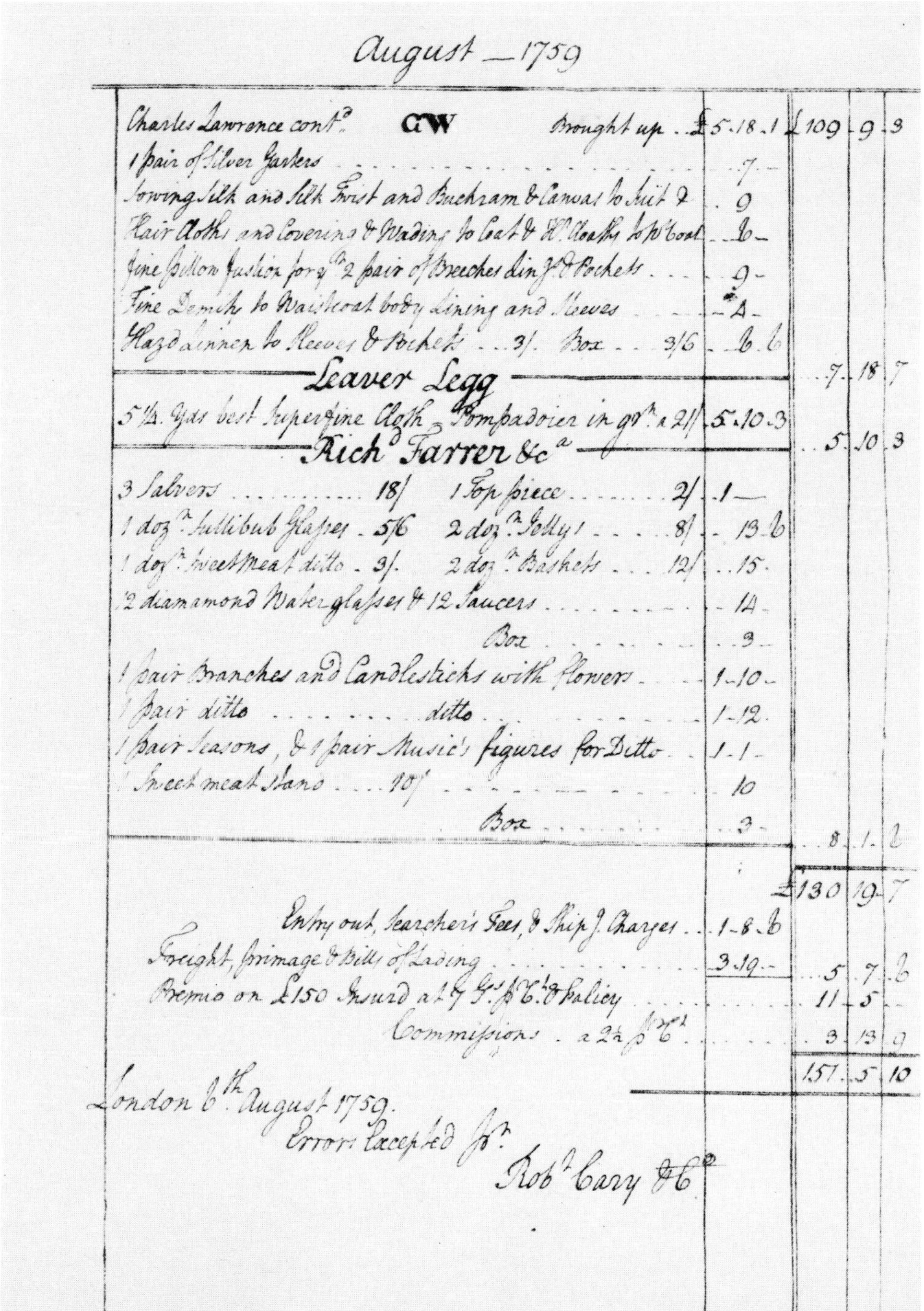

August — 1759

Charles Lawrence cont.ᵈ **GW**	brought up £5.18.1	£109	9	3
1 pair of Silver Garters	7			
Sowing Silk and Silk Twist and Buckram & Canvas to Suit &	9			
Hair Cloths and Coverins & Wading to Coat & Wt Cloaths to Wt Coat	6			
fine Cotton fustian for yᵉ 2 pair of Breeches lin'g & Pockets	9			
fine Domett to Waistcoat body Lining and Sleeves	4			
Glazd linnen to Sleeves & Pockets . . . 3/ . Box . . 3/6	6.6			
Leaver Legg			7..18	7
5¼ Yds best Superfine Cloth — Pompadoier in gr.ⁿ x 21/	5.10.3		5.10	3
Richᵈ Farrer &cᵃ				
3 Salvers . . . . 18/ 1 Top piece 2/	1 —			
1 dozⁿ Sullibub Glasses . 5/6 2 dozⁿ Jellys . . 8/	13.6			
1 dozⁿ Sweetmeat ditto . 3/ 2 dozⁿ Baskets . . 12/	15			
2 diamamond Water glasses & 12 Saucers	14			
Box	3			
1 pair Branches and Candlesticks with flowers	1.10			
1 pair ditto . . . . . . ditto . . .	1.12			
1 pair Seasons, & 1 pair Music's figures for Ditto	1.1			
Sweet meat Stand 10/	10			
Box	3		8..1	
		£130	19	7
Entry out, Searcher's Fees, & Ship.g Charges	1.8.6			
Freight, primage & Bills of Lading	3.19.		5..7	6
Premio on £150 Insur'd at 7 p Ct & ½ p Policy			11..5	
Commission . . a 2½ p Cᵗ			3.13	9
		151..5	10	

London 6ᵗʰ August 1759.

Errors Excepted pr

Robᵗ Cary &Cᵒ

28. Washington's copy of the reciprocal invoice, dated August 6, 1759,
from Robert Cary and Company, London. Richard Farrer supplied nearly
all the ceramics and glass shipped to Mount Vernon from 1759 through
1772. (Courtesy, The Library of Congress)

29. Fragment of an English brown, saltglazed stoneware mug found at Mount Vernon. The iridescent brown glaze on this fragment is usually thought to be characteristic of Nottingham wares, but such glazes are also found on Staffordshire products. In September 1760, Washington directed Robert Cary to send a dozen "strong Mugs different sizes." The return invoice, dated March 1761, listed quart, pint, and half-pint "mugs brown stone" among the other wares supplied by Richard Farrer. The impressed circle with the suggestion of a crown is probably an excise stamp, often found on English tavern mugs. Height: 2½ inches. (The Mount Vernon Ladies' Association collections)

30. Brown saltglazed stoneware mug, English, Nottingham type, ca. 1760. Height: 4 inches. (Courtesy, Colonial Williamsburg Foundation)

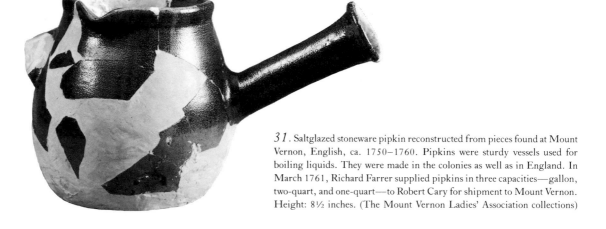

31. Saltglazed stoneware pipkin reconstructed from pieces found at Mount Vernon, English, ca. 1750–1760. Pipkins were sturdy vessels used for boiling liquids. They were made in the colonies as well as in England. In March 1761, Richard Farrer supplied pipkins in three capacities—gallon, two-quart, and one-quart—to Robert Cary for shipment to Mount Vernon. Height: 8½ inches. (The Mount Vernon Ladies' Association collections)

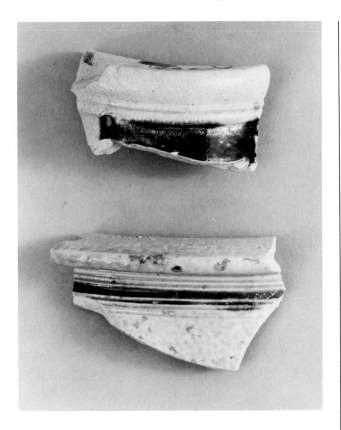

32. Fragments of a mug and chamber pot, gray, saltglazed stoneware with cobalt blue bands, probably made in the Westerwald pottery district of the Rhineland, ca. 1760. Found at Mount Vernon. A dozen "Dutch" stoneware chamber pots were sent to Mount Vernon from London in December 1771, while "stone" mugs—not designated white or brown—had been sent in December 1765 and October 1767. (The Mount Vernon Ladies' Association collections)

At the lower end of Farrer's ceramic spectrum were the common articles necessary for household and farm such as churns, earthenware pots known as pipkins, and chamber pots. In September 1760, Washington ordered seventy-two earthenware milk pans and a number of other humble objects as well as six pairs of porcelain mugs and six porcelain "potting pots." He also ordered a dozen butter plates and six milk pots on feet to supplement his large white saltglazed table service.

Farrer's corresponding invoice, dated March 1761, provides a few details of description which could be useful to future archeological identifications. The china potting pots, probably for preserving meats, were oval; four were covered and provided with stands. Washington's white stone "butter plates" were called "sweetmeat plates" by Farrer and were simply plates of a small, versatile size for table use. The "white stone hand Basons" for bedroom use show that the white saltglazed body, although usually thinly potted, was strong enough to withstand utilitarian usage. A dozen mugs of saltglazed "brown stone" in three sizes were of the type manufactured in England at Fulham or Nottingham, perhaps with the metallic glaze which characterized products usually attributed to the latter location.[66] Sherds of this material have been found at Mount Vernon. Pipkins, small pots with straight horizontal handles used to heat liquids, were also made of brown stoneware. "Blew & white stone" chamber pots may have been English saltglazed stoneware decorated by a technique known as "scratch blue," or they may have been Germanic products of the Westerwald region, which were also decorated in cobalt blue. Fragments of the latter have been found on the Mount Vernon site. The invoice for a later shipment in 1771 termed chamber pots of equal price "Dutch." By the end of the seventeenth century and through the eighteenth, a significant amount of traffic in German stonewares to England existed despite native English stoneware production.[67]

Six dozen "earthen" milk pans in six sizes had been ordered with the porcelains and stoneware by Washington in September 1760 and were shipped in March 1761. The redware milk pan—a shallow dish with straight sloping sides glazed on the inside—was used for setting milk, baking, and washing and was one of the most common ceramic products of the period. Constant use as well as size and weight accounted for the easy breakage of the brittle red earthenware pans. Probably because of such breakage, Washington ordered another six dozen in 1763. Redware was potted in the colonies at this date, and large cream or milk pans are known to have been made in quantity in Virginia in the second quarter of the eighteenth century and later.[68] However, since Washington, and undoubtedly other planters, ordered redware from London, artifacts and fragments of that material excavated at American sites should be only cautiously attributed to colonial potters.

In addition to the assortment of earthenwares, stonewares, and an inexpensive glass pyramid of eight arms, the case which was shipped in March 1761 included six Chinese porcelain mugs. Farrer described these as "Emboss'd" and charged one pound and ten shillings, the same price as one of the sets of floral candlesticks shipped in 1759.[69] Relief decoration on Chinese porcelain for the West recalls the prunus or plum blossom sprays on *blanc-de-chine* wares exported from Te-hua in China's Fukien province in the earliest years of the eighteenth century and later copied by Mennecy, Chelsea, and other European and English factories. Tendrils and flowers in relief also occurred on wares decorated in the colorful "mandarin" style at mid-century.[70]

BLUE-AND-WHITE CHINA

In 1762, the first known examples of blue-and-white Chinese export porcelain to serve the tables of Mount Vernon were acquired by Robert Cary from Richard Farrer and Company. Washington simply ordered a dozen "China breakfast cups...custard cups...[and] tart Pans," but Farrer's invoice reveals that he sent "B & W China" and that the custard cups were ribbed. Blue-and-white ware was purchased by the Washingtons at least nine times during the following thirty-five years, with the result that a variety of decorative motifs occurs on surviving examples and on excavated fragments.

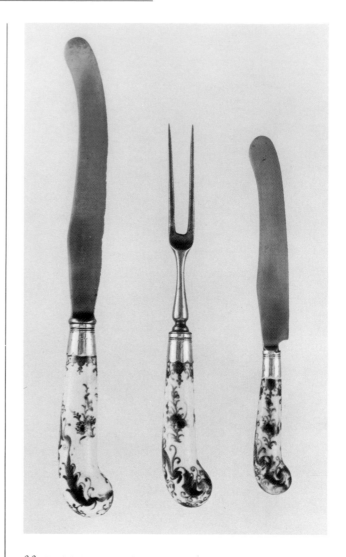

33. English knives and fork, steel blades and silver ferrules, porcelain handles probably Worcester, ca. 1760. In November 1762, Washington asked Robert Cary to send a complete set of table china with two dozen table knives and forks "with China handles" and two dozen dessert knives and forks "to suit" the set of table china. These were supplied by Richard Neale's cutlery shop in London and shipped by Cary with a set of blue-and-white china in April 1763. Blue-and-white utensil handles were also made in China for export to the West. Washington's pieces could have been either Chinese or English. (Courtesy, Colonial Williamsburg Foundation)

Shortly after the cups and patty or tart pans arrived, Washington wrote to Cary for a "very fine and compl^t sett of Table China" and eight dozen knives and forks "with China handles to suit" the service. The knives and forks and a "Compleat sett Table China fine blue & white" were shipped in April 1763.[71] According to Farrer's invoice, a complete set consisted of eleven platters, a dozen soup plates, a dozen flat plates, a covered tureen and stand, four sauceboats, and four salts.

East India Company records of that period indicate that all the above items were included in a standard set of blue-and-white Chinese export tableware with the usual addition of a salad dish. In 1755, the British ship *Prince George* sailed from Canton with 120 chests of blue-and-white china and a box of "musters," or patterns. A cargo list of these chests with the names of the Chinese merchants from whom the china was purchased reveals that Sweetia provided thirty-two chests containing seven "Table Setts Blue & W^t Octagon" consisting of dishes (platters), plates, soup plates, tureens, tureen dishes, sauceboats, salts, and salad dishes.[72] There were also "Single Plates," "Setts of Bowles," "Coffee Cups," "Half pint Basons," and "Tea Setts." The merchant Footia's fifty chests contained similar table sets of two patterns and cups and saucers of three different patterns. Chinaware which had earlier been purchased in Canton from stock was now ordered by pattern from the manufacturing center at Ching-tê Chên.[73]

Washington's blue-and-white table service, shipped in April 1763, cost an even twelve pounds for fifty-six pieces and was somewhat more expensive than the comparable but less complete service of forty-eight pieces shipped earlier by Richard Washington in August 1757. The blue-and-white service was supplemented over the years and replaced by a much larger blue-and-white table service in 1783. An inventory of Mount Vernon made in 1800 itemized the everyday blue-and-white china "In the Closet under Franks direction" and included custard cups, pickle plates, and tart pans which were probably from the 1762 and 1765 shipments since they are not known to have been purchased later. By 1800, the blue-and-white china was a conglomeration of

patterns and shapes. "All the blue and white china in common use" was bequeathed to Eleanor Parke Custis Lewis, granddaughter of Martha Washington.[74] Several pieces of Chinese blue-and-white porcelain were sold to the United States government by the Lewis family in 1878 and are now in the national collections at the Smithsonian Institution. About forty-two pieces of blue-and-white china with a traditional Washington provenance are preserved in Virginia at Arlington House in the Robert E. Lee III collection. Fragments found at Mount Vernon attest to the variety of blue-and-white landscape designs and borders used on Chinese export porcelain of the eighteenth century and to the impossibility of ascertaining exactly which patterns were used on any one of the Washingtons' many documented purchases.

"WELCH" MILK PANS, A CHINA PLATE BASKET, AND "NANKEEN" MUGS

In addition to the table service, Richard Farrer sent seventy-six milk pans in 1763, of which most were red earthenware, two were white stoneware, and a dozen were called "Welch." Certain slipware fragments unearthed at Mount Vernon may be remnants of that earthenware product which was ordered again in 1765 and which was called "Welch" by both Washington and Farrer or Cary. Welsh or "Welch" ware was an eighteenth-century term for shallow meat dishes or milk pans covered on the inside with combed or feathered slip. They were made at potteries in Staffordshire, Sunderland, and Isleworth. Milk pans thickly covered on the inside with a black lead glaze or with slip were also made in the Buckley district of North Wales. It is possible that Buckley was the source for Washington's "Welch" pans, although wares produced there are thought to have been shipped to Virginia from Liverpool rather than from London.[75]

In September 1763, Washington wrote to Robert Cary for white stoneware basins, bottles, and chamber pots and asked for a "China Plate Basket—or Basket proper for China in." Table services of blue-and-white Chinese porcelain were shipped as units from Canton to London, with each service packed in straw in a tall, cylindrical hamper. Perhaps the

34. Selection of fragments of blue-and-white Chinese porcelain table- and teawares, ca. 1760–1795, found at Mount Vernon. Washington's first identifiable acquisition of blue-and-white Chinese porcelain was made in 1762, and the last one was probably a set of "blue" mugs and dishes purchased for Mrs. Washington in Philadelphia in March 1796. There are at least nine recorded references to the purchase of blue-and-white wares in the Washington Papers. Most of the fragments illustrated display elements of the standard, underglaze-blue, painted patterns and borders imported in great quantity from Canton by the English East India Company in the third quarter of the eighteenth century. (The Mount Vernon Ladies' Association collections)

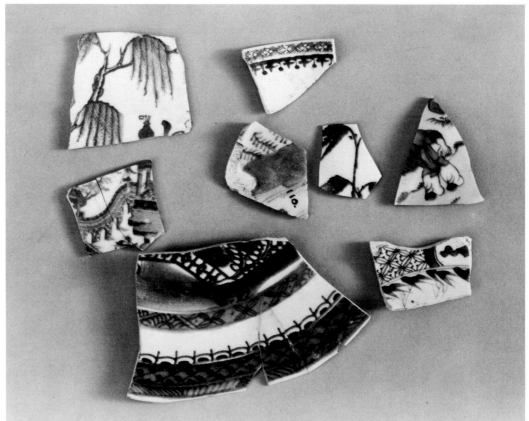

basket for Washington's new "sett Table China" was damaged or perhaps his set arrived without its basket since it had been packed with other articles. Washington obviously knew that a "Compleat sett Table China" should have a basket for storage.[76] Twenty years later when inquiring about another "compleat sett of blue and White Table China," he wrote, "They some times come in compleat setts ready packed. . . ."[77]

The white stoneware bedroom pieces were procured from James Maidment in 1764, but in February 1765, Cary again turned to Richard Farrer and Company to supply large stoneware jugs and fine table porcelain. Pickle shells were added to the blue-and-white china; and two quart-size mugs, also of blue-and-white china, were sent. Two smaller mugs designated "Nankeen" by Farrer and "2 large English Teapots" are of special interest because of the terminology employed in the invoices. Washington's order specified that the teapots be large enough to fill the quart mugs. The teapots included in Chinese services may have been too small for breakfast tea at Mount Vernon. A dozen teacups and saucers "for breakfasting" were ordered in September 1765. Breakfast tea required larger cups than evening tea, and Washington specifically ordered cups by size according to the intended function.

Farrer's reference to "Nankeen" evidently described the decoration of the pint mugs and, more specifically, of the borders, because in November 1766 he sent a large blue-and-white punch bowl with a "Nankⁿ bordʳ." Porcelains decorated in underglaze blue and white at the porcelain center, Ching-tê Chên, but shipped to merchants in Canton from the seaports of Nanking, gave rise to the term, which was used through the early part of the nineteenth century. Since much of the polychrome export ware was enameled at Canton, blue-and-white Nanking ware was thus differentiated. Landscapes with buildings in a variety of compositions were the principal motifs of Nanking porcelains, but an inner border of daggers or spearheads seems also to have been a distinctive element. The so-called spearhead motif may have developed from the *ju-i* or ceremonial scepter form used in Chinese frieze decorations or from the European *fleur-de-lis* or both.[78]

The Washingtons must have considered their ceramic supplies adequate for a time, because there was only one small order for stonewares in 1767 and no orders at all in 1768. Economies became increasingly necessary, because Washington's large debt to Cary was not easily discharged. Tobacco crops had been meager, and there had been other financial losses.[79] In order to reduce his indebtedness to the London merchant, Washington was forced to continue growing some tobacco although he had begun to convert much of his land to diversified farm crops. In July 1769, he wrote, "I only grow Tobacco to Supply my Family with Goods."[80] In fact, Washington's debt to Cary and Company was not settled until the death of Mrs. Washington's teenage daughter, Patsy, in 1773. That misfortune enabled her stepfather "to apply her money in the [stock of the] Bank [of England] to that purpose."[81]

QUEENSWARE

In the summer of 1769, Washington asked Robert Cary to send a new table service of 250 units. The requested queensware service would be comparable in numbers, cost, and function to the large stoneware service first ordered in 1757. By 1765, white saltglazed plates and dishes had been replaced on fashionable English tables by leadglazed, cream-colored earthenware in a variety of new shapes supplementing the forms created by block cutters for stoneware manufacturers. Washington's specific request for "ye most fashᵉ kind of Queen's Ware," a term originated by Josiah Wedgwood two years earlier, suggests that more than mere necessity prompted the order for the cheap, attractive tableware which was immediately popular in England with the aristocracy and consequently with the middle classes.[82]

Whatever the incentive to procure a new table service from London, Washington's request was made in the face of contemporary American sentiments against importation of all British manufactures and especially of taxed articles such as paper, glass, and paint. His sympathies lay with the supporters of the Non-Importation Agreements, to which he alluded in the historic letter accompanying the tableware order: ". . . if there are any Articles . . . which are Tax'd by Act of Parliament for the purpose of Raising a Revenue in America, it is my express desire and request, that they may not be sent, as I have very heartily entered into an Association . . . not to Import any Article which now is or hereafter shall be Taxed for this purpose untill the said Act or Acts are repeal'd. . . ."[83] Washington and the other burgesses met at the Raleigh Tavern in Williamsburg in May 1769 to consider Virginia's response to the Non-Importation Agreements. They firmly decided that nothing of British manufacture was to be purchased after September 1, 1769.[84] Prudently, Washington, who with George Mason led the effort, sent his extensive order to Robert Cary a little more than a month before the cut-off date. The American agreements were effective in Boston and Philadelphia, but they had little success in stemming the flow of British goods into trade-dependent Virginia, where imports actually increased in 1770.[85]

The protested taxes were not applied to English creamware so Richard Farrer and his new partner, Richard Garrett, supplied plates, platters, tureens, baking dishes, fish drainers, sauceboats, salad dishes, cut or pierced fruit dishes and egg cups, sugar dishes, flowerpots, pickle dishes, mugs, and tea and coffee items to Robert Cary and Company for shipment to Mount Vernon in January 1770. The variety of functional shapes in Washington's request for queensware indicates that he was ordering from a retailer's list, a pattern book, or a sample service seen in Williamsburg or Philadelphia. His designations correspond rather closely to the descriptions found in catalogues such as those published in 1774 or earlier by Josiah Wedgwood.[86] These are thought to have been enclosed with books of illustrative engravings in pattern boxes of samples which were sent to retailers in England, on the Continent, and in the colonies. Although the earliest engravings and lists of 1767–1768 do not survive, those of Wedgwood's 1774 catalogue are extant, and many of Washington's requests for such items as scalloped and oval dishes, fish drainers, sugar dishes with ladles, sauce bowls, and sauceboats are found in the illustrations of the 1774 work.[87]

Josiah Wedgwood was designated "Potter to the Queen" by 1767, following royal approval of teawares he had supplied to Queen Charlotte, wife of George III. The Wedgwood firm first used the term "Queen's Ware" for its pale, cream-colored tableware in 1767 with the initiation of an innovative marketing campaign which soon reached the colonies. Writing in 1829 of the success of Wedgwood's product, Simeon Shaw stated, "Mr. W. had as many orders for Table Services of Queen's Ware, as he could possibly manufacture, and at prices the most liberal—fifteen shillings per dozen for table plates, and all other pieces in the same proportion."[88] Wedgwood himself wrote in 1767, "The demand for the . . . *Cream-colour*, alias *Queen's Ware*, alias *Ivory*, still increases. It is really amazing how rapidly the use has spread allmost over the whole globe, & how universally it is liked. How much of this general use & estimation is owing to the mode of its introduction, & how much to its real utility and beauty, are questions in which we may be a good deal interested for the Goverm[t] of our future conduct. . . . For instance, if a Royal or Noble introduction be as necessary to the sales of an article of Luxury as real Elegance & beauty, then the Manufacturer, if he consults his own inter[t], will bestow as much pains & expence too, if necessary, in gaining the favour of these advantages as he wo[d] in bestowing the latter. . . ."[89] By 1770, Wedgwood's queensware and the cream-colored products of his Staffordshire and Yorkshire competitors were frequently listed in newspaper advertisements and estate inventories throughout the American colonies. In Virginia in 1770, for example, Anthony Hay, proprietor of Williamsburg's Raleigh Tavern, died and left a service of "Queen's china" remarkably similar in number and variety of forms to Washington's list of 1769.[90]

The creamware body and glaze had been developed in the second quarter of the century by innovators such as Thomas and John Astbury, Thomas Wedgwood, and Enoch Booth. In the 1750s, Thomas Whieldon and his partner-apprentice Josiah Wedgwood made significant improvements in the color of the paste and in the reduction of lead content in the glaze. The same clays and flint used for saltglazed tablewares were processed in two firings rather

July ---------- 1769   (37)

Invoice of Goods to be sent (under the Restriction's mentioned
in the Letter annexed of this date) by Robt. Cary Esqr. & Co. for the use of Geo.
Washington - Potomack River - Virginia - viz -

1 Pint of Universal Balsam
4 oz. Salt of Wormwood
2 oz. Mercurius Dulcis
1 lb. Blistering Plaister
1 Quart Strong Cinnamon Water
1 Pint Spirit of Hartshorne
4 oz. of Salvolatili
4 Ditto of Spirit of Lavender
1 lb. of Powder of Jirin --
½ lb. Ipecacuanha
½ lb. powder'd Jallop
4 oz. of Rhubarb powdered
4 lb. of Brimstone in powder
Two Shillings worth of black (Court or
    Sticking) Plaister
25 lb. of Whiting .... 9 lb. of Fig Blew.
4 oz. of Cinnamon ... 4 oz. of Cloves
4 do. of Nutmegs ... 4 do. of Mace
1 lb. of Allspice ..... 1 Gal. of best Sa. Oil
6 ½ lb. Bottles of best Mustard
6 Papers best Ink powder
5 ps. brown Rolls .... a 5d.
1 ps. best Oznabrigs --
1 ps. Russia Drill
2 ps. Irish Linnen a 1/.
4 ps. Do. Do. - 2/.
60 Ells of as good white Russia Sheeting
    as can be bought for 2/. p Yard.
2 lb. of fine white brown Thread
4 oz. of 6d Ditto ... 4 oz. of 8d. Do.
4 oz. of 12d Do. ... 4 oz. of 15 Do.
12 ps. fine Tape ½ Inch wide.
1 Groce flat shirt Buttons
6 fine Search bottoms
3 M. Cork p Pins ... 3 M. short wh. 2 Do.
2 M. Minikin Do.
500 best doub'd Needles -100 p w. ch. to be
    Qr. by Nest sorted from No. 6 to 10
2 oz. black Sewing Silk
4 fine Iron Combs ... 6 finer horn Do.
1 doz. Course Ivory Do. -4 Comb brushes -
2 best kind of Tooth Brushes -
1 Sett of Weavers Brushes -
2 ... Womens best Jean Stays - p Meas.
2 black Russel quilted Coat. -
1 ps. dark colour'd 6/4 Duffield not to be
    exceed 2/6. p Yard.
5 doz. p best p Hose No. 5.
4 doz. p best Do. Do. No. 4
13 Groce best Corks
9 lb. Plain & strong steel Nut Crakers
1 best Bell Mettle Skillet to hold 3 Qu. .
1 Do. Do. Do. to hold 2 Do.

1 large hunt'g Horn bound tight round a
    ... brass Wire from one end to the other
    & so in such a man. as to prev'g Wires slip
50 best Sack Bags Mark'd GW & p Yard hose
1 ps. Purple grounded Callicoe glazed with
    white to be pretty & not to exceed 2½. p Y.
6 Middle siz'd plated Stock Locks - a 9/.
1 Knife Basket lined with Tin
6 large & very strong Gardners Spades
10 lb. seiz Twine
    The following Assortment of ye most
    Fash. kind of Queen's Ware - to wit -
6 doz. shall. Plates .... 3 doz. Soup Do.
1 doz. Dessert Ditto ...
16 Oval Dishes of 4 Sizes
4 round Ditto of 2 Do.
4 Scollop'd Ditto of D. D.
4 Oval Baking Dishes
2 large Fish Drainers
2 large Tureens & Covers
4 Sauce Bowls with Stands & Covers
4 Sauce Boats ... 2 Sallad Dishes
6 fruit Dishes   12 fluted Egg Cups
2 Sugar Dishes & Ladles
2 Porringers with Stands .
6 Potting Pots of diff. sizes
12 Leaves or Shells for Pickles
1 Bottle Mug .   2 Quart Do.
2 ... Ditto   4 ½ Pint Do.
2 sett of breakfast Cups, Saucers an
    Coffee Cups of a large kind (1 doz. eac
    ... was loose ... Tea Pot &c. of high as ..
As handsome a fowling Piece & a ...
    in of Barbados can be bo. for 5 Guin.

                    Invoice of Goods to be sen
to Mr. Jos. Valentine on York River for
the use of Geo. Washington - viz -

        150 Yds. of Cotton - best kind
        150 Ells best Oznabrigs
        5 lb. brown Thread
        1 doz. p plaid hose. No. 4
        1 doz. p Do. Do. No. 5
        4 plated Stock Locks - a 3/.
        5 M. 8d. Nails - 5 M. 10d. Ditto

                Go. Washington

                July 25th. 1769.

661

Pl.7

36. Plate seven from Wedgwood's 1774 catalogue of Queen's Ware. Washington seemed to refer to a similar catalogue or list when he ordered twenty-two forms in "ye most fashᵉ kind of Queen's Ware" in July 1769. Included were tureens and covers, salad dishes, and "fluted egg cups." (Courtesy, Josiah Wedgwood and Sons, Ltd., Barlaston, Stoke-on-Trent)

than one—with a transparent, fluid, lead glaze added at the biscuit stage. Unlike saltglazed wares, which could only be colored by skillful enameling, creamware—like porcelain—could take underglaze transfer-printing and coloring which produced attractive, varied patterns with relatively low labor costs. English creamware was considerably cheaper than the increasingly standardized blue-and-white Chinese porcelains of the same period. For example, a dozen creamware breakfast cups and saucers cost George Washington only a shilling in 1770 while the same number of breakfast cups in blue-and-white porcelain had cost him fourteen shillings in 1765.

Washington may have been thinking of Wedgwood products when he ordered the most fashionable kind of queensware in July 1769, but he received 249 pieces of "fine Cream col^d . . . Earth W," according to the accompanying invoice. Richard Farrer's use of the general term could mean that some or all of Washington's creamware service was made in a factory other than that of Wedgwood at Burslem. Differences between Washington's requests and Farrer's responses indicate that the London dealer made up the order from stock in his shop. He was apparently unable to supply the scalloped dishes and porringers or broth bowls ordered by Washington, whereas Wedgwood's 1774 catalogue illustrated both forms. An unsolicited round fish drainer was sent instead of the scalloped dishes and a dozen pierced egg cups instead of the fluted ones desired by the Washingtons. Six potting pots had been ordered, but eight were shipped—perhaps to compensate for the missing porringers. Everything else was shipped as Washington had instructed, and mustard pots, pepper casters, and butter dishes were added at Farrer's discretion.

The only known piece of creamware with a Washington provenance is a fruit basket and stand in the Lewis Collection at the Smithsonian Institution. Farrer's invoice listed eight "Fruit Dishes and stands cut" among the other creamware forms shipped in January 1770. The term "cut" does not really seem appropriate for the molded basketwork elements of the Washington piece, but Farrer may have used it in the sense of "open." An open, woven basket is one of

several designs for fruit dishes found in the Wedgwood drawing book of 1804 and in the queensware catalogue of 1774. These designs are similar but not identical to the basket in the Lewis Collection.

One fragment of a feather-edge, creamware plate has been found at Mount Vernon. The deep, yellow-tan tint of the paste points to a source other than the Wedgwood factory, which used clays that fired to a lighter cream color. Other English factories known to have made creamware in the 1760s include the Rothwell, Dennison, Swinton, Kilnhurst, and Rotherham works in Yorkshire; the Turner and Whieldon factories in Staffordshire; and the Cock Pit Hill and Melbourne establishments in Derbyshire.[91] The well-known factory of Hartly and Greens in Leeds, to which so much eighteenth-century creamware is attributed, did not commence manufacturing until 1770 or later and, therefore, could not have been a source for the January 1770 shipment to Mount Vernon.[92]

English ceramics historians have attempted to assign feather-edge creamware to individual factories by matching the configuration of the feather barbs to fragments found at several manufacturing sites.[93] Of the feather borders thus identified, those from the Melbourne site most closely match the fragment found at Mount Vernon. The evidence is inconclusive, however, since wasters from other factories were apparently brought to the Melbourne grounds to facilitate drainage. It is also known that potters would make up orders with goods from other factories and that they would sell unfired wares to each other.[94]

Queensware or "Queen's China" was ordered again for Mount Vernon in the summers of 1770 and 1771. Washington must have liked the "handled" coffee cups which came earlier in 1770, because he specified small tea cups with handles to supplement the larger, presumably handleless, breakfast cups of the previous shipment. A half-dozen creamware salts and seventeen bowls in sizes ranging from one-half pint to two gallons were also sent. In 1771, cream-colored mugs and "Wash Basons & Bottles"—the latter for bedroom use—were added.

Washington purchased queensware during the Revolution

37. Creamware pickle leaf, English, ca. 1770. Washington's large order
for "Queen's Ware" in July 1769 included the request for twelve "Leaves
or shells for Pickles." Farrer and Garrett supplied a dozen "pickle leaves"
for three shillings, sixpence. The creamware leaf illustrated is a contemporary example. (Courtesy, Colonial Williamsburg Foundation)

38. English creamware fruit basket and stand, ca. 1769. Josiah Wedgwood referred to such pieces as "Twiggen baskets" in a letter of June 24, 1772, to his partner, Thomas Bentley, but this piece does not match known Wedgwood examples and catalogue illustrations, which always include a middle row of lashing. The basket is the only intact object remaining from Washington's many purchases of creamware—invariably termed "Queens Ware" or "Queens China" in his correspondence. Two "Fruit Dishes and stands cut" were sent to Mount Vernon by Richard Farrer in January 1770, and there were six fruit baskets listed among the furnishings acquired for the New York headquarters in 1776. Diameter of stand: 8½ inches; diameter of basket: 7½ inches; height of basket: 2½ inches. (Lewis Collection, The National Museum of American History, Smithsonian Institution)

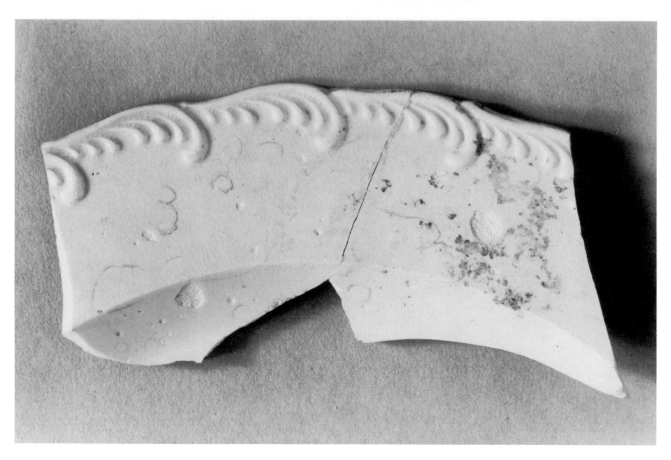

39. Fragment of English creamware plate, ca. 1767. Found at Mount Vernon. Washington ordered six dozen "Queens Ware" plates and three dozen soup plates from Robert Cary in July 1769. Although creamware continued to be purchased for Mount Vernon into the 1790s, the yellow tint of the paste in this fragment points to an early date and to the probability that it was made by a manufacturer other than Wedgwood. Length: 4¼ inches. (The Mount Vernon Ladies' Association collections)

40. George Washington in the uniform of a colonel in the Virginia militia, painted by Charles Willson Peale in 1772. (Washington–Custis–Lee Collection, Washington and Lee University) ▶

for use in several headquarters. It was also supplied for his presidential table in New York in 1789. That this ware continued to be used at Mount Vernon through the last decade of the century is revealed by entries in the cash memoranda kept by Washington's managers in 1791 and possibly as late as 1793.

LAST SHIPMENTS FROM CARY

In addition to the creamware mugs and basins mentioned above, "Dutch Chamber Potts" were sent by Farrer in December 1771 in response to Washington's request for "Stone Chamberpots." These were probably the gray-and-blue Westerwald products described previously rather than tin-enameled, delft earthenwares.

The repeated necessity for replacement of tea and coffee articles was reflected in Washington's final ceramic orders to Robert Cary and Company in 1772 for breakfast-size and smaller tea cups, breakfast and smaller coffee cups, tea pots, milk pots, sugar dishes, and slop bowls, "the whole to be of the same kind of China, of a fash'e but not of a costly sort. . . ." In response, Farrer supplied a "Comp¹ Sett Tea Equipage" with eight coffee cups and saucers and a "Comp¹ Sett Breakfast Dᵒ" also with eight coffee cups and saucers for £ 5. The pattern of both sets was designated "fine Landsᶜ," which probably was one of the many blue-and-white variations found today on fragments unearthed at Mount Vernon. "Landscape" and "New Landscape," based on Chinese prototypes, became standard blue-printed designs which were listed in the Caughley–Worcester account books of the next decade.[95]

Ceramics in use at Mount Vernon in the years just before the Revolution included a variety of English and German stonewares for table, kitchen, and bedroom; utilitarian redwares for kitchen and farm; creamware and perhaps white stoneware for daily table use; Chinese porcelains in polychrome and blue and white for table, tea, and breakfast; and ornamental English porcelain candlesticks and figures. With the exception of a few local purchases, all wares came from London or Bristol in exchange for tobacco shipped from Washington's plantations. The pivotal events of the next decade would bring about profound changes in buying patterns, availability, and taste—both for the Washingtons and for the newly united colonies.

III

THE WAR YEARS,

1774 TO 1783

"...I have asked Mrs. Cockran [sic]
and Mrs. Livingston to dine with me to
morrow; but ought I not to apprise them
of their fare?

...Since our arrival at this happy
spot, we have had a Ham (sometimes a
shoulder) of Bacon, to grace the head of
the table; a piece of roast Beef adorns
the foot; and, a small dish of Greens or
Beans (almost imperceptable) decorates
the center.

When the Cook has a mind to cut a
figure . . . we have two Beef-stake-Pyes,
or dishes of Crabs in addition, one on each side the center dish,
dividing the space, and reducing the distance between dish and
dish to about Six feet, which without them, would be near twelve
a part. Of late, he has had the surprizing segacity to discover
that apples will make pyes; and it's a question if, amidst the
violence of his efforts, we do not get one of apples instead of
having both of Beef.

If the ladies can put up with such entertainment, and will
submit to partake of it on plates once tin but now Iron; (not
become so by the labor of Scowering) I shall be happy to see
them. . . ." [From George Washington at West Point to Doctor
John Cochran, August 16, 1779 (W 16: 116–17)]

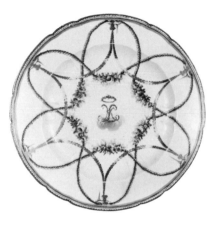

41. Plate from a service manufactured ca.
1780 for the Count de Custine at the Niderviller
factory. The gold-and-enamel decoration and the
composition of the central cipher on Custine's
plate is strikingly similar to the same elements
on the tea and coffee service presented by him
to the Washingtons in 1782 (see figs. 48–51,
54–56). (Courtesy, Musée des Arts Décoratifs,
Strasbourg)

George Washington settled his personal account with his London merchant in 1772 and never again imported ceramic tableware for Mount Vernon directly from England, although tobacco continued to be shipped to Robert Cary and Company for the Custis estates until 1774. As Washington's importance in colonial and revolutionary affairs grew, new sources for household furnishings became available to him in the urban markets of Philadelphia and New York. His accounts for Mount Vernon in September 1774, for example, included a long list of clothing, furniture, and other "sundries" purchased during his trip "to the Congress at Phil[a]."[96]

Local opportunities for furnishing Mount Vernon also existed in the years just prior to the Revolution. Isolated purchases of "Butter Boats" and "Coffee Cupps," possibly found in Williamsburg, were recorded in 1774 and 1775. Because of George William Fairfax's complicated inheritance and his and his wife's poor health, their return to England in 1774 enabled the Washingtons to acquire household furnishings and "Utensils &c." worth over £ 200 at

A View of the present Seat of his Excel. the Vice-President of the United States.

42. View of Richmond Hill, engraved by Cornelius Tiebout (1773–1832) for *New York Magazine*, June 1790. During the spring and summer of 1776, General and Mrs. Washington occupied this house, which then belonged to Abraham Mortier, paymaster general of British forces in America. (Courtesy, The New-York Historical Society, New York City)

43. Advertisement for Frederick and Philip Rhinelander's store in *Rivington's New York Gazetteer*, January 13, 1774. In April and May 1776, the Rhinelanders supplied quantities of creamware and two china bowls for Washington's headquarters in Mortier's house at the present Varick and Charlton streets in New York. Frederick Rhinelander, a loyalist, continued to receive wares from London and to advertise during the British occupation. (Courtesy, The New-York Historical Society, New York City)

LOOKING-GLASSES,

China, Glass and Earthen Ware,
A large and very elegant Assortment, to be sold,

At Rhinelander's Store

At the Corner of Burling's-Slip, just come to Hand, by the Dutchess of Gordon, Capt. Winn, and now opening,

LOOKING-GLASSES of all sizes, from 2l. to 14l. each; china ware, blue and white cups and saucers of all sizes; burnt and enamel'd ditto; blue and white sugar dishes & milk pots; burnt and enamel'd ditto; blue and white tea setts compleat; burnt and enamel'd ditto; blue and white table setts ditto; blue and white bowls of different sizes; burnt and enamel'd ditto, from half a pint to two gallons.

Also a large assortment of Glass Ware, by the Ellen, Capt. Clarke, from Bristol,

Decanters, cut, engraved and plain of all sizes; wine glasses ditto; tumblers of all sizes; quart, pint and half pint cans; caster frames and bottles; plain, engraved, cut and top'd with silver; earthen ware, a large and very general assortment. Ready money, for all kinds of shipping furrs and bees-wax. Also, common Bristol ware, and one and two quart bottles.

two sales held at the Fairfaxes' neighboring estate, Belvoir, in August and December. The sale inventory listed a small "lot of Queen's china" which Washington, by far the major buyer, may have added to the creamware service originally purchased in 1769;[97] however, there is no actual record of his acquiring Belvoir's queensware.

As impending war became a reality in 1775, Washington's attention to the furnishing of his Virginia table diminished. Although he added a spacious dining-room wing to Mount Vernon during the war, there are no records of purchases of ceramics for his own house until his last days as commander in chief in the autumn of 1783. There was no lack of attention, however, to the appointments for the commander's table at several headquarters during his eight years of service. Throughout that period, Washington maintained an account of his expenses for equipment, travel—including that of Mrs. Washington—entertaining, and household purchases in lieu of payment for services. The final settlement of the account, totaling $160,074, was made by Congress in December 1783.[98] Most expenditures for furnishings and food were supervised by four stewards: Ebenezer Austin, the first year; Maj. Caleb Gibbs with Mrs. Mary Smith, the housekeeper, in New York; and after September 1781, Lt. William Colfax.[99]

The accounts were not always itemized, but several receipts and a few entries pertaining to the spring and summer of 1776 in New York included extensive ceramic purchases. The accounts and receipts reveal a high level of comfort in dining and furnishings for the Washington household in the early months of the conflict, and the maintenance of a "tolerably genteel" table at headquarters in the later peaceful intervals.

44. Advertisement for George Ball's store in the *New York Journal or General Advertiser*, August 3, 1775. Ball supplied fine china tearwares including two sets "burnt china cups & saucers" and wine glasses and decanters to the commander in chief's household, according to the furniture account under the date May 14, 1776. (Courtesy, The New-York Historical Society, New York City)

When the center of the American war effort transferred from Boston to New York in April 1776, "a spacious house with large stables" was procured for the commander in chief and Mrs. Washington, who followed her husband from Massachusetts to spend at least a month with him in New York. The porticoed structure at the corner of the present Varick and Charlton streets then belonged to Abraham Mortier, paymaster general of British forces in America. Later known as Richmond Hill, Mortier's house became the official residence of Vice President John Adams in 1789. At that time, the architecture and the verdant, rural setting with a fine view of the Hudson were described enthusiastically by Abigail Adams in a letter to her sister, Mary Cranch.[100] It is thought that Washington, with a trip to Philadelphia in May and June, resided at Mortier's until September 1776, when he moved to the Morris–Jumel mansion at 160th Street.

The first purchases made by the housekeeper, Mary Smith, for Washington's New York quarters included a carpet, mahogany knife cases, and a damask tablecloth. In April, James Deas supplied a featherbed, bolster, and pillows as well as a tureen, eight china mugs, and two dozen plates; in May, three inexpensive fruit baskets were recorded under "bot at Sundry Places."

In the same months, glass and china merchants Frederick and Philip Rhinelander sold numerous creamware and earthenware table, kitchen, and bedroom items to the general's housekeeper. The prices on the Rhinelander list of wares supplied to Washington are those appropriate for creamware dishes, sauceboats, plates, and fluted bowls, with three relatively more expensive "china" bowls. Rhinelander's store at the "corner of Burling's Slip"—Golden Hill and Water streets—sold glass and china until May 1786, when they advertised that they were "selling off at a very low rate" and that the premises were to be rented.[101] The Rhinelanders' letterbook of 1774–1783, preserved at the New-York Historical Society, reveals the loyalist sympathies of the firm in copies of letters sent to English merchants with orders for earthenware, glassware, china, buttons, and hardware.[102] One of the correspondents included in the letterbook was Anthony Keeling of Burslem, son-in-law and successor to Enoch Booth, the developer of the leadglazing process in the manufacture of creamware.[103]

Advertisements in the New York newspapers of the 1770s reveal that much of the Rhinelanders' trade was in Oriental "China ware," especially "blue and white" and "burnt and enamel'd" china imported from London. A competitor, George Ball, also advertised "blue and white," "pencil'd," and especially "Burnt" Chinese porcelains.[104] Ball sold "burnt china cups & saucers" and a bowl with other fine tewares and glassware to the Washington household in May 1776. Apparently indicating the presence of gilding, references to "Burnt" china occur in American inventories as early as 1747 in Boston.[105] Josiah Wedgwood wrote in 1765 of ". . . gold to be burnt in, as it is upon the Chelsea china or secur'd with a varnish only. . . ."[106] The Rhinelanders' advertisement of 1774 used the phrase "burnt and enamel'd" to describe wares that were different from "blue and white" and to describe two decorative processes. In other words, "burnt" and "enamel'd" were not necessarily synonymous. The term "burnt and enamel'd" china may have referred to Chinese Imari ware with red enamels and gold added over blue underglaze designs. American archeologists think that many of the blue-and-white ceramic artifacts excavated at eighteenth-century sites originally bore red-and-gold overglaze decorations which have disappeared into the soil.[107]

"A SETT OF QUEENS CHINA"

Washington's "burnt china" tewares from George Ball and his creamware table service from Frederick Rhinelander were noted on the furniture-account document at an unknown later date as having been almost entirely lost through breakage. Whether the china traveled with him from camp to camp after the evacuation of New York in the fall of 1776 is not known. There are no further references to ceramics in his papers until February 1779, when he was settled "in peaceable quarters" at Middlebrook, New Jersey, after a month with Mrs. Washington in Philadelphia. John Mitchell, deputy quartermaster general, was asked to procure "a sett of Queens China if to be had . . . [since Washington's] plates and dishes, once of Tinn, now little better than rusty iron, are rather too much worn for delicate stomachs. . . ."

One of the delicate stomachs in question was that of Lady Kitty Stirling, wife of Maj. Gen. William Alexander. Lord Stirling was an American-born Whig whose earldom was recognized by Scottish law, but never accepted by the House of Lords. Lady Stirling informed General Washington of the availability of queensware at New Brunswick after Mitchell complained of the difficulty of finding such English products in Philadelphia. Q.M. Gen. Nathaneal Green was then asked to look for a "sett of Queens Ware" in New Brunswick, but Mitchell finally was able to procure it from two sources in Philadelphia. The exorbitant prices paid to Henry Pratt and Deborah and Hanah Mitchel—£ 12 for one tureen, for example—for Washington's tableware attest to the inflationary effects of the war and to the scarcity of English manufactured goods. The queensware service of seven dozen instead of the originally ordered eight dozen plates eventually followed Washington, sometime after March 1782, to the headquarters established at Newburgh, New York, just above West Point, after March 1782.[108] Queensware serving dishes were also purchased in Philadelphia in December 1781, according to the accounts kept by Lieutenant Colfax.

The winter of 1781–82 in Philadelphia had been peaceful and socially exuberant, with theatrical entertainments, illuminations, and banquets reflecting the success of the French alliance. The Washingtons were lodged at 110 South Third Street, the new house of their friend Benjamin Chew, where they often received and entertained visitors.[109] Their queensware plates and serving dishes, which undoubtedly saw heavy use there, continued to serve the Philadelphia diplomatic community for several months after the general and his lady moved to Newburgh in March. It was not until July that the tableware was forwarded from Philadelphia by Col. Samuel Miles and, even then, Washington complained tersely that there was a "deficiency I expect to receive by the first opportunity. . . ."[110] Miles replied that

Francisco Rendon, the Spanish agent in Philadelphia, "gave an entertainment a day or two after you had left the City, and . . . his Stewart had made use of those dishes, plates etc and had also lent part of them to the Minister of France's [Chevalier de la Luzerne] Stewart. . . ."[111] The vicissitudes of Washington's dishes and plates parallel accounts of festive Philadelphia in the early 1780s where, as one visitor noted, the French Minister "has a Ball or a Concert every week and his house full to dinner every day. . . ."[112]

The camp at Newburgh was sociable and evidently quite comfortable. Nancy Shippen Livingston wrote in June 1782 that she breakfasted there with Mrs. Washington and later dined with Lord Stirling's daughter, Lady Kitty Duer.[113] Mrs. Washington apparently left Newburgh shortly thereafter, for she was at Mount Vernon on July 20 to receive an entourage of French officers for dinner.

The last few ceramic purchases made for the "Commander-in-Chief's Table" in Newburgh included "1 Large China Tea Pott (red)." There were advertisements in New York in 1772 for red "china" teapots. There were others in Philadelphia in 1771 for "Red Engine lath China"; in 1777 for "embossed red China"; and in 1784 for "red teapots."[114] Traditional Chinese red stoneware teapots thought to brew exceptionally fine tea were exported from Yi-hsing to Europe beginning in the middle of the sixteenth century.[115] These were soon copied in The Netherlands, Germany, and England and continued to be popular through the eighteenth and early nineteenth centuries.[116] Such stoneware teapots were often polished, embellished with applied prunus or plum blossom motifs, or carved in repetitive, linear patterns by an engine-turned lathe.

A "PRESENT OF ELIGANT CHINA"

While Washington counted queensware at his headquarters in Newburgh in the summer of 1782, Martha Washington —having returned to Mount Vernon—extended a dinner invitation to a titled French porcelain manufacturer and nine other French officers who were encamped at Alexandria.[117] Adam Philibert—or Philippe—Count de Custine-

45. General Washington's headquarters at Newburgh, New York. Drawn and engraved by James Smillie (1833–1909). (The Historical Society of Pennsylvania)

Sarreck was commander of the Saintonge regiment of Rochambeau's army in the American campaign of 1780 through 1782. He was also proprietor of the porcelain and faience factory at Niderviller—sometimes spelled Niederweiler or Neidwiller—near Strasbourg. By the date of his visit to Mrs. Washington, Custine had known Washington for at least a year and a half, as revealed in the latter's letter from New Windsor, New York, to the Count de Rochambeau in January 1781.[118]

In 1770, Custine had purchased the Niderviller factory from its founder, Baron Jean-Louis de Beyerlé, and with Claude-François Lanfrey he continued the manufacture of hard-paste porcelain tableware begun there in 1765. When Lorraine became part of France in 1766, the Sèvres porce-

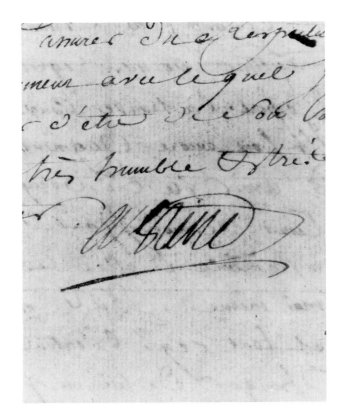

46. The Count de Custine (d. 1793), commander of the Saintonge regiment, stands third from the left in John Trumbull's historical painting of the surrender of Lord Cornwallis on October 19, 1781. Trumbull (1756–1843) painted the portraits of the French officers into the composition in 1787 in Paris, where he lived temporarily with Thomas Jefferson. (Yale University Art Gallery)

47. Signature of the Count de Custine on the second page of a letter written to General Washington, October 22, 1782. (Courtesy, The Library of Congress)

48. French porcelain sugar bowl, Niderviller, ca. 1779–1780. The tea and coffee service presented to Mrs. Washington at Mount Vernon on July 20, 1782, by the Count de Custine was probably decorated in France just before the titled porcelain manufacturer embarked with his regiment to fight in the American Revolution. General Washington's monogram in tooled gold appears on a cloud below a wreath of roses, a motif also used by Custine on a service decorated with his own cipher. Niderviller forms and decoration were influenced by the work of the Hannongs' Strasbourg factory, also in eastern France. Delicate flowers in colors and molded flowers and fruit applied as finials are similar on wares from the two establishments and on comparable German products. Overall height: 5¼ inches. (Private collection)

49. Mark in overglaze black enamel on bottom of Niderviller sugar bowl. The Count de Custine's cipher is painted above a number which corresponds to the pattern of floral swags and gilt scrollwork. A "K" incised near the painted mark is one of at least seven incised craftsmen's marks visible on several pieces of Washington's first French service.

50. French porcelain slop bowl, Niderviller, ca. 1779–1780. Decorated in pattern "No. 29" to match the sugar bowl, the slop bowl or basin was used for dregs and for rinsing cups at the tea table. This bowl and the sugar bowl descended through Martha Washington's granddaughter, Martha Parke Custis Peter, who may have acquired them in a division of property before the public sale in July 1802. The inventory made after Mrs. Washington's death listed "1 sett G.W." tea china at a value of $30. Marks: enameled $\frac{x}{N.29}$; incised $\mathrm{I}\backslash$. Height: 4¼ inches; diameter: 8 inches. (The Mount Vernon Ladies' Association collections)

lain privileges applied to Beyerlé's production and, consequently, he was restricted to single-color decoration and was prevented from selling porcelain figures. That situation had prompted the sale of the factory to Custine, whose position and title enabled him to circumvent the restrictions.[119]

The Count de Custine's later history included his return in 1783 to France, where he published several "Opinions" about military and political matters. In 1792, after renouncing his title, he was made commander of the army of the Rhine. Lack of success against the Prussians, however, and an unwise offense to Robespierre's Committee of Public Safety condemned him to the guillotine on August 28, 1793.

After Custine's death, the Niderviller factory was confiscated by the French government and subsequently sold to Lanfrey. With some interruptions, production has continued, and the factory is now part of a group of northern French faience manufacturers.

Claude Blanchard, commissary of the French forces in America, accompanied the Count de Custine to Mrs. Washington's dinner at Mount Vernon and recorded the occasion in his campaign journal kept from 1780 through 1782:

On [July] 20th 1782 we stopped at Alexandria, a city situated upon the Potomac, where ships of fifty guns can approach. . . . General Washington's residence is situated between Colchester and Alexandria. Mrs. Washington had arrived there the evening before. She invited M. de Custine, who commanded the division to which I was attached, to go and dine at her house with some officers. He proposed to me to go thither and we proceeded thither, to the number of ten persons. Mrs. Washington is a woman of about fifty years of age; she is small and fat, her appearance is respectable. She was dressed very plainly and her manners were simple in all respects; she had with her three other ladies, her relations. As to the house it is a country residence, the handsomest that I have yet seen in America, it is symmetrically built and has two stories, counting the false roofs, wherein some pretty chambers have been constructed. All the rooms are furnished with taste. . . . In the evening, we left her respectable company after having spent a very agreeable and truly interesting day. . . .[120]

Another French journalist, Baron von Closen, wrote of the visit that "M. de Bellegarde preceded him [M. de Custine], to bring on behalf of the Count, a very beautiful porcelain service from the latter's own factory at Niderviller (near Phalsbourg). It was designed in the latest style, *with General Washington's arms and monogram under a crown of laurels.*"[121]

Presentations or gifts of porcelain, an established custom among the aristocratic French, were made to Benjamin Franklin and other Americans in Paris. A gift of Sèvres cups was also sent to the Robinson family in Newport by the Viscountess de Noailles in 1783.[122] Custine's gift to the Washingtons, however, was the single known instance of eighteenth-century porcelain personalized for an American recipient by its French manufacturer.

The decoration of the Washington tea and coffee service is peculiar in that the enameled and gilt borders of ribbons, swags, garlands, bands, and trellises or scrolls vary from piece-to piece. The unifying element in the decoration is the central "GW" cipher on a cloud beneath a wreath of roses. The service appears to be a sampler of decorative schemes available at the Niderviller factory in 1780, the year Custine sailed from Brest with his regiment. The cipher and borders resemble parallel design elements on a service made for the proprietor himself. A plate in the Musée des Arts Decoratifs in Strasbourg displays the Custine cipher on a cloud with a chaplet or wreath above and border motifs of floral garlands and ropes.[123]

Existing pieces at Mount Vernon, the Smithsonian Institution, and in private collections are marked in black enamel with a cipher of crossed "c's" and numbers ranging from nine to fifty-six. A similar mark—without the numbers—was used by the Ludwigsburg factory, 150 kilometers east of Niderviller, and the products of the two factories are frequently confused. Ludwigsburg, however, marked their product in underglaze blue or, rarely, in overglaze red. Washington's Niderviller teawares also display several unidentified incised marks.

The painted number occurring next to the factory mark on each piece correlates with its border pattern. This correlation was identified by the few instances of duplicate borders and numbers. A sugar box in a private collection and a bowl at Mount Vernon are both decorated with pattern number twenty-nine: floral festoons, gilt scrollwork, and pink bands interrupted by rosettes. Pattern number nineteen is a border of bold, floral running scrolls which appears on a covered cream or milk jug at Mount Vernon and a bowl at the Smithsonian's National Museum of American History. Through the years cups have been separated from saucers so that a curious mixture of colors and borders results. In addition to the two 8-inch bowls, the sugar box, and the milk or cream jug already mentioned, several teabowls and coffee cups with appropriate saucers, and two 8½-inch plates have been preserved.

The Niderviller tea and coffee service was not mentioned in Martha Washington's will, but it was listed as "1 sett G.W. china" valued at thirty dollars in the 1802 inventory of Mount Vernon furnishings. Mrs. Washington is known to have given pieces of it to family, friends, and visitors during her lifetime. The cream jug, for example, was owned at one time by Dolley Madison, and other pieces have been returned to Mount Vernon by descendants of families to whom they were given by Mrs. Washington.[124]

General Washington did not see Custine's "present of eligant China" until he returned to Mount Vernon in December 1783; however, from headquarters at Newburgh in 1782, he sent a gracious letter of thanks for the service, "which as the product of your own Estate, I shall consider of inestimable value."[125]

A "Neat and Compleat Sett of Blue and White Table China"

The commander in chief's table continued to serve a stream of visitors to the Newburgh headquarters. In May 1783, another four dozen queensware plates and a dozen china cups and saucers were added to the stock on hand. These were acquired from Daniel Parker, merchant and auctioneer in the British-occupied city of New York.

With the news of peace and the convening of Congress at Princeton, Washington moved his headquarters to Rock-

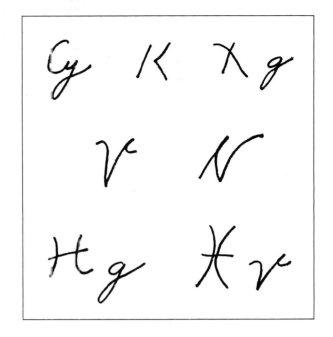

51. Incised marks on the Niderviller tea and coffee service presented to the Washingtons by the Count de Custine. (The Mount Vernon Ladies' Association collections and a private collection)

52. French porcelain teabowls and saucers, Niderviller, ca. 1779–1780. The teabowl and saucer at the left were given to Frances Dandridge Henley, third wife of Tobias Lear, by her aunt, Martha Washington. The cup bears pattern "No. 42" while the saucer displays pattern "No. 27." The other teabowl and saucer, acquired by the Mount Vernon Ladies' Association from the Peter family, are both decorated by pattern "No. 49." Marks: $\frac{X}{N.27}$ enameled $\mathcal{V}$ incised on left saucer; $\frac{X}{N^o 42}$ enameled on left cup; $\frac{X}{N^o 49}$ enameled $\mathcal{V}$ incised on right saucer; $\frac{X}{N^o 49}$ enameled on right cup. Height of cups: 2 inches; diameter of cups: 3 inches; diameter of saucers: 5¼ inches. (The Mount Vernon Ladies' Association collections)

53. French porcelain coffee cups and saucers, Niderviller, ca. 1779–1780. These cups and saucers bearing patterns "No. 21" and "No. 20" respectively were acquired from descendants of Martha Parke Custis Peter. The two border designs are composed of neoclassical foliate scrollwork which is also seen on tea- and coffeewares made by contemporary Parisian factories and on engraved source sheets of the period. Marks: $\frac{X}{N.21}$ enameled on left cup and saucer; $\mathcal{N}$ incised on left saucer; $\mathcal{V}$ incised on left cup; $\frac{X}{N^o 20}$ enameled on right cup and saucer; $\mathcal{V}$ incised on right cup. Height and diameter of cups: 2 inches; diameter of saucers: 4¾ inches. (The Mount Vernon Ladies' Association collections)

54. French porcelain slop bowl, Niderviller, ca. 1779–1780. Pattern "No. 19" of pink-and-gold floral volutes with blue triangles is enameled on one of two bowls in Custine's gift to Washington. This bowl was sold to the United States government in 1878 by the heirs of Eleanor Parke Custis Lewis, one of Mrs. Washington's three granddaughters. Diameter: 8 inches. (Lewis Collection, The National Museum of American History, Smithsonian Institution)

55. Mark enameled on bottom of slop bowl. No incised marks are visible.

◄ *56.* French porcelain cream jug, Niderviller, ca. 1779–1780. The painted decoration on this jug matches that on one of the slop bowls while the small, apple finial matches the same element on the cover of the sugar bowl. Traditionally, the jug was given to Dolley Madison by Mrs. Washington, who is known to have given several pieces of the Custine service away before she died. Mark: $\frac{x}{No_{19}}$; no incised marks. Overall height: 6¼ inches. (The Mount Vernon Ladies' Association collections)

57. Samuel Fraunces (ca. 1722–1795), keeper of the Queen's Head Tavern in New York. After "particular enquiry," Fraunces found an assortment of blue-and-white china for General Washington in September 1783. Later, he served President Washington as steward in New York and Philadelphia. (Fraunces Tavern Museum, New York City)

ingham at Rocky Hill, New Jersey. There, in early September, he gave a notable entertainment which was described by David Howell, a congressional delegate from Rhode Island: ". . . In consequence of a polite card from his Excellency the General, to his Excellency the President, the latter, with all the present members, Chaplains, and great officers of Congress, had the honor of dining at the General's Table

last Friday. The tables were spread under a marquis, or tent taken from the British. The repast was elegant but the General's Company crowned the whole. . . ."[126]

As the attention of American officers and troops turned toward their civilian futures, Washington began to search for a large set of chinaware for Mount Vernon. The units required were comparable in number to the earlier saltglazed and queensware services intended for daily use. He wrote to Daniel Parker in occupied New York and requested 'a neat and compleat sett of blue and White Table China" with six to eight dozen plates "and a proportionable number of Deep and other Plates, Butter Boats, Dishes and Tureens." Parker, a partner with William Duer and John Holker in a company formed to provision the Continental Army, turned to Samuel Fraunces, the West Indian proprietor of the Queen's Head Tavern in occupied New York. After "particular enquiry" Fraunces found 205 pieces of Chinese blue-and-white porcelain before September 18, although he could "find no compleat setts that are ready packed" as Washington had requested. With that apology and with the odd numbers of "Flatt, Soop, Dessert, and Froot" plates listed on the invoice, an assumption can be made that the china displayed a mixture of designs.

On September 18, Fraunces had also sent cut wine goblets, decanters, and two butter tubs to the Rocky Hill headquarters. The supplier was Edward Nicoll, Jr., whose father had advertised an interesting assortment of fashionable ceramics, glass, rum, and sugar "on the New-Dock" in New York in 1757.[127] It is possible that Nicoll also provided some, if not all, of the blue-and-white pieces listed by the tavernkeeper Fraunces for General Washington.

Daniel Parker shipped two barrels of "Earthen Ware" to Virginia on September 22, 1783, but, on the same day, Washington wrote to his nephew Bushrod Washington in Philadelphia to inquire about "compleat setts, amounting to a gross, or gross and a half of pieces, all kinds included" of blue-and-white table china. The numbers of plates found in New York were less than half of what Washington had requested, and his directive to Bushrod was probably for supplements. The response from Philadelphia is not pre-

58–61. Four Chinese porcelain meat dishes, made for the English market, ca. 1760–1775. Decorated at Ching-tê Chên in standard, underglaze-blue landscape scenes, these platters were probably among the "27 Dishes" assembled for General Washington by tavernkeeper Samuel Fraunces in New York in September 1783. Since "no compleat setts" could be found, a mixture of designs was sent to Mount Vernon. Three of the platters display elaborate borders composed of Chinese motifs such as the butterfly, *ju-i,* and t-pattern fret, with foliage and various diapers. Several of these elements were later combined into an underglaze border known to American collectors as "Fitzhugh." The border on the dish with an underglaze painting of pines and deer can be traced to continental European models dating to the first quarter of the eighteenth century, and the piece may have been in the April 1763 shipment to Mount Vernon of "Table China fine blue & white." The four dishes were sold to the United States government in 1878 by the heirs of Eleanor Custis Lewis, who inherited "all the blue and white china in common use" at Mount Vernon from her grandmother, Martha Washington. The landscape platters are 16 inches in length while the deer platter is 17 inches long. (Lewis Collection, The National Museum of American History, Smithsonian Institution)

served, but Washington's Ledger B recorded payments of thirty pounds in December 1783, and seven pounds in March 1784, to Bushrod Washington for "Sundries" in Philadelphia.

The variety of landscape designs on platters of the period preserved in the Lewis Collection at the Smithsonian Institution's National Museum of American History attests to the probable mixture of patterns on the Fraunces–Parker list with possible supplements from Philadelphia. Pieces of the 1783 blue-and-white porcelain table services were among the common wares listed "In the Closet under Franks direction" in the inventory made after General Washington's death.

In October 1783, Washington was still planning for future hospitality at Mount Vernon when he wrote to the Marquis de Lafayette in France for "Everything proper [in silver] for a tea-table" and stated in the same letter: "I do not incline to send to England (from whence formerly I had all my goods) for anything I can get upon tolerable terms elsewhere. . . ."[128] In late November, following the long-awaited evacuation of New York, the general "broke up housekeeping . . . discharged [his military] household," and marched into the city to receive the adulation of the citizens in speeches, fireworks, and elaborate banquets.[129] Due to the long British occupation, shops in New York could supply some of the furnishings and decorations sought for the enhancement of Mount Vernon. He purchased silver in both New York and Philadelphia in what he thought would be his "last moment . . . of public life," and departed southward on December 5, 1783, to return to domesticity and husbandry like the Roman hero Cincinnatus with whom he was so often compared.[130]

IV

CINCINNATI CHINA

AND

WORCESTER VASES,

1785 TO 1787

[November 16 and 17, 1785]
"At three, dinner was on table, and we were shewn by the General into another room, where everything was set off with a peculiar taste, and at the same time very neat and plain. The General sent the bottle about pretty freely after dinner, and gave success to the navigation of the Potomac for his toasts, which he has very much at heart. . . . the General absolutely insisted upon our staying on account of the bad afternoon. . . . I could not refuse the pressing and kind invitation of so great a General, tho' our greatest enemy, I admire him as superior even to the Roman heroes themselves. . . . After tea General Washington retired to his study and left us with the President [of Congress], his lady and the rest of the Company. If he had not been anxious to hear the news of Congress . . . most probably he would not have returned to supper, but gone to bed at his usual hour, nine o'clock, for he seldom makes any ceremony. We had a very elegant supper about that time. The General with a few glasses of champagne got quite merry, and being with his intimate friends laughed and talked a good deal. . . . At 12 I had the honor of being lighted up to my bedroom by the General himself. . . . I rose early and took a walk about the General's grounds . . . his greatest pride now is, to be thought the first

62. Chinese porcelain hexagonal planter, landscape scene painted in underglaze blue, ca. 775. According to family tradition, the planter was given to General Washington by his friend, Henry ("Light-Horse Harry") Lee. Height: 9¼ inches; width: 16 inches. (Feter family collection)

farmer in America. He is quite a Cincinnatus, and often works with his men himself. . . . The style of his house is very elegant, something like the Prince de Condé's at Chantille, near Paris, only not quite so large. . . . [He is] always keeping a genteel table for strangers, that almost daily visit him, as a thing of course. . . ." ["An Account of a Visit made to Washington at Mount Vernon, by an English Gentleman, in 1785. From the Diary of John Hunter," The Pennsylvania Magazine of History and Biography *17 (1893): 76–81]*

George Washington's most famous set of china, a Chinese porcelain table and tea service decorated with blue "Fitzhugh" borders and the arms of the Society of the Cincinnati in enamel colors, was acquired in a complicated context of events and people crucial to the history of America's newly opened East Indian trade. The Cincinnati services—Washingtons of 1784–1785 and several later ones—were intended for members of the Society of the Cincinnati, an hereditary order of French and American allied officers who had served in the Revolutionary War.

Actual organization of the Society took place in May 1783, when Washington was acclaimed "president general"

63. Membership certificate, The Society of the Cincinnati, drawn by
Augustin-Louis Belle (1757–1841) and engraved by Jean-Jacques Le Veau
(1729–1785) in Paris before the Society's first general meeting in Philadelphia in May 1784. The trumpeting figure of Fame at the right was a
motif also used by Samuel Shaw on the large Chinese porcelain service
purchased by Washington in 1786. Shaw's engravings of Fame, however,
were from a different source than that used by Belle. (Private collection)

and Henry Knox "secretary general." The idea for the Society was credited to General Knox by John Adams. On March 16, 1788, Thomas Jefferson wrote:

. . . Mr. Adams tells me that in the year 1776 he had called at a tavern in the state of N. York to dine, just at the moment when the British army was landing at Frog's Neck. Genls. Washington, Lee, Knox, and Parsons came to the same tavern. . . . They talked of ancient history, of Fabius, who used to raise the Romans from the dust, of the present contest &c. and Genl. Knox, in the course of conversation, said he would wish for some ribbon to wear in his hat or in his button hole, to be transmitted to his descendants as a badge and a proof that he had fought in defence of their liberties. He spoke of it in such precise terms as shewed he had resolved it in his mind before. . . .[131]

Jefferson, Adams, and Benjamin Franklin, who feared the creation of "an order of hereditary knights," immediately protested the elitist nature of the Society.[132] In March 1783, Lafayette wrote confidentially to Washington in response to the latter's concern about public opinion. "Most of the Americans here are indecently violent against our Association."[133] Washington may have had hesitations about the Society and its aristocratic tendencies, but his desire to recognize the honorable service of French and American officers with certificates and medals won out over the qualms expressed in his correspondence of the period.

"Ribands and Medals"

At the first meeting in 1783, appropriate iconography and mottoes for the membership certificates and badges—which came to be called Eagles—were adopted. The Roman citizen-soldier Lucius Quintus Cincinnatus, the American bald eagle, and the classical figure of Fame were selected as principal design elements for the mementoes to be presented to approved applicants.[134] The Continental Army's chief engineer, Maj. Pierre-Charles L'Enfant, who was also chief designer to the new nation, was assigned to procure the diplomas and badges in France. He had displayed his abilities by designing a spectacular fête in Philadelphia in 1782 for the Chevalier de la Luzerne. Later, in 1788, he would

create an enormous banquet pavilion in New York and, in 1791, a plan for the proposed Federal City on the Potomac.[135] L'Enfant's role in the design of the elaborate membership certificate is not certain. It was drawn by Augustin-Louis Belle (1757–1841) and engraved by Jean-Jacques Le Veau (1729–1875) in Paris, with the text added to the copper plate in Philadelphia by Robert Scott. However, L'Enfant did paint at least thirteen sketches of the proposed badge and ribbon, one for each chapter of the American Society. In Paris, during the fall and winter of 1783–84, he also supervised the fabrication of the first gold-and-enamel medallions, which were executed by goldsmiths Nicolas-Jean Francastel and Claude-Jean Autran Duval.[136] Lafayette noted in December that "Major Lenfant is employed in the execution of your [Washington's] orders. A good number of Eagles will be made in twelve days."[137] In January, Benjamin Franklin wrote from France that the "ribands and medals" had been "tolerably done."[138] The medals and certificates were ready for the first general meeting of the Society at Philadelphia the following May.[139]

"1 Sett of Cincinnati China"

After a few months at Mount Vernon, George Washington returned to Philadelphia in the spring of 1784 to preside over the first general meeting of the Society. While there, he purchased "a Cream Machine for ice" and twenty-two boxes of other manufactured goods which were sent to Mount Vernon.[140] The following year, however, he was still searching for blue-and-white china to supplement the service he had purchased from Daniel Parker in New York in 1783 when an advertisement in the *Maryland Gazette and Baltimore Advertiser* of August 12, 1785, offered a large assortment of blue-and-white and "painted" china with "Table Sets of the best Nankeen blue and white stone China" as well as "Evening blue and white stone China Cups and Saucers" and "evening" cups and saucers with "the Arms of the Order of the Cincinnati" in the cargo of the *Pallas* "direct from China." Washington wrote to his former military aide, Tench Tilghman, in Baltimore, and asked him to inquire about the conditions of sale and the prices. "If to be

64. Chinese porcelain soup plate, 1784–1785. The soup plate is one of 302 pieces in a service of "Cincinnati China" purchased in New York in 1786 by Henry ("Light-Horse Harry") Lee for George Washington, the president general of the Society of the Cincinnati. Samuel Shaw, who was the supercargo or mercantile agent on the *Empress of China*, the first American ship to enter the China trade—as well as a founding member of the Cincinnati organization—arranged for the application of the Society's Eagle with a winged figure of Fame on the porcelain in Canton. Large "table sets" or dinner services were given underglaze-blue borders at the Chinese manufacturing center, Ching-tê Chên, and then transported to Canton, where enameled decorations such as crests and arms were added in response to special orders from western traders. Armorial services with "Fitzhugh" borders identical to those on Washington's Cincinnati service are found in England. It is thought that one or more of these services, owned by the Fitzhugh family, who represented the English East India Company in Canton, inspired the popular name for the standard Chinese border pattern of butterflies, diaper, and plant forms used on export wares. Diameter: 9¾ inches. (The Mount Vernon Ladies' Association collections)

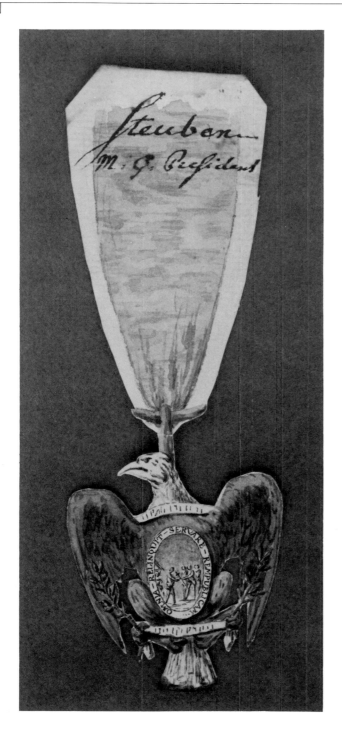

65. Insignia of the Society of the Cincinnati. Watercolor rendering by Pierre-Charles L'Enfant (1754–1825) of the proposed "Eagles." The signature at the top is that of Gen. Frederick William von Steuben (1730–1794), president of the organizing meeting for the Society, held May 10, 1783. It is believed that Samuel Shaw carried one of L'Enfant's designs to Canton aboard the *Empress of China*. Used as a model for the Chinese porcelain decorators in Canton in 1784 and 1785, this version —in which the eagle is suspended directly from its head—appears on Washington's Cincinnati service. (Courtesy, The Society of the Cincinnati)

66. Original insignia (obverse) of the Society of the Cincinnati, made in France in 1784 from dies destroyed at the time of the French Revolution. One of six Eagles ordered by General Washington for presentation to his aides-de-camp, this example was given to Col. Tench Tilghman of Maryland, volunteer aide and secretary to the general. The first Eagles were fabricated in Paris in the winter of 1783–84 and were ready for the Society's first general meeting, held in Philadelphia in May 1784. Both the obverse and reverse of the medals were copied on porcelains in Canton in the 1790s. (Courtesy, The Society of the Cincinnati)

TO BE SOLD,
By PUBLIC VENDUE,
At Baltimore, on the 1st of OCTOBER next, in
LOTS, the following GOODS, just imported
in the Ship PALLAS, direct from CHINA,—
HYSON TEAS of the first quality,
in quarter chests;
Hyson Tea, in canisters of 2¼lb. each;
Hyson Ditto, of the second quality in chests;
Confu Ditto, Ditto, in Ditto;
Hyson Skin, Ditto, Ditto;
Gunpowder, Ditto, Ditto;
Table Sets of the best Nankeen, blue and white
stone China;
Ditto of the second quality, Ditto;
Ditto, painted Ditto, Ditto;
Dishes of blue and white stone China, 5 and 3 in
a Set;
Flat and Soup Plates, Ditto,
Breakfast Cups and Saucers of the best blue and
white stone China, in Sets;
Evening Ditto, Ditto, Ditto;
Painted Ditto, Ditto, Ditto;
Ditto, with the Arms of the Order of the Cincin-
nati;
Bowls, best blue and white Stone China in sets;
Pint Sneakers, Ditto;
Mugs, best Stone China in sets;
Small Tureens with covers;
Wash-Hand Guglits and Basons;
Brown Nankeens of the first and second quality;
Plain, flowered and spotted Lustrings of all co-
lours;
Sattins, the greatest part black;
Pelongs of different colours in whole and half pieces;
Sarsnet Ditto;
Embroidered Waistcoat Pieces of Silk and Sattin;
Silk Handkerchiefs very fine, 20 in a piece;
Spotted and flowered Velvets;
Painted Gauzes;
Bengal Piece Goods and Muslins, plain, flowered
and corded;
Silk Umbrellas of all sizes;
Elegant Paper Hangings;
Japanned Tea-Chests;
Ditto Fish and Counter-Boxes;
Sago, Cinnamon and Cinnamon Flowers;
Rhubarb, Opium, Gambouge and Borax;
Very old Batavia Arrack in leaguers, with sun-
dry other articles, the enumeration of which
would take up too much room in a public paper.
The Sale to continue until the whole is disposed
of, under the following conditions:
The purchaser is immediately to pay ten per
cent. on the amount of whatever lots he may buy,
and either give undeniable and satisfactory security
for the due payment of the balance, in two months,
or leave the goods as a deposit until they are clear-
ed out, which must be at the expiration of two
months from the date of the purchase, otherwise
they are to be re-sold immediately on the first purchaser's account, who is to be answerable to the
proprietor for any deficiency, and the expences attending the second sale.—For further particulars,
enquire of MR. O'DONNEL, the Owner.
Baltimore, August 11, 1785.   29—

had," he stated, all of the china should be decorated "with the badge of the Society of the Cincinnati," although the advertisement had only listed the small cups used for evening tea as having the badge decoration.[141] Washington's subsequent correspondence with Tilghman in 1785 reveals that he probably did not purchase anything from the captain of the *Pallas*. However, his letters of 1786 show that he eventually did obtain a large "Cincinnati" porcelain service with the help of another friend, Col. Henry ("Light-Horse Harry") Lee, who was then serving in the Continental Congress in New York.

On July 3, 1786, Lee wrote to Washington at Mount Vernon, "If you should be in want of a new set of china it is in my power to procure a very gentele set, table & tea —What renders this china doubly valuable & handsome is the order of the eagle engraved on it, in honor of the Cincinnati. . . ." Authorizing Lee to purchase the service for $150, Washington responded that he was "much obliged . . . for the information respecting the China which is for sale in New York." To conclude the transaction, Constable, Rucker and Company, the New York mercantile firm, gave Colonel Lee a receipt, dated August 7, to acknowledge payment of £ 60 for "1 Sett of Cincinnati China Cont^g, 1 Breakfast, 1 Table, 1 Tea Service of 302 p^s." By early September, the china was on its way to Norfolk, and on September 23, it was sent from Norfolk to Mount Vernon.

The documents immediately involved in Washington's acquisition of the famous Cincinnati service are interesting in themselves, because they emanate from historically important people such as Henry Lee, Tench Tilghman, and William Constable. However, Samuel Shaw, who actually directed the placement of the Cincinnati emblem and the figure of Fame on the service in Canton in 1784, and who brought the service to New York on the *Empress of China* in

67. Advertisement placed by Capt. John O'Donnell in the August 12, 1785, *Maryland Gazette and Baltimore Advertiser* for goods he planned to sell on his own account in Baltimore. The *Pallas* also carried a cargo of tea procured by Thomas Randall and Samuel Shaw. The tea was sold to Robert Morris in Philadelphia. (New York Public Library. Astor, Lenox and Tilden Foundations)

*Invoice of Goods to be purchased,
by Tench Tilghman Esq.ᵈ on Acc.ᵗ of George
Washington, agreeably to the letter accompanying this, of equal date. —*

A sett of the best Nankin Table China
Ditto — best Evening China Cups & Saucers
* A set of large blue & White China
    Dishes — say half a doz.ⁿ — more or less
* 1 Doz.ⁿ small bowls — blue & White .
* 6 Wash hand Guglets & Basons
  6 large Mugs — or 3 Mugs & 3 Jugs.
A Quart.ʳ Chest, best Hyson Tea.
A Leaguer of Battavia Arrack
    if a Leaguer is not large —
* About 13 y.ᵈ of good bla. Paduasoy
* a p.ᵒ of fine Muslin — plain
* 1 p.ᵒ of Silk Handkerchiefs
  12 p.ˢ of the best Nankeens.
  18 p.ˢ of the second quality — or
    coarsest kind. for servants.

17. Aug.ᵗ 1785.   G. Washington

68. Supplement to letter from George Washington at Mount Vernon to Tench Tilghman, merchant, in Baltimore, August 17 1785. Washington, the president general of the Society of the Cincinnati, desired the Society's badge—"if to be had"—on table and tea china as well as on mugs and "Wash hand Guglets & Basons." Subsequent correspondence reveals that his request for china brought from Canton to Baltimore by Captain O'Donnell on the *Pallas* was not fulfilled. (Manuscript Department, The Historical Society of Pennsylvania)

69. Henry ("Light-Horse Harry") Lee (1756–1818) painted ca. 1782 by Charles Willson Peale (1741–1827). Lee, who served in the Continental Congress in New York, wrote on July 3, 1786, to Washington at Mount Vernon, "If you should be in want of a new set of china it is in my power to procure a very gentele set, table & tea—What renders this china doubly valuable & handsome is the order of the eagle engraved on it, in honor of the Cincinnati." (Independence National Historical Park Collection)

1785, is not mentioned in the invoices and correspondence between New York and Mount Vernon in 1786. By then, Shaw had embarked on his second voyage to the Chinese port city.

SAMUEL SHAW AND THE *EMPRESS OF CHINA*

Samuel Shaw, one of the charter members of the Society of the Cincinnati, should have been at the May 1784 general meeting in Philadelphia. Earlier he had been an aide to the founder, General Knox, and secretary to the Society's constitutional committee. Shaw, however, had sailed from New York as commercial agent aboard the *Empress of China* on February 22, 1784. In Canton, he would procure tea and china to sell in New York, and he also planned to have a commemorative service of porcelain decorated. As he noted in his journal of the voyage, he carried a "copy of the [Cincinnati] emblems"—probably one of L'Enfant's painted sketches—and three engravings of figures to be used by the Chinese enamelers.[142]

Financed primarily by Robert Morris of Philadelphia, William Constable of New York, and Daniel Parker, the New York merchant and auctioneer at 23 Wall Street, the *Empress of China* was the first American ship to trade directly with Canton.[143] Returning to New York on May 11, 1785, the ship and her cargo embodied American hopes for a mercantile lift to the depressed postwar economy. New Jersey poet Philip Freneau sang of these expectations in an ode written to commemorate the departure of the *Empress* from New York:

> . . . *She now her eager course explores*
> *And soon shall greet Chinesian shores.*
> *From thence their fragrant* TEAS *to bring*
> *Without the leave of Britain's king;*
> *and* PORCELAIN WARE, *enchas'd in gold,*
> *The product of that finer mould. . . .*[144]

Leaving his partner, Thomas Randall, in Canton, Shaw returned on the *Empress* with a cargo of tea, fabrics, cassia, and 962 "piculs," or about 64 tons, of porcelain.[145] Capt.

79. Chinese porcelain tureen, blue "Fitzhugh" border with polychrome Cincinnati motifs, 1784–1785. Blue-and-white dinner services of the period generally included large soup tureens and smaller tureens used for sauces, stews, and potted meats. Overall length: 7 inches; overall height: 5 inches. (Private collection)

John Green of the *Empress* had purchased—on his own account—"ombrellas," "satin breeches," 600 "Ladies Silk Mitts," fans, fabrics, and "Sundry China Ware" worth over $800 from merchants Synchong, Sayhoun, Winchong, Anyong, and Exchin, all of whom were listed in the record book of F. Molineaux, Green's clerk, as "China Merchants" at Canton.[146] More than half of Green's china was purchased from Exchin, whose receipt, dated November 17, 1784, stated: "for Acc't of Capt. Green four hundred and thirty seven Dollars six Mace five Candereens four Cash being in full for several Invoices of China Ware."[147] Like Green, Capt. John O'Donnell, the English master of the *Pallas*, brought hundreds of "piculs" of assorted luxury goods, including china, to sell in Baltimore for his own profit. It was his advertisement for a "Public Vendue" to be held October 1 that Washington read in the August 12, 1785, Baltimore newspaper. The *Pallas* had been chartered by Samuel Shaw and his associate, Thomas Randall, to bring a quantity of teas for speculative sale through Robert Morris in Philadelphia.

The advertisement for O'Donnell's merchandise listed sets of cups and saucers "with the Arms of the Order of Cincinnati" painted on them, and it is probable that similar teawares had arrived in New York aboard the *Empress of China*. Also aboard the *Empress* was at least one set of Fitzhugh-bordered china decorated with the Cincinnati Eagle and a winged figure of Fame. In a journal of the first American voyage to Canton, Shaw wrote of his frustration in trying to elicit an ambitious composition of three classical figures and the Eagle from the Chinese enamelers:

There are many painters in Canton, but I was informed that not one' of them possesses a genius for design. I wished to have something emblematic of the institution of the order of the Cincinnati executed upon a set of porcelain. My idea was to have the American Cincinnatus, under the conduct of Minerva, regarding Fame, who, having received from them the emblems of the order, was proclaiming it to the world. For this purpose, I procured two separate engravings of the goddess, an elegant figure of a military man, and furnished the painter with a copy of the emblems which I had in my possession. He was allowed to be the most eminent of his profession, but, after repeated trials, was unable to combine the figures with the least propriety; though there was not one of them which singly he could not copy with the greatest exactness. I could therefore have my wishes gratified only in part. . . .[148]

Four Designs on Cincinnati China

During nine years of voyaging to and from Canton, Shaw procured at least two Cincinnati services for himself and several services for friends. His use of the Cincinnati insignia on porcelains shipped to America evolved from the early Fame and badge composition and simple copies of L'Enfant's preliminary sketch for the Eagle badge, to exact copies of the obverse and reverse of the fabricated medals brought from Paris in 1784 and later. The first two designs appear on Shaw's service or services of 1784–1785, one of which was acquired by George Washington in 1786, while the third is found on later Cincinnati services of about 1790 made for Shaw himself and for his associates Henry Knox, William Eustis, Benjamin Lincoln, and others.[149] A fourth arrangement, the later copy of the actual medal suspended from a bow held by two chubby "Fames," is found on a tea and coffee set made for Governor William Eustis of Massachusetts.[150]

The Mount Vernon service with Cincinnati insignia can be identified by pieces which have descended from George Washington Parke Custis of Arlington House. Mrs. Washington bequeathed "the sett of Cincinnati tea and table China" to her grandson, and "several pieces" were seen at Arlington House by Benson Lossing in 1859.[151] Forms from the Washington–Custis table service which have survived include dinner plates, soup plates, 7½-inch dessert plates, salad bowls, oblong platters or stands in five lengths from 10½ inches to 17¼ inches, round platters, insets or drainers for the larger platters, tureens of two heights —12¾ inches and 5 inches—sauceboats which were 7½ inches long, and leaf-shaped stands for the sauceboats. Teawares have not survived in comparable numbers. One saucer is in a private collection, and a teapot as well as a

71. Chinese porcelain cup, 1786–1793. The cup, which bears an exact copy of the reverse of the Cincinnati badge, is from a large service made to order for Samuel Shaw during his second (1786–1788) or subsequent voyages to Canton. Shaw died at sea in 1794. (Courtesy, The Henry Francis du Pont Winterthur Museum)

72. The Cincinnati badge and two figures of Fame on a Chinese porcelain saucer, ca. 1795, made for Governor William Eustis of Massachusetts. (Courtesy, The Henry Francis du Pont Winterthur Museum)

73. Chinese porcelain salad bowl, blue "Fitzhugh" border with polychrome Cincinnati motifs, 1784–1785. Square salad bowls for western
table services were copied from delftware bowls of 1740–1750, according
to D.F. Lunsingh Scheurleer. Blue-and-white salad dishes were included
in the table sets imported from Canton by the English East India Company
as early as 1755, and Washington had previously received salad "dishes"
in 1770 and 1783. Although George Washington Parke Custis inherited
the Cincinnati service from his grandmother, this bowl belonged to the
Peter family and attests to the sharing of memorabilia among Mrs. Washington's descendants. Height: 4¼ inches; length: 10 inches; width: 9¼
inches. (Peter Collection, The National Museum of American History,
Smithsonian Institution)

74. Chinese porcelain teapot, blue "Fitzhugh" borders and polychrome Cincinnati motifs, 1784–1785. The cylindrical body and strap handle with floral terminals are similar to the same forms in contemporary English creamware examples. Teapots of this shape continued to be exported to the West well into the nineteenth century. Washington's large "Sett of Cincinnati China" was described on the invoice from Constable, Rucker and Company to Henry Lee as "1 Breakfast/1 Table/1 Tea" service, but notably few of the teawares survive. His Cincinnati teapot at Mount Vernon is thought to be the single teapot among the 130 or so surviving pieces from the service. Overall height: 5 inches. (The Mount Vernon Ladies' Association collections)

75. Chinese porcelain custard cup and breakfast teabowl, blue underglaze borders and enameled Cincinnati Eagle within a wreath, 1784–1785.
The version of the Eagle based on L'Enfant's watercolor sketch rather than
on the actual medal which was first fabricated in France in 1783–1784 is
used here without the figure of Fame, which appears on larger pieces in
Washington's Cincinnati service. The invoice accompanying the sale of the
302-piece service of Cincinnati china to Col. Henry Lee on August 7,
1786, recorded breakfast, table, and tea sets, but did not itemize the three
divisions. The custard cup presumably was part of the dinner set while the
large teabowl was intended for breakfast use. In 1769, Washington ordered a set of breakfast cups "of a large kind" in queensware, and in 1772
he requested a dozen "large Breakfast Tea Cups" in china from his agent
in London. Smaller teacups or bowls were often called "evening" cups in
contemporary invoices and advertisements. Overall height of custard cup:
3½ inches; diameter of teabowl: 5 inches. (The Mount Vernon Ladies'
Association collections)

large cup used for breakfast tea are preserved at Mount Vernon. The latter bears only the early, wreathed Eagle, lacking the figure of Fame, but the Washington–Custis provenance is strong—as it is for two covered custard cups also bearing only the Eagle.

WAS THERE ONLY ONE SERVICE WITH FAME AND EAGLE?

Based on the evidence of the Custis inheritance, all Cincinnati china with the trumpeting Fame holding the early version of the Eagle and ribbon has usually been assigned a Washington provenance by collectors and curators. The documents engendered by Samuel Shaw's voyage to Canton and Washington's acquisition of Shaw's table and tea service seem to support the assertion that there was originally one large "valuable & handsome" service, but the Lee family tradition that Henry Lee purchased a second service in New York in 1786 can also be bolstered by the mercantile records of the firm which sponsored the voyage.[152]

When Henry Lee first wrote from New York to George Washington on July 3, 1786, that it was in his "power to procure a very gentele set, table & tea . . . [with] the order of the eagle engraved on it, in honor of the Cincinnati" for $150, only the *Empress of China* and the *Pallas* had returned to American shores directly from Canton.[153] China brought by the *Empress* was advertised for sale in New York by "Constable, Reeker & Co." in May 1785,[154] while ceramics carried in the *Pallas*, the Baltimore-bound ship chartered by Shaw and Randall to carry tea, were advertised shortly after she docked in July. John O'Donnell, British captain of the *Pallas*, undertook to sell "the greater part of [his portion of] the Cargo" including "Cups and Saucers . . . with the Arms of the Order of Cincinnati" at auction in large lots, as Tench Tilghman's letters to Washington and the advertisement reveal. The sale, however, proved a disappointment for all concerned, because O'Donnell "held his goods so extravagantly high" that little or nothing was sold at the October auction. As Tilghman reported, "he [O'Donnell] has an Idea they will be in great demand in the Spring, and therefore holds them up. . . ."[155] Tench Tilghman's death in

the spring of 1786, however, ended Washington's connection to Tilghman's mercantile firm and, evidently, his quest for bargains in chinaware in Baltimore.[156]

A business associate of Tilghman, Robert Morris, the "financier of the Revolution," had been one of the principal backers of the *Empress* with Daniel Parker and William Constable. He was also a partner in the Constable, Rucker firm which billed Henry Lee for Washington's "1 Sett of Cincinnati China" of 302 pieces on August 7, 1786. Robert Morris and Gouverneur Morris had signed articles of co-partnership with William Constable in May 1784, nine months before the *Empress* left New York harbor, and in June they took on another partner, John Rucker, who would act as agent for the firm in Europe.[157] Tench Tilghman, until his death in 1786, acted as purchasing agent in the south for the firm, which was active in the decade after the war in the French tobacco trade.[158] Although the tobacco venture was never very successful, Robert Morris's investment in the *Empress of China* enterprise realized a net profit of more than twenty-five percent after the eventual sale of the "India goods" brought to New York. Morris had also commissioned Capt. John Green to purchase special "paper Hangings" and borders, lacquered fans, and a "dressing Box" with painted glass for his elegant Philadelphia townhouse, which would later be Washington's presidential residence.[159]

In the introduction to the journal of his second voyage to Canton on the *Hope* in 1786, Shaw wrote of the financial complexities described above which delayed the sale of much of the cargo of the *Empress*.[160] Those delays may have accounted for the availability more than a year later of what Henry Lee wrote Washington was a "very gentele set" of tableware with "the order of the eagle engraved on it, in honor of the Cincinnati." Constable and Rucker's business ledger for the year 1786 contains two pages recording sales of unidentified Chinese goods from the "Empress of China's Cargo" to individuals and to other firms.[161]

According to the ledger, Robert Morris spent more than £1,300 at one time, and other large purchases were made by Joshua Jones, James Stewart, and William Whiteside and Company during the period from January 1786 to

January 1787. Smaller amounts were charged to Alexander Macomb, Anthony Bleecher, Israel Navarro, Alexander Hamilton, and Henry Lee. Hamilton's expenditure of £2.8. and Navarro's of £1.6. were especially small. Lee made two purchases which were recorded on June 3 and August 16—each for £60. The August purchase undoubtedly referred to the receipt for a set of Cincinnati china at £60, dated August 7, from Constable, Rucker and Company which Lee enclosed in his letter of the same date to Washington. Lee's unidentified purchase on June 3 is remarkable in that it also cost exactly £60.

This evidence of two sales—each at £60—to Henry Lee does seem to support the tradition that there were originally two Cincinnati services; however, in Samuel Shaw's own description of having "something emblematic of the institution of the order of the Cincinnati executed upon a set of porcelain," he consistently referred to one set decorated with a composition, including the figure of Fame. It is possible that Lee and Washington divided one exceptionally large service of Cincinnati china which Shaw had originally intended for his own use. He may have used the entire set during his brief stint in 1785 in New York as part of Henry Knox's Department of War preceding his appointment as consul to Canton and his return voyage to China in 1786. Realizing that he could now obtain the more precise work found on the later Cincinnati services by having in hand the previously unavailable medal which the Chinese enameler "could . . . copy with the greatest exactness," Shaw may have sold the "Fame" service to Constable, Rucker and Company. It is noteworthy that in his first letter on the subject, Lee stressed that the service was "offered at the prime [original] Cost, 150 dollars."[162] If Cincinnati table services had been generally available, a profit would surely have been sought by Constable.

Thus, the documentary evidence and the mercantile context point to the existence of one large set of Cincinnati "Breakfast, table, and tea" china with the figure of Fame and the early version of the Eagle. It was brought to New York in May 1785 on the *Empress of China* and was sold at a bargain price by Constable, Rucker and Company to Henry Lee and George Washington after Samuel Shaw had returned to China as American consul in 1786. There had also been teawares "with the Arms of the Order of Cincinnati" advertised in Baltimore in August 1785. These probably displayed only the early L'Enfant sketch version of the Cincinnati Eagle in a green wreath topped by a bow. The early Eagle began to be replaced on Cincinnati china by exact copies of the obverse and reverse of the metal badges as soon as Shaw returned to Canton. He then procured a large service for himself and tea services for several comrades. These later services were brought on his return voyages to America in 1789 and 1792.[163] The early version of the Eagle without the figure of Fame continued to be used occasionally, for it appears on a punch bowl made for Col. Richard Humpton in about 1790 and on a matching tea caddy.[164]

THE CINCINNATI CHINA AFTER WASHINGTON'S LIFETIME

Washington obviously prized his Cincinnati service, and he used it in New York and Philadelphia. Mrs. Washington, who inherited her husband's personal property, left the Cincinnati service to her grandson, George Washington Parke Custis. Custis used the service at Arlington House, where Benson J. Lossing saw much of it in 1858. In 1928, Henry Francis du Pont purchased more than sixty pieces from the heirs of Mary Custis Lee. Miss Lee, the daughter of Gen. Robert E. Lee and Mary Anna Randolph Custis, had received—by order of President William McKinley—what remained of the Cincinnati china which had been removed from Arlington House by the federal government during the Civil War.[165] Other pieces had been damaged during the war, and a few plates came into the possession of Union troops. Due to these unusual circumstances, pieces emerge now and then from unlikely or anonymous sources. There is also evidence that Mrs. Robert E. Lee, and perhaps her father, George Washington Parke Custis, gave or sold Cincinnati china to friends. In 1847, Mrs. Lee wrote to a Mrs. Stiles in Austria: "I send you a small tureen of the Cincinnati which you must value very highly as they are getting very rare and it is almost like parting with one of my family to send it so far. . . ."[166] Several of the thirteen pieces at Mount Vernon were at one time in the collection of Governor Caleb Lyon, who, according to Alice Morse Earle, was a frequent visitor to Mount Vernon and Arlington House in the mid-nineteenth century.[167] Other public collections where Cincinnati china with the figure of Fame can now be seen include the Smithsonian Institution's National Museum of American History, the Metropolitan Museum of Art, the Museum of the American China Trade, the Diplomatic Reception Rooms of the Department of State, the White House, the Lee homes—Arlington House and Stratford Hall—and especially the Henry Francis du Pont Winterthur Museum.

"JARRS . . . EXCEEDINGLY HANDSOME"

The Cincinnatus allegory of the warrior's return to the simple agricultural life was repeatedly applied to Washington during his years of temporary retirement from public life at Mount Vernon. In 1788, a French visitor rhapsodized that "the comparison [to Cincinnatus] is accurate. This famous general is now merely a good countryman entirely devoted to the care of his farm, as he calls it. . . . Everything was simple in the general's home. He provides a good table but not a sumptuous one. . . ."[168] After the war, as Brissot de Warville noted, Washington had turned his attention to agricultural and architectural improvements at Mount Vernon, especially to the adornment of the large dining room he called the "New Room." His plans for the New Room were elegant rather than simple, however, and the simplicity emphasized by Brissot was contradicted by an English visitor who wrote with some exaggeration that the general's "revenues enabled him, as well as the presents he received from all parts, to have all the luxuries of every clime. . . ."[169]

Among the presents "from all parts" were the French tea and coffee service received in 1782 and an elaborate "marble chimney piece and pair of glass Jarendoles" for the New Room.[170] The mantel of "Sienna jasper and statuary marble" had been sent from England in 1784 by Samuel Vaughan, an amateur architect and exceptionally enthusiastic Wash-

ington admirer who had met the general during the latter's triumphal tour of Philadelphia in December 1783.[171] At that time, they had discussed the New Room and the appropriate treatment of its plaster, "which is the present taste in England," as well as Washington's intention to place a marble mantel there.[172] A successful merchant in the West Indian trade and a member of Franklin's Club of Honest Whigs in London, Vaughan had come to Philadelphia in 1783 with his American-born wife and some of his children. He stayed in Philadelphia until 1790 and during his extended visit contributed considerably to the city's literary and architectural life.[173]

In November 1786, Vaughan sent a painting and three elaborately painted Worcester vases to adorn the mantel which Washington had feared was "too elegant and costly for my room and republican stile of living."[174] Protestations aside, the mantel was accepted and the "Jarrs" deemed "fine and exceedingly handsome . . . they shall occupy the place you have named for them." The mantel had been removed from Wanstead, the Vaughan country seat near London, and shipped to Mount Vernon by Benjamin Vaughan, who had remained in England when his father left for Philadelphia in 1783.[175] It had been installed in the Wanstead library in 1770, and the vases with manly scenes of lions in African landscape settings were probably purchased at that time.[176]

The forms and decoration of the Worcester factory-marked vases are consistent with a 1770 date. Furthermore, the signature of Jefferyes Hamett O'Neale (1734–1801), who lived in Worcester from 1768 to 1770, appears three times on two of the vases.[177] The scene of lions and leopards on the central vase is signed "ONeale pinx" and the landscape scene on the opposite side is signed "ON. Pinxt." The animal and landscape scenes on one of the side vases are signed "ON inu^r &c."

O'Neale specialized in animals, landscapes, and mythology on products of the highest level of achievement at Chelsea and Worcester.[178] The lions and landscapes of the Vaughan–Washington vases are particularly characteristic of the artist's decorative compositions. His animals in fables

76. Samuel Vaughan (1720–1802) by Robert Edge Pine (1730?–1788). Vaughan, an English Whig and a member of the American Philosophical Society, gave Washington a marble mantel, a painting, and a garniture of Worcester porcelain vases from Wanstead, his house near London. (The American Philosophical Society, Philadelphia)

and exotic settings usually display a humorous countenance which appears to derive from the graphic source sheets published by English illustrator Francis Barlow.[179] Using such models, O'Neale probably worked as an independent porcelain painter, miniaturist, and illustrator throughout much of his career. Chelsea and Wedgwood factory records and correspondence indicate that he was paid on a piecework basis after 1770.[180] His relationship to the Worcester factory may have been similar during the period of his known residency in that city.

Several Worcester baluster-shape vases with scroll handles and underglaze "mazarine" blue grounds surrounding gilt-framed reserves are preserved in English collections.[181] The reserved areas on these luxurious pieces were painted over the glaze by artists such as O'Neale and John Donaldson during a period of strong European influence at the Worcester porcelain factory. The decoration is also stylistically indebted to earlier works of the Chelsea factory, which had temporarily ceased manufacturing in 1768. At that time, several Chelsea artisans transferred their skills to Worcester. When the Chelsea factory reopened under William Duesbury in 1770, many of the former Chelsea workers, including O'Neale, are thought to have returned to London from Worcester and elsewhere.

77. Mantel of "Sienna jasper and statuary marble" given to Washington
in 1784 by Samuel Vaughan. The mantel, removed from Wanstead,
was installed in the large dining room, which Washington often called
the "New Room," at Mount Vernon. The garniture of Worcester vases
was sent by Vaughan in 1786 to adorn the mantel (The Mount Vernon
Ladies' Association collections)

78. English soapstone porcelain garniture of three vases, Worcester, first or "Dr. Wall" period, 1768–1770. In November 1786, Samuel Vaughan sent a luxurious set of vases from his country house near London to adorn the mantel he had previously sent to Washington for the "New Room" at Mount Vernon. On each of the baluster-shape vases, an underglaze "mazarine" blue ground and elaborate gilt scrollwork surround large reserve panels which contain humorous, fable-style paintings of lions, leopards, and tigers. Jefferyes Hamett O'Neale (1734–1801), an Irish miniaturist who signed the animal scene on the center vase, "ONeale pinx," and that on the left vase, "ON inuʳ&c," worked for the Chelsea factory before and after his brief time in Worcester. Height of side vases: 12¾ inches; overall height of center vase: 18¾ inches. (The Mount Vernon Ladies' Association collections)

79. The opposite sides of Washington's Worcester vases. O'Neale signed the landscape scene on the vase at the left, "ON inuʳ&c" and that on the center vase, "ON. pinxt." The mauve clouds, flocks of birds, and foreground rocks are recurring images in O'Neale's landscape compositions.

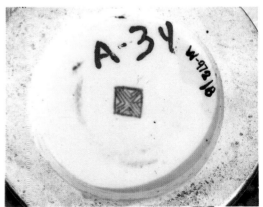

80. Detail of the reserve panel on the central vase in Washington's Worcester garniture. O'Neale, whose signature appears on the embankment, derived his expressive animals from the work of an English illustrator, Francis Barlow.

81. Worcester square or fret mark, painted in underglaze blue, used ca. 1755–1775. The mark appears under the base of each of the three vases.

The gilding methods in use at Chelsea and Sèvres were also adopted at the Worcester factory. Gold was applied to the Vaughan–Washington vases in foliate scrollwork around the reserves, in bands at the rims, and in transparent butterflies on the bases by means of a flux after having been ground in honey, washed, and dried.[182] All of the preserved Worcester vases decorated by O'Neale display similar foliate gilt motifs as well as butterflies or friezes of arcs and triangles.

The Worcester vases from an important Whig family followed Custine's Niderviller service in a series of porcelain presents from Washington's Old World admirers. To them, he was the embodiment of a political ideal and Mount Vernon the geographic and architectural focus for their hopes of a new order of government. Samuel Vaughan's elegant Italian mantel and luxurious porcelain "Jarrs" undoubtedly nourished the predilection for fashionable furnishings already present in the Washingtons' earliest choices of household goods. The final expression of that taste would become visible on the presidential dinner tables in New York and Philadelphia as Washington attempted to balance his professed republican style of living with the expectations of urbane associates and his own concern about setting proper social precedents for a new nation.

V

ORNAMENTS

FOR THE

PRESIDENT'S TABLE,

1789   TO   1790

"The centre of the table contained five or six large silver or plated waiters, those of the ends, circular, or rather oval on one side, so as to make the arrangement correspond with the oval shape of the table . . . and the whole of these waiters were filled with alabaster figures, taken from the ancient mythology, but none of them such as to offend in the smallest degree against delicacy. On the outside of the oval, formed by the waiters, were placed the various dishes, always without covers; and outside the dishes were the plates. . . ." [Ashbel Green, in Benson J. Lossing, George Washington's Mount Vernon or Mount Vernon and Its Associations, *Alexandria, Va.: The Fairfax Press, 1977, pp. 298–99]*

82. French biscuit-porcelain table ornament, ca. 1790, perhaps representing "fall" in a set of allegorical figures. Height: 6½ inches Mark (incised on base): "No. 1" (see page 14). (Peter family collection)

the serious business of strengthening the confederation of states. According to the diary he kept that summer, Washington lodged and often dined sumptuously with Robert Morris in his elegant house at 190 High Street, which would later become one of Washington's three presidential residences. There were dinners with Philadelphia's leading families—the Chews, Willings, Mifflins, Penns, and Vaughans—and frequent evening teas at the fashionable house of Samuel and Elizabeth Powel on Third Street.[184]

On May 21, Washington noted especially that he "dined and drank tea at Mr. Bingham's, in great Splender."[135] A mercantile aristocrat and probably the wealthiest American of that time, William Bingham had furnished his house at Third and Spruce

Reluctantly abandoning his retirement from public matters, George Washington "yielded . . . to the earnest wishes of . . . friends" and agreed to be a delegate to the Constitutional Convention in Philadelphia.[183] From his arrival in May 1787 until September, a regular social schedule accompanied

with purchases made during a tour of France, where his wife Anne found "the Mind . . . continually gratified with the admiration of Works of Taste."[136] An estate auction of Bingham's personal property at the "Mansion House" in 1804 included an astounding list of ornamental and useful

83. Drawing room from the house of Samuel and Elizabeth Powel on
Third Street in Philadelphia. General Washington was a frequent guest
there for evening tea during the Constitutional Convention in the summer
of 1787. (Philadelphia Museum of Art)

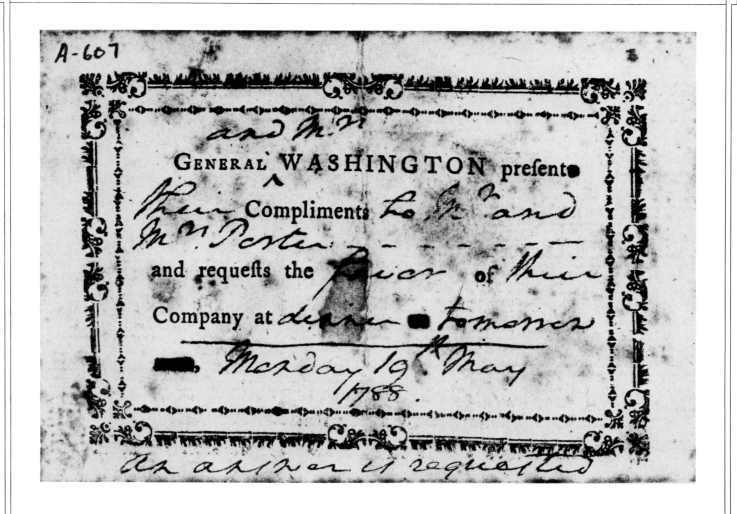

84. Invitation to dinner at Mount Vernon, issued by General and Mrs. Washington to Mr. and Mrs. Porter for May 19, 1788. Dinner was served in the afternoon at three or four o'clock. The invitation is in Washington's hand. (The Mount Vernon Ladies' Association collections)

85. House at the corner of Pearl and Cherry streets, New York, lithograph in Valentine's *Manual of the Corporation of the City of New York*, 1853, opp. p. 304. This house was leased in April 1789 from Samuel Osgood for President and Mrs. Washington. Mrs. Osgood and "Lady" Kitty Duer managed the furnishing of the house with a substantial appropriation from Congress. The Osgoods' niece exclaimed that there was the "best of furniture in every room, and the greatest quantity of plate and China that I ever saw before. The whole of the first and second Story is papered, and the floor covered with the richest kind of Turkey and Wilton Carpets." (Courtesy, The New-York Historical Society, New York City)

luxuries, among which were several sets of "French china," and two "save" (Sèvres) tureens.[187]

FIXING "THE TASTE OF OUR COUNTRY"

Impressions of mercantile "Splender" in Philadelphia persisted through Washington's election and inauguration in New York as he began to set precedents in the social obligations of the presidency or "to fix the taste of our Country properly," as his friend Gouverneur Morris suggested. The president protested to friends at home that "... pride and dignity of office, which God knows has no charms for me ... for I can truly say I had rather be at Mount Vernon with a friend or two about me, than to be attended at the Seat of Government by the Officers of State and the Representatives of every Power in Europe...."[188] Nevertheless, he also recognized the necessity of presenting the new nation properly and of responding in some measure to the desire for official pomp expressed by several members of his cabinet.

A precise schedule of formal receptions and dinners at the president's house on Cherry Street was soon established. The president held "levees" for callers every Tuesday while Mrs. Washington, with the president attending, received visitors of both sexes at eight o'clock on Fridays. For the Tuesday levees, a virtual uniform of black with silver or gold knee buckles and black cockades with silver or gold eagles on tricorn hats was worn by the president and his cabinet. After attending a levee with General Knox, one woman described these costumes and concluded, "I thought that an injudicious effort was made to surround our republican President with the trappings of royalty."[189] No refreshments were served on Tuesdays, but Abigail Adams wrote that on Fridays, "The company are entertained with Ice creems & Lemonade."[190] Invitations for Thursday dinners were issued in rotation to members of Congress and government officials. One such dinner was recorded by Pennsylvania's Senator William Maclay on August 27, 1789:

At a little after four I called on Mr. Bassett, of the Delaware State. We went to the President's to dinner. The company were: President and Mrs. Washington, Vice-President and Mrs. Adams, the Governor and his wife, Mr. Jay and wife, Mr. Langdon and wife, Mr. Dalton and lady (perhaps his wife), and a Mr. Smith, Mr. Bassett, myself, Lear, Lewis, the President's two secretaries. The President and Mrs. Washington sat opposite each other in the middle of the table; the two secretaries, one at each end. It was a great dinner, and the best of the kind I ever was at. The room, however, was disagreeably warm.

First was the soup; fish roasted and boiled; meats, gammon, fowls, etc. This was the dinner. The middle of the table was garnished in the usual tasty way, with small images, flowers (artificial), etc. The dessert was, first applepies, pudding, etc.; then iced creams, jellies, etc.; then water-melons, musk-melons, apples, peaches, nuts.

It was the most solemn dinner ever I sat at. Not a health drank; scarce a word said until the cloth was taken away. Then the President, filling a glass of wine, with great formality drank to the health of every individual by name round the table. Ev-

erybody imitated him, charged glasses, and such a buzz of "health, sir," and "health, madam," and "thank you, sir," and "thank you, madam," never had I heard before.[191]

The small images and artificial flowers on the table observed by Senator Maclay were either molded of sugar by a confectioner or they were the unidentified "Table Ornaments" purchased for the president's house on July 7, 1789, from Thomas Burling, whose china shop was at 70 Water Street.[192] These were charged to "House Expense" rather than to the president's account and, thus, joined the china and queensware purchased by Congress through Samuel Osgood, owner of the Cherry Street house which had been leased for the Washingtons.[193] As Martha Washington reported in a rare letter written soon after her arrival in New York, "...the House...is a very good one and is handsomely furnished all new for the General...."[194] To Washington's taste, however, the congressionally supplied tableware was insufficiently "genteel" for state occasions. Tobias Lear, Washington's chief secretary, would later use the term "Common China" to differentiate these objects from the president's own, finer porcelains.[195]

Washington probably used his large Chinese table and tea service decorated with the Cincinnati insignia for at least some Thursday dinners in 1789 and early 1790. Correspondence between Lear and Washington reveals that the Cincinnati service must have been present in New York, because it was sent from there to Philadelphia when the seat of government was moved in the fall of 1790.[196] The Cincinnati china was soon supplemented by purchases of other fine table- and teawares used for official entertaining but acquired personally by the president and charged to the "contingency fund," which was actually his $25,000 annual salary.[197]

NEAT AND FASHIONABLE ORNAMENTS

President Washington was particularly persistent about acquiring a fashionable French centerpiece, or *surtout*, of silver and glass *plateaux* to ornament the table on public

86. Tobias Lear (1762–1816) by Constantina Coltellini (dates unknown). Lear became Washington's secretary at the beginning of the presidency. He supervised household expenditures and the movement of furnishings as well as the acquisition of articles such as the president's *surtout*. (Courtesy, The R.W. Norton Art Gallery, Shreveport, Louisiana)

days. Less than two months after the inaugural celebrations in New York, he asked Tobias Lear to find a set of "waiters, salvers, or whatever they are called. . . . Mr. Morris & Mr. Bingham have them, and the French & Spanish Ministers here, but I know of no one else who has. . . ." The Morris and Bingham *plateaux* in Philadelphia were probably remembered from Washington's numerous visits in 1787. The 1804 sale catalogue of Bingham's estate included "1 Large plateau with 17 marble figures" among the numerous entries of splendid French tableware.[198]

By 1789, the desire for French luxury furnishings had permeated American mercantile and diplomatic society.[199] In Paris, Americans, guided by French advisers, soon patronized fashionable shops for porcelain tableware and ornaments while goods manufactured in France were transported to American ports by merchants such as William Constable, whose sloops carried raw materials or provisions to Le Havre. As ambassadors to the French court, Benjamin Franklin and his successors, Thomas Jefferson and Gouverneur Morris, enjoyed a social intimacy with leading members of the French bourgeoisie and aristocracy. Such associations could not fail to impart elements of French taste and manners. An elaborately planned and equipped dining table with porcelain serving dishes and ornaments made of confection or porcelain, symmetrically arranged in patterns evoking formal gardens, was often the focus for the social and political occasions enjoyed by French and American officials. Franklin returned to Philadelphia in 1785 with 128 boxes of acquisitions, including porcelain, and Jefferson followed in 1789 with eighty-six cases, including tableware and biscuit-porcelain figures listed in a packing invoice.[200]

In June 1789, Tobias Lear asked Clement Biddle to inquire about the availability of *plateaux* "at French Stores" in Philadelphia. Porcelain figures to stand on the mirrored surfaces would not be necessary since "The President has a French man with him who is said to be a compleat confectioner, & professes to understand everything relative to those ornaments. . . ." Colonel Biddle found two sets of "glasses," or *plateaux*, in the shop of confectioner Joseph de la Croix in Philadelphia, but neither was considered large enough for the table in the Cherry Street house. Equally unsuccessful were the skills of the president's French confectioner, whose craft stemmed from a European tradition of decorating dining tables with sculptures compounded of wax, tragacanth, and sugar.[201] In July 1789, the "Table Ornaments" which may have decorated the table in Senator Maclay's description were purchased locally; however, Washington soon realized that a *surtout* and porcelain figures for it would have to be imported from France. Relying on the sophisticated taste of Gouverneur Morris—then in Paris negotiating tobacco sales for his associate Robert Morris—Washington wrote in October for "mirrors for a table, with neat and fashionable but not expensive ornaments for them." As an example of what the president desired, Gouverneur Morris should "recur to what you have seen on Mr. Robert Morris's table for my ideas *generally*. . . ."

The fulfillment of the president's wishes was recorded by Gouverneur Morris in the detailed journal he kept during four of his ten years in France. On January 11, 1790, shortly after receiving Washington's letter, Morris inquired at "the Porcelaine." This was probably the Royal Manufactory at Sèvres, which he had visited twice during the previous fall.[202] The prices and the length of time for delivery at Sèvres were discouraging, however, so four days later Morris called upon his mistress, Adèle, countess de Flahaut, to "go to look for a Surtout. Afterwards to the Manufacture of Angoulême. We agree that the Porcelaine here is handsomer and cheaper than that of Sève. I think I shall purchase for General Washington here. We are to go on Monday to see the Person whom we first visited."[203]

In 1781, the Angoulême salesrooms were located at rue de Bondy and from March 1789 at the corner of boulevard du Temple and rue Meslée. They obviously impressed American visitors. After his first visit to the new salesrooms, Gouverneur Morris described Christophe Dihl as "the Principal [who] is a German or Swiss and boasts much of his Work. He has Reason. Tis a Pity that some Vases of most exquisite Workmanship should be of brittle China Ware. In Spite of Reason a Person possessed of Money would I

think be obliged to make some Purchases. Am to go again for the Purpose of seeing the Work in its different Stages."[204]

Dihl, born at Neustadt in 1753, was a porcelain modeler who came to Paris in 1779 to sell his figures, vases, and medallions.[205] With Antoine Guérhard as financial partner, he procured the protection of the Duke d'Angoulême and established an extremely successful factory which produced tableware and ornaments until 1828. Dihl himself seems to have been the factory's leading modeler of biscuit figures, although designs were provided to all French factories by sculptors and designers such as Boucher, Falconet, Lemire, and Cyfflé.[206] There was also a great deal of copying among factories and substantial pirating of the models created at Sèvres, where the taste for biscuit-porcelain figures originated after 1750 at the instigation of Madame de Pompadour.[207] Sèvres figures and sculptural groups can be identified, but unless a piece bears a mark, assignment to a particular factory other than that of Sèvres is usually impossible.[208]

Neoclassical imagery, the wellspring for French fine and applied arts during the reign of Louis XVI, was especially appropriate for the marblelike purity of flawless biscuit porcelain left in an unglazed state after only one firing. Sets of table ornaments were often composed of allegories using figures of the Greek and Roman pantheon with attributes which cultured people could easily recognize. As Grimod de la Reynère noted in 1805, one could learn mythology without leaving the table.[209]

Gouverneur Morris's diary for January 18, 1790, recorded the actual "purchase at the Manufacture of Angoulême which will cost him [Washington] ab.^t 100 Louis."[210] The president's manuscript account of furnishings for his official residences in New York and Philadelphia recorded 2,384 livres for "Porcelaine etc Table" on June 3 and duties of £ 17.1.4., with £ 20.4.9. to merchant William Constable for freight. Duties of ten percent ad valorem "on all china, stone and earthen ware" and on a long list of other manufactured products such as silver, looking glasses, buttons, and knee buckles had been levied by an act of Congress in 1789.[211] The cost of the *plateaux* with the porcelain figures, therefore, was about 170 New York pounds. The porcelains,

however, were far costlier than the *plateaux*. A list of plate and plated ware "Purchased by G. W." during his two terms as president states that "7 Plateaux—G Morris cost in Fr: 378 Livres."[212] The difference between that figure and the total of 2,384 livres is 2,006 livres or "ab.ᵗ 100 Louis," just as Morris had estimated.

The letters which Gouverneur Morris wrote to the president in January 1790 described the proper placement and care of the biscuit sculptures and set forth—with fervor —the rationale for a classical iconography appropriate to the American republic. On the twenty-fourth, Morris wrote a note to accompany

three cases containing a Surtout of seven Plateaus and the ornaments in Biscuit. . . . There are in all three Groups two Vases and twelve figures. The Vases may be used as they are or when occasion serves, the Tops may be laid aside and the Vases filled with natural flowers. When the whole Surtout is to be used for large Companies the large Group will be in the middle the two

87. Gouverneur Morris (1752–1816) and Robert Morris (1734–1806) painted in 1783 by Charles Willson Peale (1741–1827). The men were business associates, not relatives. Washington lived in Robert Morris's house during the Constitutional Convention in Philadelphia in 1787. The house was later the presidential residence. Gouverneur Morris chose President Washington's *surtout* and biscuit figures at the Angoulême factory in Paris. In 1792, he was appointed Ambassador to France. (Pennsylvania Academy of the Fine Arts, Bequest of Richard Ashhurst)

smaller ones at the two Ends—the Vases in the Spaces between the three and the figures distributed along the Edges or rather along the Sides. . . . To clean the Biscuit warm water is to be used and for any things in the Corners a Brush such as is used for painting in Water Colours.

On the same day, Morris wrote another remarkable letter to Washington in which he attempted to justify his apparent extravagance.

I could have sent you a Number of pretty Trifles for very little Cost, but the Transportation and the freight would have been

88. One of three biscuit-porcelain groups which with single figures and vases stood on President Washington's mirrored centerpiece, or *surtout-de-table*. The ensemble was purchased by Gouverneur Morris on January 18, 1790, at the popular factory of Christophe Dihl and Antoine Guérhard on the boulevard du Temple in Paris. In a note accompanying the packing cases which contained the *surtout* of seven *plateaux* and the biscuit ornaments, Morris described the latter as "three Groups two Vases and twelve figures," and suggested that "when the whole Surtout is to be used for large Companies the large Group will be in the middle the two smaller ones at the two Ends—the Vases in the Spaces between the three and the figures distributed along the Edges or rather along the Sides." The only known group among the three sent by Morris is an allegory of love and youth portrayed by *amours* and Venus with a ewer as the identifying attribute. It was one of the two pieces intended for the rounded ends of the *surtout*. Incised mark: *A* Height: 15¼ inches; length: 13½ inches. The factory enjoyed the patronage and protection of the Duc d'Angoulême from 1781 until the French Revolution. (The Mount Vernon Ladies' Association collections)

89. Biscuit-porcelain figures of Minerva and Venus, Paris, Guérhard and Dihl's Angoulême factory. These are two of the twelve porcelain figures representing the arts and sciences which were sent from Paris to stand along the sides of the *surtout*. Referring to the classical sources for the images, Gouverneur Morris wrote to the president on January 24, 1790, that the figures had been "fashionable above two thousand years" and that "they stand a fair chance to continue so during our time." Height of Minerva: 6¼ inches; height of Venus: 6½ inches. (Peter family collection)

more, and you must have had an annual Supply, and your Table would have been in the Style of a petite Maitresse of this City, which most assuredly is not the Style you wish. Those now sent are of a noble Simplicity, and as they have been fashionable above two thousand years, they stand a fair chance to continue so during our time. . . . I think it of very great importance to fix the taste of our Country properly, and I think your Example will go so very far in that respect. It is therefore my Wish that every Thing about you should be substantially good and majestically plain; made to endure. . . .

Three pieces of Washington's seventeen table ornaments, a group probably representing an allegory of Love and Youth,

now at Mount Vernon, and two of the twelve single figures —Minerva and Venus—owned by the Peter family reveal that Morris meant classical models by his allusion to eternal stylishness. Although the "Love and Youth" group at Mount Vernon has usually been considered the central piece, letters from Washington to Clement Biddle in Philadelphia in 1797 and 1798 reveal that it was one of the two intended for the rounded ends of the *surtout*. After his last term as president, Washington had left several objects in Philadelphia to be sold, including "A Platteau in nine pieces. three large groupes with glasses over them, two vases, and twelve small single figures, of Porcelain." By January 1798, the *plateaux* and figures were still unsold, and Washington asked Biddle to send the *plateaux* to Mount Vernon "together with the two smallest of the large groups of Porcelain, and the twelve single images (Arts and Sciences) with which my Table, on Public days, was ornamented. The large group (Apollo instructing the Shepherds) and the two Vases, may be sold for what ever they will fetch." Unfortunately, no record of that sale, if it occurred, is known.

The "table images" were mentioned often in correspondence between Washington and Tobias Lear in the fall of 1790, when the presidential entourage moved from New York to Philadelphia. In a letter of October 31, Lear suggested that "the large Images stand on the Side Boards in the Dining Room [of the Philadelphia house]. The Glasses which cover will preserve them from the dust, and prevent delicate parts from being touched. They will likewise be an ornament to the Room. . . . The small Images can be put in the closets with the China. . . ."

The porcelain figures were admired by Theophilus Bradbury, a Massachusetts congressman who attended one of the president's Thursday dinners. In a letter to his daughter, he described "a piece of table furniture about six feet long and two feet wide rounded at the ends. It was either of wood gilded, or polished metal, raised only about an inch, with a silver rim round it like that round a tea board; in the centre was a pedestal of plaster of Paris with images upon it, and on each end figures, male and female of the same. It was very elegant and used for ornament only. The dishes were

90. The large, central, biscuit-porcelain group which Washington described in 1798 as "Apollo instructing the Shepherds"—and which he directed to be sold in Philadelphia—was briefly noted by a Massachusetts congressman as a "pedestal of plaster of Paris with images upon it." The group in the Museo Arqueológico Nacional in Madrid is probably the same model as the largest of the "substantially good and majestically plain" table ornaments sent from Paris by Gouverneur Morris in 1790. A lyre and several sheep—attributes of Apollo Nomius, the pastoral aspect of the god—are present in the composition which, as *Apollon instruisant les bergers*, was among the subjects for large biscuit groups in an inventory of the Guérhard and Dihl factory after the death of the latter in 1830. An impressed factory mark proclaiming the protection of "le Duc d'angoulême à Paris" places the manufacture of the Madrid group in the years just prior to the French Revolution.

The following four photographs are of French biscuit-porcelain table ornaments, ca. 1785–1795. The presidential accounts record three "contingency expense" purchases of "table images" or "figures" in January 1790, February 1797, and March 1797. The figures illustrated here and the one on page 103 are owned by descendants of Martha Parke Custis Peter, granddaughter of Mrs. Washington. (Peter family collection)

91. Oriental cymbal player and shepherdess. The molded Niderviller mark, which is found on both figures, was used at the factory after the death of the Count de Custine and the assumption of management by his former partner, Claude-François Lanfrey, in 1793. Marks: NIDERVILLER in relief on a raised lozenge on bases of both figures; "F no. 1.63" incised on the base of the cymbal player. Height: 6¼ inches.

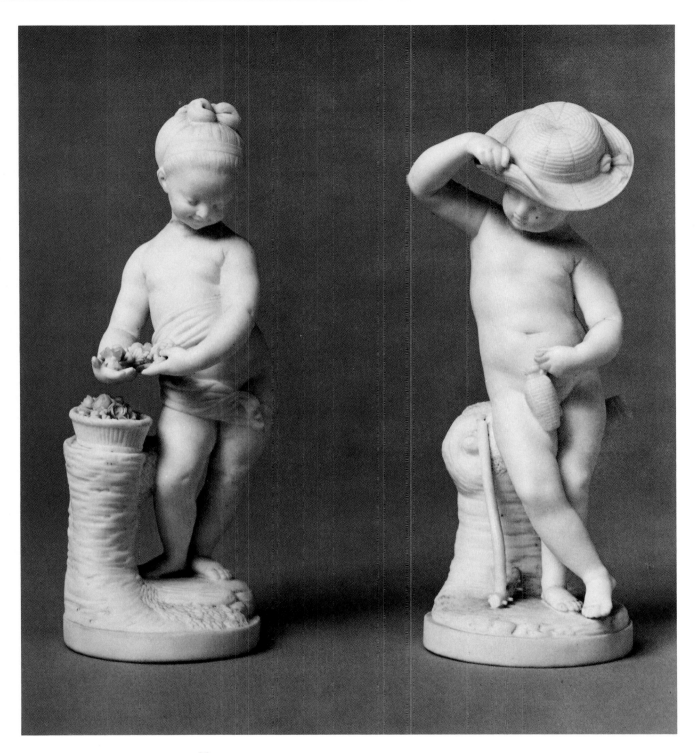

92. Pair of children, probably representing spring and fall. Sets of *saisons* and *enfants nus* were included in a 1789 Niderviller factory price list which was reproduced by Tainturier in 1868. Many of the Niderviller models made before the Revolution continued to be used in the nineteenth century. Marks: NIDERVILLER in relief on a raised lozenge and "E. no. 70" incised on base of male figure; "E. no. 69" incised on base of female figure. Height: 6¾ inches.

93. Two identical groups of country dancers. Several *groupes* or composi-
tions of *paysans* and *bergers* engaged in rustic activities were included in the
Niderviller list of 1789. These figure groups, however, are unmarked.
Height: 11½ inches.

94. Winged *amours* with attributes of Bacchus and Eros. The Niderviller price list of 1739 included *Amours et Saisons nus* and *Divinités et Saisons demi-nues* of six inches, but these figures are unmarked and cannot be attributed to that factory without additional evidence. Height: 6½ inches.

placed all around and there was an elegant variety of roast beef, veal, turkeys, ducks, fowls, hams, &c.; puddings, jellies, oranges, apples, nuts, almonds, figs, raisins, and a variety of wines and punch. We took our leave at six, more than an hour after the candles were introduced. No lady but Mrs. Washington dined with us. We were waited on by four or five men servants, dressed in livery."[213]

Four other purchases of table ornaments were recorded in the presidential account books from 1789 through early 1797. In New York, Thomas Burling supplied forty-three New York pounds'—$107.50—worth of "Table Ornaments" in July 1789; John and Nicholas Roosevelt added "Table Images" worth eleven pounds—$27.50—in January 1790.[214] After the arrival of the Angoulême groups, figures, and vases, there were no comparable purchases until the last month of Washington's presidency in Philadelphia, when table ornaments were supplied by two French china

and glass dealers, Pasquier and Company and Madame Decamps at $58 and $25 respectively, the latter for two figures and packing.[215] All of these ornaments except those purchased from Burling were charged to "contingent expenses," which was the president's personal account. Therefore, Washington's removal of the ornaments to Mount Vernon in March 1797 was legally proper.

In addition to the Angoulême pieces, there are nine other biscuit-porcelain figures which are now owned by the Peter family, descendants of Martha Parke Custis, second granddaughter of Martha Washington. Of these, four figures bear Niderviller marks. The marks, NIDERVILLE or NIDERVILLER on a raised lozenge or incised in the paste, were introduced at the factory after the Count de Custine's death in 1793, when Lanfrey became sole owner.[216] New models were introduced, but figures of the Custine period were also repeated.

VI

NEW YORK

AND

MOUNT VERNON,

1790

"Since my last to you ... I have removed to a larger house (the one lately occupied by the Count de Moustier), enlarged my table, and of course my Guests; let me therefore request the favor of you to add two pieces to the number of plateaux required in the above letter, and ornaments equivalent, for it will take these in addition to what I before asked, to decorate the present Table.

I would thank you also for sending to me at the same time fourteen (of what I believe are called) Patent lamps, similar to those used at Mr. R. Morris's, but less costly, two or at most three guineas a piece...." [George Washington in New York to Gouverneur Morris in Paris, March 1, 1790 (W 31:15)]

95. Sèvres hard-paste porcelain mustard pot and Nast cover, ca. 1778 and 1785. One of four "mustard pots" listed in the 1790 inventory of tableware sold to President Washington by the Count de Moustier, the pot lacks its original cover. See fig. 113. Height of pot: 2¾ inches. Marks: see fig. 96. (Peter collection, The National Museum of American History, Smithsonian Institution)

Moustier, continued the course of lavish balls and banquets from his appointment in 1787 until his recall to France in October 1789.

At the beginning of the search for a French *surtout*, Tobias Lear had mentioned the example of Moustier's table ornaments, which the president may have seen in New York on May 14, 1789, at the French legation on lower Broadway. The *Gazette of the United States* reported the following day: "Last Thursday evening, His Excellency THE MINISTER OF FRANCE, gave a Ball to THE PRESIDENT OF the UNITED STATES, which was uncommonly elegant, in respect both to the company and the plan of the entertainment. . . ."[217] Congressman Elias

The dining tables of Robert Morris and William Bingham had inspired President Washington to seek French ornaments for the nation's early state dinners in New York. Examples of stylish entertainments had also been offered by the French diplomatic corps beginning in 1780 with the Chevalier de la Luzerne in Philadelphia; Luzerne's successor as French minister, Éléanor-Françoise Élie, Count de

Boudinot of New Jersey described the "splendid Ball" to his wife: ". . . Three rooms were filled, and the fourth was most elegantly set off as a place of refreshment. A long table crossed this room, in the middle, from wall to wall. The whole wall, inside, was covered with shelves, filled with cakes, oranges, apples, wines of all sorts, ice creams, etc, and highly lighted up. A number of servants from

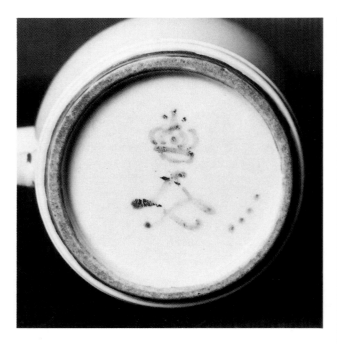

96. Marks on bottom of mustard pot, blue overglaze royal cipher with crown designating hard-paste porcelain. Four dots in a row were the mark of gilder Théodore, who was active at Sèvres from 1765 until 1771 or later. Incised marks visible near the footring to the left of the cipher: *ρℎ ⊂ ℬ.*

behind the table supplied the guests with every thing they wanted, from time to time, as they came to refresh themselves. . . ."[218]

Moustier, who came to New York highly recommended by both Lafayette and Jefferson, seems to have become a personal friend of the Washingtons.[219] Accompanied by his sister-in-law, Madame de Bréhan, the French minister had spent several days at Mount Vernon in November 1788. At that time, Madame de Bréhan, an accomplished amateur artist, began a miniature profile of the retired general. The portrait was completed at a sitting in New York on October 3, 1789, and was graciously judged "exceedingly like the Original" by the president.[220] Moustier's correspondence with the French minister of foreign affairs also emphasized his friendship with the American president. Of the reception honoring Washington's arrival in New York, Moustier, who was a teetotaler, wrote: "There was a great provision of wine and punch, which the President himself offered to

me; but I reminded him how I had objected, in Mount Vernon to that usage."[221]

Evangelistic abstinence was only one of many eccentricities displayed by the Count de Moustier. A vivid picture of his unusual behavior was included in a recollection of dinner on September 27, 1789, at Richmond Hill, the New York residence of Vice President John Adams: "in the centre of the table sat Vice President Adams, in full dress. . . . On his right sat Baron Steuben. . . . On his left was Mr.

97. Profile of Washington, painted by the Marchioness de Bréhan (dates unknown), sister-in-law of the French minister to the United States, the Count de Moustier (1751–1817). Mme de Bréhan and the count visited Mount Vernon in November 1788, and thereafter seemed quite intimate with the Washingtons. In New York on October 3, 1789, President Washington wrote in his diary that he sat "for Madame de Bréhan to complete a miniature profile of me. . . ." Less than two weeks later, the Washingtons paid a farewell visit to the marchioness and the count, who had been recalled to France. Mme de Bréhan took the original ivory miniature, now in the Mabel Brady Garvan Collection at Yale, to France, but copies and engravings were sent to Washington in 1790. The watercolor copy pictured here was given to Mrs. William Bingham by President Washington in 1791. (The Mount Vernon Ladies' Association collections)

98. President Washington's dinner table as it might have appeared on "public days," when members of Congress, the cabinet, and the foreign ministers dined at his New York and Philadelphia residences. The silver-plated centerpiece, or *surtout*, and the Angoulême biscuit-porcelain ornaments were sent from Paris by Gouverneur Morris in 1790. The large Sèvres table service was purchased from the Court de Moustier in the same year. In addition to plates, Sèvres pieces visible on the table include an oval serving dish, a sauceboat, a broth bowl or *écuelle*, and a small casserole or *poêlon*. The butter dish at the right was made at Dihl and Guérhard's Duc d'Angoulême factory. (The Mount Vernon Ladies' Association collections)

99. No. 39 Broadway, built in 1786 by Alexander Macomb, lithograph in Valentine's *Manual of the Corporation of the City of New York*, 1855, opp. p. 582. On January 30, 1790, President Washington decided to lease this property, which had been the French legation, and, therefore, the residence of the Count de Moustier until his recall to France in October 1789. On February 3, Washington visited the legation and decided to purchase furniture, mirrors, and a large service of Sèvres porcelain left behind by Moustier. (Courtesy, The New-York Historical Society, New York City)

Jefferson, who had just returned from France, conspicuous in his red waistcoat and breeches, the fashion of Versailles. Opposite sat Mrs. Adams... next to... the courtly Count du Moustiers, the French ambassador, in his red-heeled shoes and ear-rings. ..." Moustier took no food at all until "at length his own body cook, in a clean white linen cap, a clean white *tablier* before him, a brilliantly white damask *serviette* flung over his arm, and a warm pie of truffles and game in his hand, came bustling eagerly through the crowd of waiters, and placed it before the Count, who reserving a moderate share to himself, distributed the rest among his neighbors."[222]

American objections to Moustier's odd manners and his questionable relationship with Madame de Bréhan, who reportedly kept a pet monkey and a Negro child for her own amusement, helped bring about the diplomat's recall in October 1789.[223] President and Mrs. Washington, however, esteemed the couple highly enough to pay them a farewell visit on October 14, and Washington and Moustier exchanged letters for the next two years.[224]

In need of more space for his large presidential family, Washington decided to move to the house still occupied by the French legation after Moustier's departure. On January 30, 1790, he agreed to rent the lower Broadway property, which was larger than his Cherry Street residence and also more convenient to Federal Hall on Wall Street. Washington's diary for February recorded a month-long preoccupation with details of improvement and furnishing, including the acquisition of furnishings left behind by Moustier. On February 3, he "fixed on some furniture of the Ministers," which included mirrors, sideboards, and chairs as well as a large service of white Sèvres porcelain with gold dentate —*dent-de-loup*—borders.[225] The manuscript account of furnishings for the official residences in New York and Philadelphia reveals that "C^t de Moustier" was paid £ 665.16.6. for "Stoves, China etc., etc."[226] That figure is

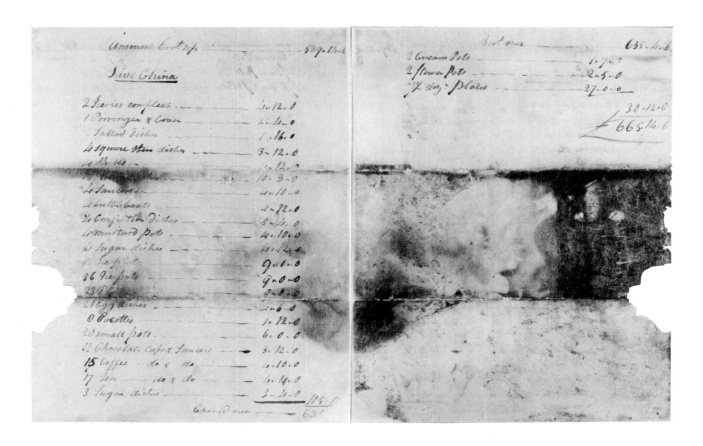

100. Invoice for "Save" china purchased by President Washington from the Count de Moustier in February 1790. All of the china was white with gold rims which were either simple or dentate, but not all of the pieces were Sèvres. Surviving examples reveal that Moustier had supplemented a basic Sèvres dinner and dessert service with pieces from other French factories. (Archives of the Mount Vernon Ladies' Association)

101. French porcelain chiller, Locré factory, 39 rue Fontaine-Roy, La Courtille, Paris, ca. 1785. One of two "iceries compleat" listed in the March 4,
1790, inventory of 309 pieces of white-and-gold table porcelain sold to
President Washington by the Count de Moustier. Although most of the
service was Sèvres, there are many surviving pieces which bear the marks
of other factories. Chillers—*seaux à glace*—were used at dessert to keep
ices and fruit cold. Height: 8½ inches. (Peter Collection, The National
Museum of American History, Smithsonian Institution)

102. Crossed-torches mark, underglaze blue, of the Locré factory at La
Courtille, on the bottom of the chiller. Jean–Baptiste Locré de Roissy
opened his factory of "German porcelain" and registered his mark in 1773.

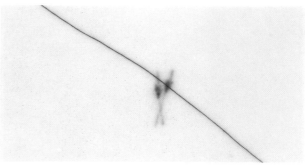

103. *Plateau à deux pots à confiture*, Sèvres, 1778. Listed as "confection dishes" in the 1790 inventory, three of the original four purchased by President Washington survive. Covered cups—attached to a tray—held preserves for the dessert course. Length: 10 inches; overall height: 3½ inches. (The Mount Vernon Ladies' Association collections)

104. Overglaze mark on the bottom of the tray with confection pots. The crown above the royal cipher indicates a hard-paste porcelain body, and the letters within the cipher are a code for the year of manufacture, 1778. The initials "HP" are the mark of gilder Prévost aîné, who worked at Sèvres from 1754 until 1793. An identical gilder's mark and date letters also appear on the *écuelle* in Washington's service. In 1778, the Count de Moustier purchased a table service and ornaments at the royal manufactory at Sèvres. Among the items listed on his bill of sale were "4 *Plateaus à deux pots*" and "1 *Ecuelle.*"

also given in an inventory of the purchases, but in the latter document, now at Mount Vernon, the Sèvres or "Save" China was itemized for a total cost of £ 136.3., or about $340, for 309 pieces. At about thirty-five New York pounds less than the Angoulême biscuit figures, Washington's elegant secondhand Sèvres seems to have been something of a bargain.

The Washingtons moved into the former French legation on February 22, and the first Thursday dinner served to all twenty-six senators took place on March 4. Senator Maclay, who fortunately kept a diary, described the occasion as "a dinner of dignity," but the president seemed bored or distracted for "at every interval of eating or drinking he played on the table with a fork or knife, like a drumstick."[227] Obviously, the new rooms and furnishings accommodated an increase in the number of guests at the weekly formal dinners. Although the *plateaux* and ornaments had not yet arrived from France, Washington wrote to Gouverneur Morris on March 1 for two more *plateaux* because "I have removed to a larger house . . . enlarged my table, and of course my Guests."[228]

A survey of Washington's white-and-gold porcelain in several collections reveals that at least 122 pieces have survived.[229] In addition to many of the seven-and-one-half-dozen original dinner and soup plates, there are one or more examples of each form listed in the March 4, 1790, inventory with the exception of flowerpots and cream pots. In the following list, surviving pieces of Washington's Sèvres have been identified—when possible—with original factory models.[230]

Inventory	Sèvres Model
2 Iceries Compleat	not Sèvres
1 Porringer & Cover	*écuelle rond*
2 Sallad dishes	*saladier*
4 square stew dishes	*compotier carré*
4 shells	not Sèvres
15 Round dishes	*assiettes de dessert*
4 Saucers	*saucière*
4 butter boats	*beurrier*

4 Confection dishes	*plateau à deux pots à confiture*
4 mustard pots	*moutardier*
4 Sugar dishes	*sucrier de Monsieur le Premier*
12 Ice plates	*plateau Bourette*
36 Ice pots	*tasse à glace*
23 Pl[atters]	several models
21 Egg dishes	*coquetier de 1776*
8 Cocottes	*poêlon* or *cocotte*
20 small pots	*pot à jus*
12 Chocolate cups & saucers	possibly a larger *tasse litron*
15 Coffee do	*tasse litron*
17 Tea do	*gobelet Bouillard*
3 Sugar dishes	*pot à sucre Calabre*
2 Cream Pots	
2 flower Pots	

The archives of the Manufacture Nationale de Sèvres retains a sale document naming "Mr. le comte de Moutier" as buyer on May 9, 1778, of a similar service of tableware with additional ornamental pieces.[231] The bill of sale does not describe the decoration so that identification of that service with the pieces Moustier sold to President Washington is not certain. Significantly, however, the only Sèvres date-letters found on existing pieces of Washington's service are "AA"—for 1778—on the *écuelle* and the confection dishes. These are two of the forms listed on Moustier's 1778 Sèvres invoice.

Between 1778 and 1788, Moustier enlarged his original Sèvres service with white-and-gold pieces from other French factories and possibly procured additional pieces from Sèvres. For example, Moustier purchased six dozen plates from Sèvres in 1778, but he sold seven-and-one-half-dozen Sèvres and Angoulême plates to Washington in 1790. The crossed-torches mark of the La Courtille factory appears on one of Washington's chillers; the stenciled Angoulême mark of the Dihl and Guérhard partnership is on several plates and serving pieces; the mark of the Nast factory is on two large cups; and that of the Count d'Artois factory at Limoges is found on a *cocotte* or casserole.

French inventories of the 1770s reveal that a taste for plain, well-made furnishings, including undecorated white porcelain tableware, existed among members of the French urban and rural aristocracy.[232] Connoisseurs of today also consider minimal gilt decoration on eighteenth-century white porcelain "the supreme triumph of any factory, for it demands faultless pieces."[233] In the case of Moustier's Sèvres, the lack of decoration beyond gold borders and a few gold dots and flourishes means that all craftsmen's painted marks on the reverse of extant pieces are those of gilders. The following occur with the Sèvres cipher, which is surmounted by a crown on the hard-paste pieces:[234]

Mark (all overglaze blue unless noted)	Gilder
H P (in red)	Prévost aîné (active 1754–1793)
2ooo	Vincent jeune (1753–1806)
••••	Théodore (1765–1771 or later)
K	Girard (1772–1817)
△	Capelle (1746–1800)
A (in red)	C.E. Asselin (1765–1804)
g (occurs most frequently)*	unidentified
⌒	unidentified
m : f	unidentified
7'	unidentified
⌣	unidentified
Y	unidentified
m : w	unidentified

Mark	Gilder
'T'	unidentified
M a	unidentified
Y	unidentified
B D **	unidentified

*Perhaps Mlle Julie Gremont, who was listed as a gilder at Sèvres in 1775.
**Perhaps Baudouin père (active 1750–1800).

Washington's Sèvres service contained most of the forms of comparable table services produced by that factory in the 1770s and 1780s. A variety of shapes had been developed to serve a formal dinner in which each of about four courses would be placed on the table in a symmetrical pattern based on units of four. In this method of service, often called "French" by Americans, each diner would help himself and his neighbors to the nearest dishes. Servants carried the filled or clean plates to guests and periodically removed dirty ones. Senator Maclay, dining once again in New York with President Washington on Thursday, January 20, 1791, recorded a humorous instance of French service gone awry: "At dinner, after my second plate had been taken away, the President offered to help me to part of a dish which stood before him. Was ever anything so unlucky? I had just before declined being helped to anything more, with some expression that denoted my having made up my dinner. Had, of course, for the sake of consistency, to thank him negatively. but when the dessert came, he was distributing a pudding, he gave me a look of interrogation. and I returned the thanks positive."[235]

In France, the first course would have included a mixture of meats in stock or broth served in tureens and various *compotiers* or dishes. The second course would have included a roast, meat juices served in small cups, vegetables, and salads. A third course might have featured pies, salads, eggs. and ragouts in small casseroles called *poêlons*. The dessert course was always the most spectacular, with both

105. *Plateau Bourette* with three *tasses à glace*, Sèvres, ca. 1778. Twelve "ice plates" and thirty-six "ice pots" were listed in the 1790 inventory of tableware sold to President Washington by the Count de Moustier. These pieces would have been placed at intervals on the table to be served from dishes of frozen confection in the "iceries" during the dessert course. Fruit ices and ice creams were served in a partly melted state to be sipped as well as spooned. Moustier purchased twenty-four ice cups and twelve trays from the royal manufactory in 1778. The tray in the picture bears the overglaze blue mark "2000" of gilder Vincent jeune (active 1753–1806), while the cups display a triangle in overglaze red for gilder Capelle (active 1746–1800). All four pieces have the royal cipher mark but no crown or date letters. Greatest width of tray: 8½ inches; height of cups: 2½ inches. (The tray is in the Peter family collection. The center cup is in a private collection. The other two cups are in the Mount Vernon Ladies' Association collections.)

106. *Saucière*, Sèvres, ca. 1780. Four sauceboats were simply called "saucers" on the 1790 inventory. Another of Washington's four sauceboats is preserved in the White House China Room. Although this Sèvres form, a simplified version of an earlier model by Jean-Claude Duplessis, was usually accompanied by a lozenge-shape tray, no such dishes are known among the surviving pieces in Washington's French table service. Height: 3½ inches; length: 8¾ inches. (Peter family collection)

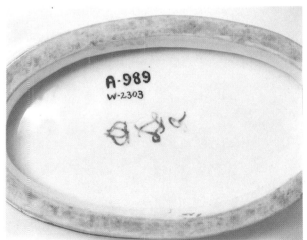

107. Sèvres mark painted over the glaze on the bottom of Washington's sauceboat. The crown above the royal cipher indicates hard-paste porcelain while the script "g" below is the mark of a gilder—possibly Mlle Julie Gremont, who was listed in the factory records in 1775. The "g" occurs more frequently on pieces in the Moustier-Washington service than any other gilder's mark.

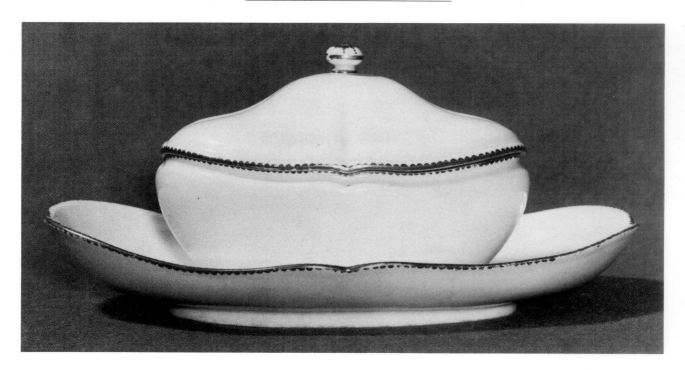

108. Sèvres porcelain sugar dish of the form called *sucrier de Monsieur le Premier* in the factory archives. These were table sugar dishes used for sugar and sweet sauces at dessert, as opposed to coffee and tea sugar dishes, which were smaller and nearly cylindrical in form. Marks: ⅌ in overglaze blue below the Sèvres cipher; ⅌ ⅌ incised. Overall height: 4¼ inches; overall length: 10 inches. (The Mount Vernon Ladies' Association collections)

109. French porcelain coffee cup and saucer, Paris, Nast factory, ca. 1785. These cups may have been purchased by Moustier to use with the larger Sèvres coffee cups, which they nearly match in size. Mark: NAST stenciled in overglaze red. Height: 3¼ inches; diameter of saucer: 5¼ inches. (The Mount Vernon Ladies' Association collections)

dried and fresh fruit in pyramids, preserves and ices, the latter served barely frozen in footed cups on special plates called *plateaux Bourette*. Senator Maclay's description of an earlier presidential dinner in August 1789 indicated that Washington served comparable courses at his Thursday dinners.[236]

The Moustier dinner and dessert service was taken to Philadelphia from New York when the seat of government was transferred in late 1790 and to Mount Vernon when Washington retired in 1797. There, the family continued

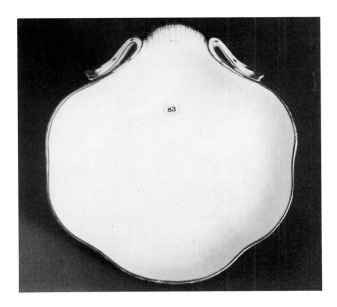

110. French porcelain dish, Paris, Duc d'Angoulême factory, ca. 1785. One of four "shells" listed on the invoice of March 4, 1790, the dish was one of the pieces evidently purchased by Moustier to supplement his Sèvres service. (Peter family collection)

111. Stenciled mark in red on the reverse of the shell dish. Under the patronage of the Duke d'Angoulême until the French Revolution, the partnership of Christophe Dihl and Antoine Guérhard manufactured hard-paste porcelain at their factory on rue de Bondy in Paris from 1781 until 1789, when they moved to the boulevard du Temple. The factory closed in 1828.

112. Two coffee cups and one teacup, Sèvres, ca. 1775. The coffee cups or cans are the form called *tasse litron*, or *gobelet litron*, in the factory archives while that of the teacup was called *gobelet Bouillard*. *Tasse* and *gobelet* were interchangeable terms for cups of any form. Among the pieces of Washington's Sèvres service now at Mount Vernon are two sizes of coffee cup. The inventory of pieces he bought from Moustier listed coffee, tea, and chocolate cups which may have been simply the larger coffee cups.

Moustier's 1778 bill of sale from the Sèvres factory listed thirty-six *tasses à thé* at four livres each, eighteen *gobelets* at four livres each, and twelve—presumably larger—*gobelets* at five livres each. All six pieces bear the royal cipher with a script "g" below in overglaze blue. Height of coffee cups: 2¼ inches and 2¾ inches; height of teacup: 2 inches; diameter of saucers: 5 inches, 5½ inches, and 5¼ inches. (The Mount Vernon Ladies' Association collections)

113. French porcelain covered cup, Paris, probably Nast, ca. 1785. Moustier had evidently augmented the Sèvres gravy cups in his original service with these, which bear an obscured mark, apparently that of the Nast factory (1780–1835) on rue des Amandiers Popincourt. Overall height: 3¼ inches. (The Mount Vernon Ladies' Association collections)

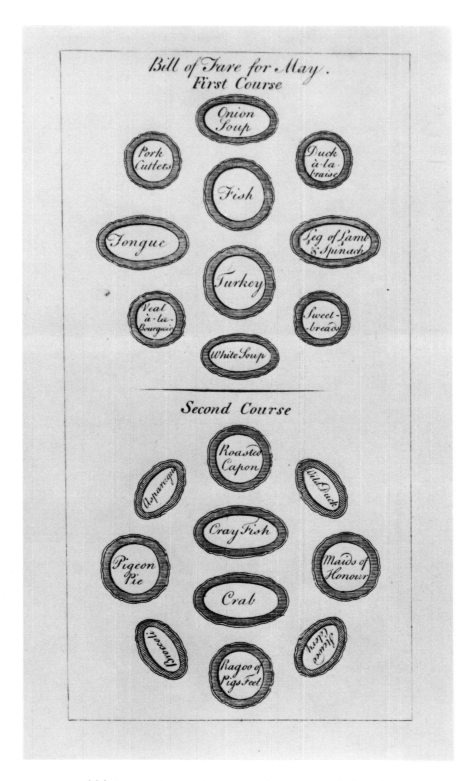

114. A suggested menu and arrangement for two courses of a dinner in John Farley, *The London Art of Cookery and Housekeeper's Complete Assistant*, London, 1785. Symmetrical placement of dishes on the table required serving pieces in multiples of two or four. (Courtesy, The Library Company of Philadelphia)

115. Sèvres egg cup and covered gravy or custard cup, soft-paste porcelain, ca. 1778. Listed as "21 Egg dishes" and "20 small pots" on the March 4, 1790, invoice, these forms are a *coquetier de 1776* and a *pot à jus*, names for designs found in the archives of the Manufacture Nationale de Sèvres. On May 9, 1778, Moustier purchased twenty-four "Coquetiers" and the same number of "Pots à jus" at the royal manufactory. Both pieces are marked with the royal cipher and a script "g" below. Height of egg cup: 1¼ inches; overall height of covered cup: 3¼ inches. (The Mount Vernon Ladies' Association collections)

to use the French porcelain for "genteel dinners," one of which was described by a Polish visitor in his diary on June 13, 1798: "On our return we found a notable and unexpected company from Alexandria. The table in the great hall was set out with a Sèvres porcelain service with places for 20."[237]

After Mrs. Washington's death, the white-and-gold French porcelain was evidently divided into thirds and purchased by her granddaughters, Eliza Parke Custis Law, Martha Parke Custis Peter, and Eleanor (Nelly) Parke Custis Lewis, at the sale of her personal estate on July 20, 1802.[238] Many pieces have been acquired by Mount Vernon from the Peter, Lewis, and Law descendants, and nineteen pieces were purchased by the United States government from the Lewis family in 1878.

116. English soaprock porcelain coffee cup and saucer, transfer-printed in blue under the glaze, possibly Liverpool, ca. 1790–1795. In July 1790, Tobias Lear ordered three dozen teacups and two dozen blue-and-white coffee cups from Philadelphia for Mrs. Washington. He specified that they be "handsome, but not of the highest price, as they are for common use," and that they should be sent directly to Mount Vernon. Although the cups and saucers from Philadelphia have never been identified, they may have been these English pieces, which were printed to imitate Chinese wares of the same period. Diameter of saucer: 5¼ inches; height of cup: 2¼ inches. (The Mount Vernon Ladies' Association collections)

SUMMER AT MOUNT VERNON

With Congress in recess while the national government was being transferred from New York to Philadelphia, the Washingtons returned to Virginia for three months in the late summer and early fall of 1790.[239] The Cincinnati and Sèvres table services were left behind to be moved with the other presidential furnishings. As the china supplies at Mount Vernon were somewhat depleted, Mrs. Washington —through Tobias Lear—asked Clement Biddle, a Philadelphia merchant and agent for the president, to look for "handsome blue and white china Tea and Coffee Cups and Saucers" to match china at Mount Vernon. Lear requested that they should not be too expensive "as they are for common use."

Although Biddle's replies have not been located, it is evident that he found the requisite number of tea cups—three dozen—and coffee cups—two dozen—with three or four slop bowls in "enameld" china and that he thought it probable they could also be obtained in blue and white. Mrs. Washington authorized the purchase of either type, with preference for the blue and white, and on August 8, 1790, Lear acknowledged Biddle's invoice of August 5 for the "China sent to Mount Vernon."

Meanwhile, at Mount Vernon, anticipation of the family's return brought about some refurbishing. Silk thread and blue silk cording were purchased for the chairs and settee in the parlor. The cash memorandum kept by George Augustine Washington, the president's nephew and manager, also recorded the purchase of two "Burnt China" sugar dishes from Thomas Poultney in Alexandria on August 7.[240] These may have been purchased to use with the cups, saucers, and slop bowls which had just arrived from Philadelphia.

Two English porcelain coffee cups and several saucers, which would have been available in Philadelphia at the time of Biddle's shipment, were given to Mount Vernon in 1938 by J. P. Morgan, who had purchased them from descendants of Martha Parke Custis Peter. The cups are transfer-printed, bone-ash porcelain with designs imitating the popular blue-and-white Nanking wares imported by the English East India Company. Such products from the Caughley factory and several Liverpool establishments in the last two decades of the eighteenth century were meant to supplement and replace Chinese services. Chinese and English articles bearing similar patterns were also mixed in table services in England. For example, in 1796 the Phillips auction house in London offered "A Capital and extensive Table service of Nankin porcelain . . . an oval Salopian Caughley dish and fish tray nearly to correspond in pattern."[241]

Although these Mount Vernon pieces have previously been given a Caughley attribution, they are unmarked and are more likely to have been Liverpool products.[242] A group of Liverpool porcelain factories, including those of Seth and James Pennington and Thomas Wolfe, exported most of their wares to the United States and, therefore, have not been extensively studied by English ceramics historians. Characteristics shared by the Washington teawares and known or attributed Liverpool examples include a highly reflective glaze; dense, dark blues in the transfers; and a consistent lack of factory marks.

Soon after the Washingtons arrived at Mount Vernon on September 11 for their three-month respite, the president began to worry about the packing and shipping of his costly French table ornaments from New York to Philadelphia. During September and October, he sent a stream of instructions and cautions to Tobias Lear with final ap-

◄ *117*. Biscuit-porcelain bust of Jacques Necker, Sèvres, 1790. In March 1790, the Count d'Estaing, commander of French naval forces in the American Revolution, sent the bust of Necker, a briefly popular French political leader, to Mount Vernon, where President Washington discovered it the following October. Jean Antoine Houdon sculpted the marble original, and Louis-Simon Boizot made the Sèvres master model in late 1789 or early 1790. Washington's figure bears a partly obliterated, incised mark: *JR 21* , probably that of Josse-François-Joseph Le Riche, who was active at Sèvres as a modeler and sculptor from 1757 until 1801. The bust of Necker was placed on a bracket over the door in Washington's study at Mount Vernon. Height, including marble base: 23 ½ inches. (The Mount Vernon Ladies' Association collections)

proval on November 7 for the placement of the large bis-cuit images on the sideboards in the dining room of the Philadelphia house.

During the family's stay at Mount Vernon, queens-ware plates and mugs were purchased from Col. Philip Marsteller in Alexandria. That purchase and two later addi-tions of queensware platters, plates, and soup plates entered in the August 1791 cash memoranda of Mount Vernon's managers, George Augustine Washington and Anthony Whiting, reveal that English cream-colored earthenware continued in service there in the 1790s.[243] With the blue-and-white china "in common use," queensware would serve the daily needs of the residents of Mount Vernon until and beyond the final return of the Washingtons in 1797.

A MEMENTO OF THE FRENCH REVOLUTION

A "package from Baltimore" containing "a Bust of Mr. Necker" in biscuit porcelain and a number of prints sur-prised and obviously puzzled President Washington early in his sojourn at Mount Vernon. On October 3, he wrote to Tobias Lear to ask him to search the letters from the Count d'Estaing, commander of the French naval forces in the American Revolution, for information about the gift. A plaque on the bust had been inscribed: "Presented to George Washington, President of the United States of America, by his most dutiful, most obedient, and most humble servant,

ESTAING, a citizen of the state of Georgia, by an act of 22d Feb., 1785, and a citizen of France in 1786."

The bust of Jacques Necker, popular French comptroller general at the outbreak of the Revolution in 1789, thus joined the Key to the Bastille, "the token of victory gained by Liberty over Despotism," which Lafayette had pre-viously sent to Washington through the courtesy of Thomas Paine, as tributes to "the patriarch of Liberty."[244] Jean Antoine Houdon had executed the original marble sculp-ture by December 30, 1789, and Sèvres began producing biscuit-porcelain copies soon thereafter.[245] The Sèvres model was made by Louis-Simon Boizot, who had become head of the biscuit-porcelain studio in 1773.[246] Portrait busts were extremely popular in revolutionary France; as Prudhomme stated in 1806, one saw the bust of the current idol on every mantelpiece. Portraits of Necker and Lafayette were soon succeeded by those of Mirabeau, Bailly, and finally Marat and Robespierre.[247]

The silver label on the base of the Necker bust bears the words QUI NOBIS RESTITUIT REM (who put our affairs in order), which only temporarily applied to Necker, who had fled to his native Geneva before Washington received the bust in October 1790.[248] The Count d'Estaing himself would be destroyed by the excesses of revolutionary terror. He shared the fate of the Count du Custine, another of Washington's admirers, on the guillotine in 1793.

VII

THE

PHILADELPHIA

YEARS,

1791 TO 1797

118. Biscuit-porcelain plaque, Bristol, 1777–1778. The porcelain portrait of Benjamin Franklin given to George Washington by Richard Champion was probably identical to this one (see page 147). Champion also made plain, circular medallions with the same bust of Franklin. One of these—marked with the Bristol incised cross—was formerly thought to be Sèvres. (Copyright British Museum)

"*He devoted one hour every other Tuesday, from three to four, to . . . visits. He understood himself to be visited as the President of the United States, and not on his own account. He was not to be seen by any body and every body; but required that every one who came should be introduced by his secretary, or by some gentleman, whom he knew himself. He lived on the south side of Market Street, just below Sixth. The place of reception was the dining room in the rear, twenty-five or thirty feet in length, including the bow projecting into the garden. Mrs. Washington received her visitors in the two rooms on the second floor, from front to rear.*

At three o'clock, or at any time within a quarter of an hour afterwards, the visitor was conducted to this dining room, from which all seats had been removed for the time. On entering he saw the tall manly figure of Washington clad in black velvet; his hair in full dress, powdered and gathered behind in a large silk bag; yellow gloves on his hands; holding a cocked hat with a cockade in it, and the edges adorned with a black feather about an inch deep. He wore knee and shoe buckles; and a long sword,

with a finely wrought and polished steel hilt, which appeared at the left hip; the coat worn over the sword, so that the hilt, and the part below the folds of the coat behind, were in view. The scabbard was white polished leather.

He stood always in front of the fireplace, with his face towards the door of entrance. The visitor was conducted to him, and he required to have the name so distinctly pronounced, that he could hear it. He had the very uncommon faculty of associating a man's name, and personal appearance, so durably in his memory, as to be able to call any one by name, who made him a second visit. He received his visiter with a dignified bow, while his hands were so disposed of as to indicate that the salutation was not to be accompanied with shaking hands. This ceremony never occurred in these visits, even with his most near friends, that no distinction might be made.

As visiters came in, they formed a circle around the room. At a quarter past three, the door was closed, and the circle was formed for that day. He then began on the right, and spoke to each visiter, calling him by name, and exchanging a few words with him. When he had completed his circuit, he resumed his first position, and the visiters approached him, in succession, bowed and retired. By four o'clock this ceremony was over.

On the evenings when Mrs. Washington received visiters, he did not consider himself as visited. He was then as a private gentleman, dressed usually in some colored coat and waistcoat, (the only one recollected was brown, with bright buttons) and black, on his lower limbs. He had then neither hat nor sword; he moved about among the company, conversing with one and another. He had once a fortnight an official dinner, and select companies on other days. He sat (it is said) at the side, in a central position, Mrs. Washington opposite; the two ends were occupied by members of his family, or by personal friends." [Recollection by William Sullivan (1774–1839) in Familiar Letters on Public Characters and Public Events, *Boston: Rusell, Odione, and Metcalf, 1834, pp. 75 and 76]*

In the summer of 1790, the Philadelphia City Corporation selected the house of Robert Morris at 190 High—now Market—Street for the new presidential residence. Since he had spent several weeks with the Morris family during the Constitutional Convention in 1787, Washington was familiar with the arrangement of rooms and outbuildings on the property.[249] While at Mount Vernon, he wrote to his secretary, Tobias Lear, "It is, I believe, the best Single house in the City; yet without additions, it is inadequate to the commodious accommodations of my family."[250] Lear had remained in New York to supervise the move to Philadelphia and, from September through early November, the president sent him at least ten long letters with detailed instructions. These included Washington's suggestions for additions such as bow windows to lengthen the state dining and drawing rooms; for the "appropriation of the furniture"; and for the storage of the "Images, Save [Sèvres] China, and other things of this sort."

By December 7, 1790, the Washington household, which included Eleanor Parke Custis—known as Nelly—George Washington Parke Custis, Mr. and Mrs. Lear, the president's three secretaries, and about twenty servants, was sufficiently settled in the Philadelphia house for the president to hold his first levee in the new capital.[251] The New York schedule of Tuesday levees, Thursday dinners for diplomats and members of Congress, and Mrs. Washington's Friday drawing rooms continued in Philadelphia until the end of the second administration in March 1797. Sally McKean, daughter of Pennsylvania's chief justice, wrote chauvinistically to a friend in New York that the December 24, 1790, drawing room was "brilliant beyond anything you could imagine, and though there was a good deal of extravagance, there was so much of Philadelphia taste in everything that it must be confessed the most delightful occasion of the kind ever known in this country."[252] By February 1791, Abigail Adams observed that Philadelphia was ". . . one continued scene of Parties upon Parties, Balls and entertainments equal to any European city. . . ."[253]

Thursday dinners were held at four o'clock in the state dining room, which had been lengthened to thirty-four feet by the bow window overlooking the backyard.[254] Furnishings of the carpeted dining room included "Crimson Persian" curtains and the sideboards purchased in New York from the Count de Moustier.[255] Tobias Lear proposed to place one of the large biscuit figure groups under protective glass domes on each of the sideboards so that they would be convenient to the sectional dining tables for what the president called "public days" as well as being "an ornament to the Room."

With windows facing High Street, the family dining room, used for all meals except the formal Thursday dinners, was adjacent to the state dining room. "Blue furniture" and matching curtains were used there, according to Lear's letter of November 14, 1790.[256] In the family dining room, breakfasts of toast or cornmeal cakes, honey, and sliced tongue or ham were followed at three by dinner. A light supper or tea was usually served at eight in the evening.[257]

EARLY PURCHASES

The china and queensware brought from New York apparently were adequate for the state and family tables through 1791 and most of 1792. Recorded expenses for tableware in those years included only cheap cups, saucers, and bowls

The Residence of Washington in High Street — 1795-6.

2ᵈ door below 6ᵗ Street south side of Market St

for the servants in the High Street residence; $1.44 for mending a tureen and china dishes; and $62.57 to James Gallagher in late 1792 for glass and china. Gallagher, whose shop was between a grocer and a brush manufacturer near the corner of High and South Second streets, four squares east of the presidential mansion, continued to sell small amounts of china and glassware to the president through March 6, 1797, when he supplied "China & Glass to send to Virgª."[258]

Early in Washington's second administration, on June 18, 1793, "a sett of China" at a relatively high $211 was acquired from John Bringhurst, "fancy-goods merchant," on South Third Street. The china from Bringhurst cost

119. The Residence of Washington in High Street, watercolor, painted ca. 1810 by W.L. Breton (1775–1856). A note below the title adds that the house was "2ᵈ door below 6ᵗ Street south side of Market St," as High Street is now called. At one time owned by a grandson of William Penn, the house was rebuilt in 1785 by Robert Morris. Washington stayed there with the Morrises for several months in the summer of 1787. In 1790, the house was selected by the Philadelphia City Corporation as the best available for the president when the seat of government was transferred from New York to Philadelphia. Morris then moved to the house next door—just visible at the right. The Washingtons occupied 190 High Street until March 1797, and President and Mrs. John Adams lived there until 1800, when they moved into the new presidential mansion in the Federal City. The building was removed in 1832. (Manuscript Department, The Historical Society of Pennsylvania)

Juſt Imported, and To be Sold, By

James Gallagher,

At his China and Glaſs-Ware

STORE,

In Second-ſtreet, the third door below Market-ſtreet, and oppoſite the Quaker's Meeting-houſe.

CHINA, Blue and White, and Enameled.
GALLON, three quart, two quart, one quart, and pint Bowls.
Round and oval Diſhes and Plates.
Tea and Coffee Pots of different ſizes.
Tea and Coffee-Cups and Saucers, ditto.
Sugar Diſhes and Milk Pots.
Pudding Pans and Sop Bowls.
Brown and blue Tea Cups and Saucers.
Brown, burnt china Tea Pots, Sugar Diſhes and Cream Pots.

QUEEN's-WARE.

ROUND and oval Diſhes, of all ſizes.
Flat and Soup Plates.
Sallad Diſhes and Fiſh Drains.
Pudding Diſhes and Diſh Covers.
Pepper and Muſtard Pots, and Salts.
Round and oval Tureens, of all ſizes.
Wiſh Hand Baſons and Bottles, and quart Mugs.
Quart, pint, and half pint Bowls.
Tea Pots and Slop Bowls.
Tea Cups and Saucers.
Sugar Diſhes and Cream Pots.

GLASS, ſingle and double Flint, plain and cut.

GALLON, half gallon, quart, pint, and half pint Decanters.
Flowered and plain Goblets, Mugs.
Half gallon, quart, pint, half pint, jill and half jill Tumblers.
Quart, pint, and half pint, cut and ſtemed, plain and labelled Punch, Grog, and Beer Glaſſes, with and without Covers.
Cut, flowered, and plain Wine Glaſſes, of all ſizes.
Table Waſh Baſons, Cream Pots, Vinegar Cruets, Pepper and Muſtard Pots, and Salts.
Eleven by 9, 10 by 8, 9 by 7, and 8 by 6, Engliſh, French, and Spaniſh Window Glaſs, by the box or ſmaller quantity.

A neat ASSORTMENT of

CUTLERY AND HARD-WARE,

Conſiſting of,

WHITE and ſtained ivory, real and ſham buck, bone, cam wood, and ebony handled Knives and Forks.
Torrois ſhell, real buck, and ſtained horn Penknives.
Beſt cap'd and plain Raizos and Lancets.
Cutteau, ſhoe, and butchers Knives.
Siſſars and taylors' Sheers,
Hand Axes, claw and lathing Hammers.
Augers, Gouges, Chiſſels, Files, and Raſps.
Jointer and Plane Irons, and two feet Rules.
Cheſt, H and HL Hinges, of different ſizes.
Stock, cheſt, common, and bag Padlocks.
Gimblets, Braſs Cocks, and Snuffers.
Knitting, ſail, and ſewing Needles.
Mens and womens Thimbles.
Fiſh Hooks of all ſorts and ſizes.
Leather Ink Pots, common and temple Spectacles.
Plated, pinchbeck, yellow, and white metal, and ſteel Shoe and Knee Buckles; Chapes.
Coat, veſt and ſleeve, metal and horn Buttons.

---

more than any other ceramic purchase charged to the president's contingency fund except Moustier's Sèvres, which cost \$340, and the Angoulême figures at \$450. Unfortunately, this service has not been identified.[259]

INTERVALS IN NEARBY GERMANTOWN

To escape the yellow fever epidemic then raging in the city, Washington spent most of November 1793 and six weeks in the summer of 1794 in Germantown, northwest of Philadelphia. The house of Col. Isaac Franks, now within the city of Philadelphia at 5442 Germantown Avenue, was leased to the Washington family. Franks agreed to rent the house furnished, but two loads of supplementary furniture had to be sent from 190 High Street, according to the president's account book under August 16, 1794. Sometime after December 20, 1793, Franks submitted an "Account of Extraordinary . . . Expense to Accomodate the President of the United States."[260] Attached to the bill was an inventory of the furnishings left in the house for the use of the Washingtons. Ceramics were listed in five rooms as follows:

First Right Hand Room: a Doble Sett of Nankin China 72 pieces

First Left hand room: 1 Sett Mantle China

In the Back Room adjoining: China in the closett,[261] *9 china plates . . . China Choklet Pot . . . 1 large China Tureen, 1 China Punch Bowl, 1 China Bowl, Do sugar dish*

In the first Kitchen: 1 Black pitcher . . . 1 China coffee pot . . . 6 Cups & Saucers, 1 Milk Pot, 1 Mustard Pot, 1 Slop Bowl, 32 Plates, 4 Large Dishes, 2 Gravy Tureens, 1 Salt Box, 1 Sallet Dish

In the Back Kitchen Adjoining: 1 Quart Black mug . . . 23 Cups & 23 Saucers, 7 cups & 7 saucers, 16 Cups & 16 saucers, 12 Coffe Cups.

120. Advertisement in the *Pennsylvania Packet*, Philadelphia, November 20, 1781. Six purchases of china at Gallagher's store for the presidential household are recorded as well as one in 1797 "to send to Virgᵃ." (The Historical Society of Pennsylvania)

One Sugar Dis one Cream Jug 2 Tea pots—Two Stands for Do 2 Cake plate 1 Small Do—2 slop Bowls a Spoon Tra all of Nankeen China

Damage noted after the president and his party left included four plates valued at one shilling each.

LATER PURCHASES

With the cold weather of December 1793 the yellow fever epidemic diminished, and the Washingtons returned to the presidential mansion on High Street. Three sets of tea china and six chocolate cups were purchased just before the new year from "House Expense" funds. The "House Expense" designation indicated that these teawares were considered government property and that they supplemented or replaced the china and queensware bought by Congress for the use of the president in New York in 1789. Additional small expenditures for "house" china were recorded in December 1795 and February 1796, the latter for two pitchers and four chamber pots purchased by Frederick Kitt, the steward.

Before leaving office in March 1797, President Washington noted that the "China and Glass-ware which was

121. The Washingtons spent most of November 1793, and six weeks in the summer of 1794 in this house in Germantown, northwest of Philadelphia, to escape the recurrent epidemics of yellow fever which plagued the city in the last decade of the century. Col. Isaac Franks leased his house and furnishings to the government. His inventory of 1793, including many references to ceramics, survives. The house, at 5442 Germantown Avenue, is now administered by Independence National Historical Park in association with the Germantown Historical Society. (Independence National Historical Park Collection)

furnished at the expence of the United States . . . have been worn out, broken, stolen and replaced (at private expence) over and over again. . . ." With that situation as well as the precedents set by the first president in mind, John Adams lamented that he would have to purchase "all the glasses, ornaments, kitchen furniture, the best china, settees, plateaus, &c. . . . all the china, delph or wedgwood, glass and crockery of every sort. . . ."[262]

Nothing can be identified with certainty from the twelve contingency-fund purchases of table-, tea-, and ornamental-wares made during Washington's second administration, although two sets of the biscuit figures now at Mount Vernon may have been acquired from Pasquier and Company in February 1797 and Decamps and Company in March just before the Washingtons returned to Virginia.[263] China had been purchased from Pasquier the previous year "p.ʳ order of Mrs. W," and a "set" of blue mugs as well as a set of blue dishes or platters had also been purchased by the steward, Frederick Kitt, "for Mʳˢ Washington." In February and March 1797, four entries for china, one of which specified "to send to Virgᵃ," were recorded in the household account book and charged to contingency expenses. Finally, on March 13, R. Lindsay was paid $15 to pack the tableware and ornaments for shipment to Mount Vernon.

Tableware of late-eighteenth-century manufacture with a tradition of Washington ownership has often been ascribed by collectors to the miscellaneous purchases made in Philadelphia. For example, three Caughley dessert pieces in the

122. On March 7, 1797, Mme Decamps, a French china seller and glass engraver, sold "2 table ornaments" to the Washingtons just prior to their departure from Philadelphia for Mount Vernon. Her advertisement in the *Aurora,* April 4, 1800, describes the wares and services available in her shop (see page 114). (The Historical Society of Pennsylvania)

123. English porcelain square dish, Caughley, ca. 1785–1795. This dish is from a dessert service decorated with the blue-and-gold pattern known as "Dresden Flowers and border" in Caughley factory records. With two matching dessert plates, one of which is in a private collection, it is traditionally assigned to the purchases made for the Washingtons in Philadelphia. Mark: "S" in blue, painted underglaze. Width: 8½ inches. (The Mount Vernon Ladies' Association collections)

124. Chinese porcelain cooler, liner, and cover, underglaze-blue river scene, with gilt handles and rims, made for the English and American markets, ca. 1790–1810. The standard pattern, sometimes called "inclined pines" after motifs in the background, with a trellis-diaper and spearhead border usually termed "Nanking," decorates a large service of table- and dessertware said to have been given to Mrs. Samuel Powel by President and Mrs. Washington in 1797. Overall height: 12 inches. (The Mount Vernon Ladies' Association collections)

125. French porcelain mug, Paris, Christopher Potter, ca. 1790–1795. The pattern of a yellow band and intertwined ribbons of leaves and flowers with cornflower sprigs is also known on other pieces produced by Potter's factory on the rue de Crussol. Washington's presidential household accounts list a purchase of three pairs of china mugs from an unidentified source in Philadelphia on June 6, 1796. In the same year, other china was purchased in Philadelphia from Pasquier and Company, obviously a French firm. Although the mug's provenance (traced to Nelly Custis Lewis) is traditional rather than documented, the date of manufacture agrees with the period of the Philadelphia acquisitions. Mark: $_{Pott}^{B}$ in overglaze red. Height: 4¼ inches. (The Mount Vernon Ladies' Association collections)

126. Chinese porcelain tea caddy, ca. 1760. Traditionally ascribed to ownership by Martha Washington, the small canister displays polychrome enamel decoration which shows Japanese influence in the borders and the bamboo motifs. The silver cap is engraved "M W." The piece came to Mount Vernon from the Kountze collection at Yale University, but it is probably the same tea caddy which was lent to the exhibition at the Metropolitan Opera House in New York in 1889 celebrating the centennial of Washington's inauguration. Height: 4¼ inches. (The Mount Vernon Ladies' Association collections)

"Dresden Flowers" pattern, used from 1785 to 1795 and with an undocumented Washington provenance dating to the nineteenth century, were formerly in the collection of William Wilson Corcoran.[264] Mr. Corcoran gave two of the pieces to Mount Vernon in 1879, while another plate is now in a private collection. These pieces traditionally date to the Washingtons' years in Philadelphia. The Philadelphia "contingency expence" purchases are a convenient but uncertain catch-all for traditionally attributed Washington pieces, and are a possible source for otherwise undocumented entries found in the inventories made after the deaths of General and Mrs. Washington.

PORTRAITS IN PORCELAIN

In the spring of 1791, the president undertook a tour of the southern states. He was greeted by banquets, processions, and receptions throughout the journey, but the high point was the week he spent in Charleston, South Carolina. Northwest of Charleston, the town of Camden celebrated Washington's arrival on May 25. The president's diary for that date noted that he arrived at "Cambden" and "Dined late with a number of Gentlemen & Ladies at a public dinner."[265]

Leaving Rocky Branch, ten miles north of Camden, Richard Champion, former English "china manufacturer," joined Washington's admirers in town and submitted a long political and commercial essay for the president's consideration. Introducing himself and his views, Champion wrote, "Many years have now elapsed since I became a Citizen of this State. A Period almost wholly spent in Retirement devoted to literary pursuits."[266] Champion's letter and "a printed volume of . . . observations on the commercial connexion between G.B. and the U.S." were delivered to Washington at Camden, according to the latter's note of thanks written after his return to Philadelphia.[267]

Inexplicably, the president's note did not mention a parcel which accompanied the book and which, according to Champion's letter of transmittal to Maj. William Jackson, Washington's aide, contained "two Reliefs in a very fine porcelain exquisitely wrought round with flowers. The one of Dr. Franklin. The other taken from a Relief, (a good

127. Richard Champion (d. October 7, 1791), engraved by W.T. Davey, ca. 1870, from a miniature then owned by Richard Champion Rawlins. Frontispiece in Hugh Owen, *Two Centuries of Ceramic Art in Bristol*, Gloucester, England, 1873. (Courtesy, The Library Company of Philadelphia)

likeness, as he was informed of the President when young,) which Mr. Champion directed a Statuary to make." After seeing Washington in person, however, Champion informed Major Jackson that he found the likeness disappointing and that he therefore merely presented it "as a Curiosity, made from a beautiful native Porcelain, which is to be found in America." He added that he had taken a "similar Liberty during the War, in sending these Reliefs to the President, by way of Paris, but he never knew whether they arrived safe. These were finished, the ornaments having been enamelled with Gold, which he laments is not the Case with these. But being two which he had by him, he brought them out England with him, and through forgetfulness or accident omitted it." Diffidently, Champion concluded that he would have been pleased to have been presented to the president, but that he was "unwilling to break in upon the hour before Dinner."

Champion's American connections dated to the decade before the Revolution. Members of his wife's family had been residents of South Carolina since the 1760s, and Champion himself was entered in the Bristol Port Books as a shipowner whose vessel, the *Lloyd*, made several trips between Bristol and Charleston in 1768 and 1769.[268] In 1775, Champion and other "American Merchants" unsuccessfully petitioned the English government to adopt a friendlier attitude toward the colonies. As an active Whig in Bristol and a strong supporter of Edmund Burke, Champion favored the American cause during the war, and it is not surprising that in 1783—after the failure of his porcelain factory—he settled in South Carolina.

The short period of Richard Champion's proprietorship at the "china works," 15 Castle Green, Bristol, began in 1774 with his assumption of William Cookworthy's patents for the manufacture of porcelain by methods and materials "of the same Nature as those of which the Asiatic and Dresden Porcelain are made."[269] Champion's hard-paste or true porcelain was, he asserted, superior to the typical English "frit or false porcelain," which would melt at temperatures used to fire the Bristol product. From 1774 until his patent rights were sold in 1781 to a company of Staffordshire potters at New Hall, the Bristol factory manufactured tea and coffee services and ornamentalwares of high quality for the luxury market. Actual production, however, ceased in 1778; and only wares in stock were decorated and sold until 1781. Bristol porcelains, which are relatively rare today, included vases and tea sets made for influential members of Parliament such as Edmund Burke and Thomas Pitt, and armorial biscuit plaques, given in hopes of favors or orders to members of the House of Lords.[270]

Biscuit-porcelain plaques encrusted with flowers and ribbons in high relief were a unique product of Champion's Bristol factory. Sèvres and Wedgwood manufactured portrait profiles on smaller plaques contemporary with Champion's portraits of 1774–1778, but the armorial and monogram compositions bearing wreaths of flowers are thought to have been introduced at Bristol by a former Derby craftsman, Thomas Briand, who signed and dated a flower-monogram plaque in 1777, or by a French modeler known as Le Quo.[271]

Most of the surviving Bristol plaques were presented by Champion to members of the House of Lords and to other personages such as Queen Charlotte and Benjamin Franklin.[272] Plaques portraying Benjamin Franklin and one thought to be George Washington are preserved in the British Museum.[273] The profile portrait on the so-called Washington plaque in London, however, looks like that of a Roman military hero and does not resemble the three-quarter bust portrait given to the president in 1791.

Champion either copied the profile of Franklin from a small Sèvres biscuit medallion of 1778 or his statuary modeled the original.[274] Prints depicting Franklin were available in Europe at that time, but the source from which the modeler took Washington's portrait has not been determined. A fictitious mezzotint of Washington was published in London in September 1775 by one Alexander Campbell, and French engravings after Charles Willson Peale's 1776 portrait of Washington may have been made as early as 1777. Engravings after a miniature painted from life in 1777 by Charles Willson Peale and after a drawing by Eugène du Simitière were not made in Europe before the 1780s—too late to have been used as sources for Champion's version.[275] The Washington family arms are furnished below the portrait so that there could be no doubt about the identity of the subject, but the features only vaguely resemble those of the American leader.

Josiah Wedgwood, who also produced ceramic plaques or medallions, regarded Champion's efforts to manufacture commemorative and table porcelains in Bristol as a threat to the commercial superiority of the Staffordshire firm.[276] Wedgwood's vehement but unsuccessful attacks "on behalf of himself and the manufacturers of earthenware in Staffordshire" to defeat Champion's renewal of his patent in

128. Biscuit-porcelain plaque, Bristol, 1777–1778. In May 1790, Richard Champion, former proprietor of the English porcelain factory at Bristol, wrote that he had sent plaques bearing portraits of Washington and Franklin to the American commander in chief during the Revolutionary War. However, fearing that those had been lost, he now sent duplicates which he had brought with him to South Carolina in 1783. The portrait of Washington, from an unidentified graphic source, is surrounded by nearly three-dimensional flowers and foliage. Above the portrait are modeled a snake and a liberty cap, symbols associated with the movement for independence, while the Washington family arms are presented on an oval shield against crossed banners at the bottom. The crown hovering above the composition may have symbolized Champion's ambitions for the American leader. Overall height: 8¼ inches; width: 7 inches. (Peter family collection)

Parliament revealed the depth of his concern.[277] His efforts did succeed, however, in forcing Champion to include his formulas for Bristol's porcelain body and two glazes in the final patent document. In spite of the granted renewal, Champion failed to produce porcelain wares commercially and as Wedgwood noted cheerfully on August 24, 1778, "Poor Champion, you may have heard is quite demolished; it was never likely to be otherwise, as he had neither professional knowledge, sufficient capital, nor scarcely any real acquaintance with the materials he was working upon."[278]

Washington's two Bristol plaques were described by Joshua Brookes, a dinner guest at Mount Vernon on February 4, 1799, as "a miniature marble likeness of G. Washington [and] one of Dr. Franklin" over the fireplace in the "sitting parlor, a small back room with the chimney in the corner."[279]

The plaque of Washington is now owned by a member of the Peter family. The Franklin plaque was mentioned in the will of Eleanor Custis Lewis in 1852 as the "Profile in flowers of B. Franklin" and, later, in 1890, it was sold to an A.G. Murphy at the Lawrence Lewis estate sale in Philadelphia.[280] The present location of Washington's Franklin portrait is not known. The fate of the plaque which Champion had given to Franklin in 1778 is also unknown.[281]

Two Punch Bowls

Just before Washington left Philadelphia for a brief visit to Mount Vernon in June 1793, he received a large, antique china bowl from Col. William Fitzhugh. Fitzhugh, who had been born in 1721, revealed in the accompanying letter that the bowl was "much older than himself." The donor's second wife, Ann Frisby Rousby Fitzhugh, had died in March, and the widower, in anticipation of his own death, may have been giving certain of his possessions to old friends.[282] The bowl, which Washington graciously esteemed "more as a memento of . . . friendship than for its antiquity or size," may have originally belonged to Colonel Fitzhugh's great-grandfather, the first American Fitzhugh in the line, or to one of his descendants.[283] One Chinese porcelain punch bowl among several preserved at Mount Vernon

bears inexplicably early *famille-rose* decorations of about 1725, but lacking further evidence, identification of a particular bowl with the Fitzhugh gift is mere speculation.

Another punch bowl, called "the bowl that has a ship in it" in Martha Washington's will, was inherited by George Washington Parke Custis upon his grandmother's death in 1802. The bowl was seen at Arlington House in 1859, but was removed during the Civil War by a Union soldier. It is now in the museum at Mount Vernon.[284]

The exterior of the Chinese export porcelain bowl displays a simple, dark blue and gilt border. A blue-and-gold mantle draped around a shield bearing Washington's initials is also enameled on the exterior. Such pseudo-armorial framing for initials became increasingly popular in the American China trade after about 1790. Standardization of decoration resulted, and sample plates were used by dealers to facilitate the placement of orders. One such sample plate —bearing a central shield and ermine mantling similar to the same motif on Washington's bowl—is now at the Henry Francis du Pont Winterthur Museum.[285] The plate also displays four sample borders, one of which matches the border on the rim of Washington's bowl.

The interior of the bowl is nearly covered by a three-masted frigate drawn in black. Flying from the ship's masthead, a blue pennant with fifteen stars and red-and-white streamers marks the vessel as American. If the number of stars and the number of portholes are meant to represent the states in the Union, the date of the bowl could be placed between 1792, when Kentucky was admitted as the fifteenth state, and 1796, when Tennessee came in as the sixteenth. "DEFENDER" is painted below the ship, but the word may refer symbolically to Washington himself since no American naval or merchant ship of that name is known. Whether there was a ship named *Defender* or not, the depiction in the bowl is copied from a frigate in an engraving in Thomas Truxtun's *Remarks, Instructions, and Examples Relating to the Latitude and Longitude; also, the Variation of the Compass . . .*, published in 1794. Printed design sources—especially the frontispiece of Hutchinson's *Naval Architecture*, an English publication—were frequently used as patterns for Chinese

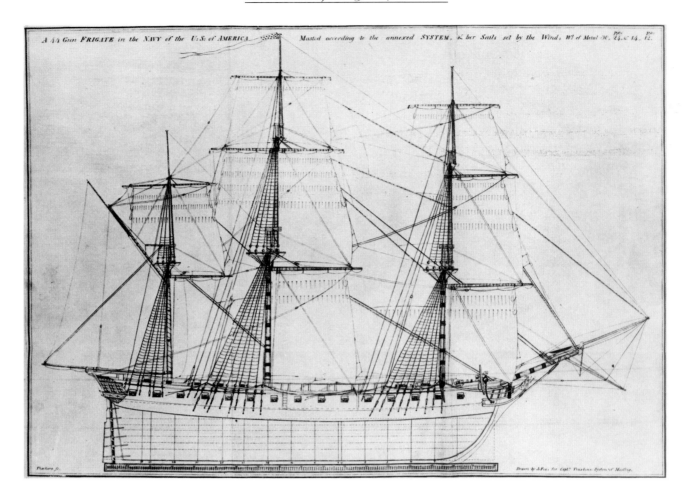

copyists even when a particular ship was meant to be com-memorated.[286] Truxtun (1755–1822), whose privateers sailed in the Revolutionary War, captained the ship *Canton* in one of the first East Indian ventures from the port of Philadelphia. Perhaps referring to a second voyage, President Washington wrote on May 6, 1792, of the "return of Captain Truxton from the East-Indies which is expected to be sometime next Spring, or Summer."

Recently, a punch bowl at the Naval Historical Foundation in Washington, D.C., has been found to be identical to the Washington bowl except that the initials within the blue mantling on the side are "T.T." for Thomas Truxtun. It is almost certain that Truxtun, who was appointed a captain in the United States Navy in 1794, was the donor of the historic bowl at Mount Vernon. He visited Mount Vernon, at

129. "A 44 Gun FRIGATE in the NAVY of the U.S. of AMERICA," drawn by Josiah Fox (1763–1847) for "Capt.ⁿ Truxtuns System of Masting," and engraved by James Thackara (1767–1848), 1794. In November 1794, Thomas Truxtun wrote to Fox and instructed him to draw a picture of one of the Navy's new frigates "complete with spars and sails" for Truxtun's *Remarks, Instructions, and Examples Relating to the Latitude and Longitude; also, The Variation of the Compass, &&& to which is annexed a general chart of the globe . . .*, printed in Philadelphia by T. Dobson in 1794, according to the title page. The engraving was obviously the source for the Chinese artist who painted the ships in the Truxtun and Washington bowls (see fig. 131). (Courtesy, The Library Company of Philadelphia)

Washington's invitation, on September 12, 1799, and possibly presented the bowl at that time.

"A Box of China for Lady Washington"

Custine's porcelain, Vaughan's Worcester vases, d'Estaing's Sèvres bust, Champion's plaques, and Fitzhugh's bowl had all been given to George Washington, but in 1796 the First Lady also received a porcelain gift. "The set of tea china that was given me by Mr. Van Braam, every piece having M.W. on it," was in "A Box of China for Lady Washington," listed in the supplement to the manifest of the *Lady Louisa*, which arrived in Philadelphia from Canton via Capetown on April 24, 1796.[287]

Mrs. Washington's Dutch–American benefactor, Andreas Everardus van Braam Houckgeest (1739–1801), had chartered the *Lady Louisa* to bring a vast collection of furnishings, works of art, and several Chinese servants to Philadelphia, where he proposed to establish himself in Oriental splendor. As director of Canton operations for the Dutch East India Company from 1790 to 1795, he had designed, commissioned, and collected nearly 2,000 watercolor views of Chinese life and architecture as well as wallpaper, porcelains, furniture, and extravagant ornaments including a "surtout de table executed . . . according to the ideas of M. Van-Braam" in silver and precious stones representing "rocks interspersed with pagodas, human figures, bridges, trees, fruit, flowers, quadrepeds, birds, insects. &c."[288] With the addition of fish and "crustaceious animals" in pools and streams of water, the assemblage on van Braam's table must indeed have presented "the most brilliant and striking appearance" described by his publisher and editor, Moreau de Saint-Méry, in the appendix to van Braam's account of his journey to the court of Emperor Ch'ien Lung in Peking.

After his arrival in Philadelphia, van Braam displayed his collection of art and natural history for the edification of curious citizens. He became something of a celebrity and was elected to membership in the American Philosophical Society. In 1797, he built "China's Retreat" three miles below Bristol on the Delaware River.[289] The house and its contents soon attracted tourists such as Julian Ursyn Niemcewicz, a Polish visitor, who commented in his journal about the omnipresence of porcelain in the house and dairy:

April 19, 1798: We arrived finally at the house of Mr. Van-braam. He is a Dutchman who made an immense fortune in China and the Indies and has come to establish himself in this country. . . . He then showed us his house. It is immense, surmounted with a cupola and decorated with golden serpents in the Chinese manner. Six tabourets of porcelain were arranged in a circle in the peristyle. The cellars are immense and the floor alone, made with great flags of stone, cost him 3,000 doll. In the dairy there are twenty porcelain bowls a foot and a half in diameter; they were filled with milk and cream. In the larder there were tubs also in porcelain, for keeping fresh and salt meat. In truth everything was so much in porcelain that I thought for a moment that his wife was made of the same material, she was so pale and still. . . . We entered a hall filled with different objects from China, more curious than useful . . . many chests in sandalwood, containing dessert services: they portrayed rocks amidst waterfalls, houses, horses, men, etc. . . . Mr. Vanbraam, thoroughly discontented with this country, is selling everything and is embarking for Europe. . . .[290]

Born in Holland in 1739, van Braam had gone to China in the service of the Dutch East India Company in 1758. After returning to Europe in 1773, he watched the events of the American Revolution unfold and became so enthusiastic about the cause that he moved with his family to Charleston, South Carolina, in 1783 and became an American citizen in 1784.[291] Business losses and the deaths of four of his children prompted van Braam's return to Holland in 1788 and his acceptance of another post with the Dutch East India Company in 1790. By 1795, he decided to return to America. Flaunting "an Asiatic luxury," van Braam soon landed in debtor's prison according to Niemcewicz, because he had left "all his good sense and all his prudence" in China.[292] Later, in 1798, van Braam took his collection to London, where part of it was sold at Christie's auction house on February 15 and 16, 1799.[293] He died in Amsterdam in 1801.

130. Chinese porcelain punch bowl, made for the United States market, ca. 1795. George Washington's monogram is painted in gold on a shield surrounded by blue-and-gold mantling. The scalloped blue border with gold dots and the pseudo-armorial frame for initials were standard decorations on bowls which the china merchants in Canton kept in stock. Initials and other decorations would be added to order. Thomas Truxtun (1755–1822), who was appointed in the summer of 1794 by Washington as captain of the *Constellation*, one of the new United States Navy's six frigates, probably presented the bowl to the president in 1795 or 1796. A matching bowl with Truxtun's initials is in the collections of the Naval Historical Foundation, Washington, D.C. Diameter: 15¼ inches. (The Mount Vernon Ladies' Association collections)

131. Interior of the bowl which Mrs. Washington's will described as "the bowl that has a ship in it." An American frigate, painted in the black pigment *encre de chine* to simulate the engraving from which the Chinese craftsman worked, covers the bowl's interior. The ship had originally been drawn by Josiah Fox for Capt. Thomas Truxtun's book about international navigation, published in Philadelphia in 1794. In November 1794, Truxtun instructed Fox to draw a picture of one of the Navy's new frigates "complete with spars and sails" for the book. Truxtun's own bowl, now at the Naval Historical Foundation, portrays the same ship on its interior, but lacks the word "DEFENDER," visible below the rim on Washington's bowl. "Defender" seems to be Truxtun's honorary appellation for the president since no ship of that name is known.

132. Second page of van Braam's supplement to the master's declaration of entry for the ship *Lady Louisa*, James Cooper, captain, from China and the Cape of Good Hope, Philadelphia, April 25, 1796. Van Braam declared a striped "Ass skin covered Trunk cont.ᵍ Presents from the Emperor" (Ch'ien Lung), furniture, table ornaments, and thirty-three chests of chinaware in addition to the "Box of China for Lady Washington." (Courtesy, The National Archives Trust Fund)

Undoubtedly, van Braam himself designed the service he gave to Mrs. Washington. Moreau de Saint-Méry wrote that the Dutch merchant was "doubly a painter, his pen and his pencil were constantly employed in depicting whatever he saw," and that "during five years [he] constantly employed two Chinese draughtsmen in forming this numerous and curious assemblage of all kinds of objects."[294]

Sources for van Braam's program of text and symbols, enameled on every piece of the service, are found in graphic and literary material of his time. Martha Washington's initials are presented as the central motif on a gilt, green-rimmed disc set upon a gold aureola or sunburst within a closed circle of chain-links, each containing the name of a state. The latter configuration has given the china its popular name, the "States" service. The same arrangement of sunburst and chain was printed on fractional dollars issued for the Continental Congress in Philadelphia in 1776. Using that design, van Braam simply added Vermont and Kentucky to the original thirteen states and elongated the links of the chain to fit the borders of plates, cups, and saucers.[295]

The chain, symbolizing strength and union, is paralleled on the rims by a blue serpent. Forming an eternal circle by grasping its tail in its mouth, the serpent was an image used by the Egyptians and repeated by European illustrators of sixteenth-century emblem books. Any of the editions of the *Emblematum Libellus* by Andreas Alciatus or later editions of similar emblem books could have been used by van Braam.[296]

The motto DECUS ET TUTAMEN AB ILLO on a floating red ribbon below the central disc evidently echoed van Braam's sentiments about defensive strength achieved in the union of states. Translated as "A glory and defense from it," the motto derives from Vergil's *Aeneid*. In speaking of the magnificent leather cuirass or protective breastplate which Aeneas awarded to the victor at the funeral games honoring Anchises, Vergil wrote that it was *decus et tutamen in armis* (a glory and defense in battle).[297]

Although Martha Washington called van Braam's gift a "set of tea china," the only known cups of the service are

133. "China's Retreat," the house on the banks of the Delaware River built by van Braam in 1797. A visitor in 1798 described the Dutch trader's Chinese curiosities and furnishings in the dwelling and dairy, including such an astonishing amount of porcelain that "in truth everything was so much in porcelain that I thought for a moment that his wife was made of the same material." Hand-colored engraving in William Birch, *The Country Seats of the United States of North America*, designed and published by W. Birch, enamel painter, Springland near Bristol, Pa., 1808. (Manuscript Department, The Historical Society of Pennsylvania)

134. Fractional dollars displaying the sunburst and chain of states which were motifs used by van Braam on the Chinese porcelain service he presented to Mrs. Washington in 1796. The currency had been printed for the Continental Congress in Philadelphia in 1776. (The Historical Society of Pennsylvania)

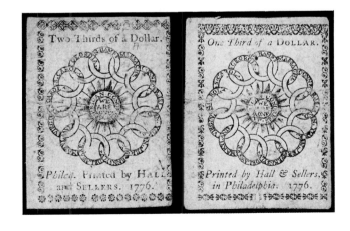

135. Chinese porcelain chocolate or caudle cup and saucer, 1795. Included in "A Box of China for Lady Washington," which arrived in Philadelphia aboard the *Lady Louisa* on April 24, 1796, the symmetrical, two-handle, covered cup was a form intended for cabinet display rather than for serving chocolate or caudle, a warm, spiced drink made with wine or ale. Andreas Everardus van Braam Houckgeest (1739–1801), agent for the Dutch East India Company, designed the enameled decoration himself and directed its application to Mrs. Washington's service in Canton. Overall height of cup: 5 inches; diameter of saucer: 6 inches. (The Mount Vernon Ladies' Association collections)

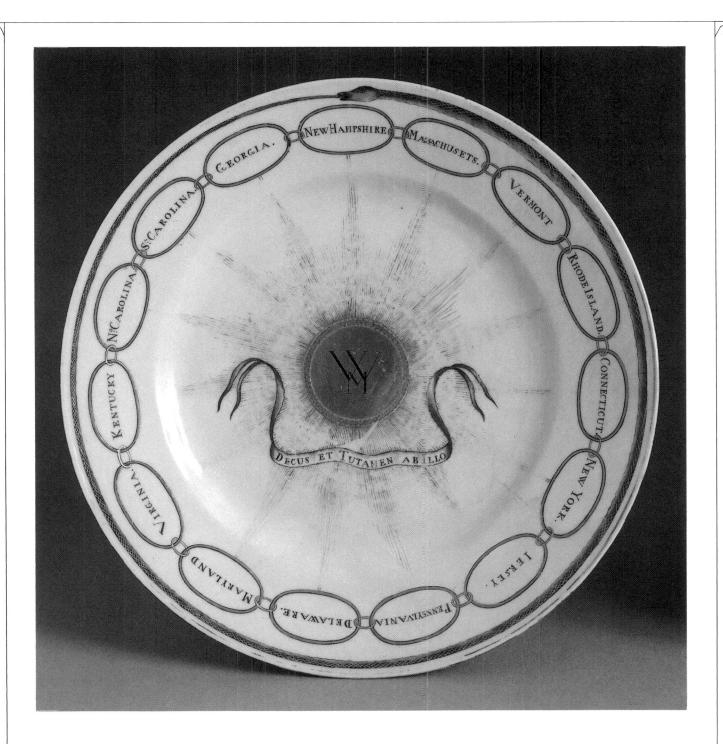

136. Chinese porcelain plate, 1795. The program of enameled text and symbols designed by van Braam for Mrs. Washington's service includes a chain enclosing the names of the states. That configuration represents strength in union, an attribute which is the subject of the motto DECUS ET TUTAMEN AB ILLO (a glory and defense from it). The outer rim bears a blue serpent which grasps its tail to form a never-ending circle representing eternity. Diameter: 9½ inches. (Private collection)

two-handle, covered caudle or chocolate cups with saucers displaying a molded footring on the upper side. At least four such cups and seven saucers exist as well as a sugar bowl, one 14-inch plate, and four 9-inch plates.[298] With its elaborate program of symbolic imagery, van Braam's service was probably meant for cabinet display rather than for daily use.[299]

Mrs. Washington gave at least one piece of the van Braam service away during her lifetime. Julian Niemcewicz wrote to thank her in June 1798 before returning to Poland with "a cup marked with her initials" in his baggage. George Washington Parke Custis, who inherited the service upon the death of his grandmother, also gave pieces away. A plate in the Massachusetts Historical Society and two saucers at Mount Vernon have histories as gifts to antecedents of the donors from Custis or his wife, Mary Fitzhugh Custis.

George Washington Parke Custis left the van Braam china to his daughter, Mary Custis Lee, wife of Gen. Robert E. Lee. During the Civil War, according to family tradition, barrels of china were rolled down the hill from Arlington House by Union troops to storage in the United States Patent Office. Such treatment may account for the poor condition of every piece of the "States" china, although as early as 1847, Mrs. Lee wrote of breakage in the van Braam and Cincinnati services. As author Samuel Woodhouse, Jr., noted in 1935, ". . . no porcelain is more highly prized in American collections than are surviving pieces of this service. Nearly all such pieces . . . are damaged, many even badly broken, yet they hold their first-rank position."[300]

The popularity of the "States" service, due to its obvious association with Martha Washington, has inspired numerous reproductions by French, English, and American manufacturers from the last quarter of the nineteenth century to the present. "Martha Washington China" was sold at the American Centennial Exposition in Philadelphia in 1876, and reproductions of van Braam's design on tea cups and other forms not found in the original service soon followed.[301]

VIII

THE RETURN

TO

MOUNT VERNON

137. Black stoneware coffeepot, English. John Turner, Lane End, Longton, Staffordshire, ca. 1795. Said to have been acquired by the Washingtons in Philadelphia, this coffeepot may have accompanied the "Egyptian China" teapot inventoried in the butler's closet after the death of Washington in 1799. Height: 8¼ inches. Mark (impressed): TURNER. (The Mount Vernon Ladies' Association collections)

for "the President elect . . . the foreign characters, the heads of departments, &c." followed by Mrs. Washington's last drawing room.[302] After John Adams was inaugurated on March 4, the merchants of Philadelphia gave "a most sumptuous entertainment" at Rickett's Circus for the Washingtons. According to *Claypoole's Advertiser* of the following day, Samuel Richardet, master of the City Tavern, supplied for the merchants and their guests "four hundred dishes of the most choice viands which money could purchase or art prepare." Five days later, the Washingtons were ready to leave the presidential residence on High Street for their return to Mount Vernon.

"All the Diplomatic Corp (except France) dined with me," President Washington wrote on January 12, 1797. His diary included brief references to several other social events during his last months in office. On February 17, Mrs. Washington was hostess to "A very crouded drawing Room," and on Friday, March 3, the Washingtons gave a farewell dinner

Once more, Tobias Lear, the president's personal secretary, was left behind, this time to oversee the separation of personal property from the congressional purchases which would be left in the house for the new president. "The furniture of the Green Drawing Room & other Articles" deemed unnecessary or unsuitable for Mount Vernon were sold at auction by Footman and Company on March 10 for $501.45,[303] and on March 25

No 539.   EDWARD POLE, auctioneer.

Sales of Elegant Furniture,

On Friday Next the 10th instant, at 1 o'clock, will be sold by public Auction, at the House of the late President of the United States, in Market street,

A QUANTITY of Valuable Household FURNITURE, belonging to General Washington, among which are, a number of Elegant Chairs with Sattin Bottoms, sattin Window Curtains, a Beautiful Cut Glass Lustre, and a very complete Mahogany Writing Desk, also, a Coach and Phaeton.

Footman & Co. auctioneers.

138. The day after the Washingtons left Philadelphia for Mount Vernon, Footman and Company, auctioneers, held a sale "of Elegant Furniture . . . belonging to General Washington," which the new president, John Adams, had declined to purchase. Advertisement in *Claypoole's American Daily Advertiser*, March 8, 1797. (The Historical Society of Pennsylvania)

Mrs. Samuel Powel bought a desk which the president had purchased from Thomas Burling in New York in 1790.[304]

The sloop *Salem* sailed out of Philadelphia bound for the Potomac on March 15. Her cargo included the household items used in the presidential residences, but considered personal property by the Washingtons. Among the ninety-seven boxes, forty-three casks, two plate baskets, and other bundles aboard were remnants of the eighteen recorded ceramic purchases made from the former president's "contingency fund" between January 12, 1790, in New York and March 7, 1797, in Philadelphia. Unfortunately, the long bill of lading which specified many interesting objects from Venetian blinds and a carpet to "one Tin shower bath"

139. Chinese porcelain bottle and washbowl, made for the English market, ca. 1775–1785. The underglaze-blue painting of a Chinese garden pavilion near a river with two birds above the trees and borders of trellis-diaper edged by a frieze of daggers was popular in England and in the United States in the early years of American shipping from Canton. The design was copied on English blue-printed teawares made at the Caughley factory in the 1780s. River scenes and landscapes painted in underglaze-blue with simple dagger-and-diaper or complex "Fitzhugh" borders characterized "Nanking" dinner- and teawares decorated at Ching-tê Chên from the 1760s through the 1780s. "Wash hand Guglets & Basons," as Washington called them in 1785, were often listed in the invoices from London and in his later accounts. On February 22, 1786, for example, four "Wash Basons" and a "Water Jugg" were purchased in Alexandria. However, many of the basins mentioned in the documents were stoneware and creamware, and none can be identified with existing objects. Washbasins and pitchers or bottles were inventoried in several rooms after the death of General Washington. Height of bottle: 9¾ inches; diameter of bowl: 11¾ inches. (Lewis Collection, The National Museum of American History, Smithsonian Institution)

and a bidet does not disclose the contents of the casks and plate baskets which held the Sèvres dinner and dessert service, the Cincinnati china, van Braam's gift to Mrs. Washington, and the table-, tea-, and ornamentalwares supplied by shopkeepers Gallagher, Bringhurst, Pasquier, McCall, Decamps, and Inskeep in Philadelphia.

The porcelain brought home on the *Salem* and the blue-and-white china and the queensware which had remained at Mount Vernon and had been augmented during the presidential years were evidently adequate for the family's dining needs in the year and eight months remaining in Washington's life. The only ceramics known to have been acquired during that period were useful wares entered in Ledger G, an account book for his farms and the "Mansion." Robert Gordon, an unidentified merchant in Alexandria, supplied earthen and stoneware mugs and earthen flowerpots and milk pans.

A DINNER IN 1799

Joshua Brookes (1773–1859), an English businessman who traveled in the United States in 1798, left a revealing description of the furnishings of Mount Vernon as well as the menu of a three-course dinner served there on February 4, 1799. His manuscript journal at the New-York Historical Society tells of visiting General Washington on that date.[305] Brookes and his friends, Samuel and Robert Campbell, were greeted by Tobias Lear, who had stayed on as Washington's secretary, and Nelly Custis, Mrs. Washington's granddaughter. At about two-thirty, the general returned from his daily round of farm business in clothes "all of American manufacture" and "bespattered boots," and Mrs. Washington, dressed in "a Mazareen blue satin gown," soon joined the group in the sitting room. The visitors were pressed to stay for dinner and, after Washington changed his clothes, they dined about four o'clock. Brookes described the meal.

Mrs. Washington at the head [of the table], the General on her right, Miss Custis on her left, next I came, then Samuel Campbell, Mr. Lear at bottom, next him Robert Campbell and Mr.

Craig next [to the] General.[306] At dinner wine, porter and beer. After it we drank about three glasses when we took our leave. The General and Lear came to the door and waited till we were on our horses. The General gave no toasts, he had the horses brought to the door.

At dinner we had two pint globular decanters on table, after dinner large wine glasses. Port was brought in claret bottles. Wood fire, very mean dogs [inferior andirons]....

[Menu] Leg [of] boil[ed] pork, top [at head of table]; goose, bot [at foot of table]; roast beef, round cold boil[ed] beef, mutton chops, hommony, cabbage, potatoes, pickles, fried tripe, onions, etc. Table cloth wiped, mince pies, tarts, cheese; cloth of[f], port, madeira, two kinds [of] nuts, apples, raisins. Three servants.

With only eight for dinner on that February afternoon, the family dining room was probably used, not the large dining room which Washington often called the "New Room." Larger groups like "the notable company from Alexandria" seen by Niemcewicz on June 13, 1798, would be served at the "table in the great hall . . . set out with a Sèvres porcelain service with places for 20." Joshua Brookes also described the "elegantly furnished," multipurpose dining hall or drawing room which had been added to the mansion during the Revolution and finished in 1785. Mahogany chairs with yellow damask seats and white chintz curtains with "deep festoons of green satin" were noted, as was a glass chandelier and the sculptured marble mantel which had been a present from Samuel Vaughan. On the mantel were "marble jars and blue china ones in which were placed some blue and red bachelor's buttons."[307] The blue china jars were probably the Worcester vases which Vaughan had also sent in 1786, while the marble jars may have been the two flowerpots which accompanied Moustier's white-and-gold table service[308] or the two biscuit-porcelain vases which accompanied the ornaments for the presidential *surtout*. Washington had attempted to sell the biscuit vases with the largest of the three figure groups, "Apollo instructing the Shepherds"; but by June 1798, Clement Biddle still had not sold them, and their fate is unknown.

In the "sitting parlor, a small back room with the chimney in the corner," Brookes observed several prints and, over the fireplace, "a miniature marble likeness of G. Washington, one of Dr. Franklin and other pieces." Again confusing biscuit porcelain with marble, Brookes thus pointed out the location of Champion's Bristol plaques at Mount Vernon.

GENERAL WASHINGTON'S WILL AND INVENTORY

After having enjoyed less than two years of the private life for which he longed, Washington died within a year after the visit from Brookes. Excepting a few specific bequests, none of them ceramics, he left his real and personal estate to his widow for the remainder of her life. Household furnishings and supplies were left to her discretion for use and eventual distribution or sale, and an inventory of the contents of Mount Vernon was soon begun. Later filed in the Fairfax County Courthouse, the inventory is now at Mount Vernon after having been removed from the courthouse during the Civil War. It was eventually published in 1909, when it was in the collection of W. K. Bixby of Saint Louis.

. Several of the entries in the inventory confirm what has been suggested about the ceramics at Mount Vernon after March 1797. Two sideboards which had been made in Philadelphia by John Aitkin in February 1797 were "In the New Room" with one of the biscuit-figure groups and a flowerpot or vase on each. Five "China Jarrs," perhaps the same arrangement of the Worcester and biscuit or "marble" vases noted by Joshua Brookes in February 1799, and "All the Images" were in the same room.[309] However, identification of the various "Jarrs" in the inventories of 1800 and 1802 is difficult, if not impossible. Two jars bought at the sale of Mount Vernon furnishings in 1802 by Judge Bushrod Washington were possibly the pair of Chinese jars seen at Mount Vernon on the Vaughan mantle in 1858 by Benson Lossing. If these were added to the Worcester vases, a garniture of five units would have resulted.

In the inventory, the *plateaux* were identified, but the Sèvres, Cincinnati, Custine, van Braam, and other special table- and teawares were simply grouped into "Glass & China in the China closet up Stairs & that in the Cellar" and given a total value of $850. The only china listed by form or function other than wash basins, pitchers, and a bottle in the bedrooms was found "In the Closet under Franks direction," probably the pantry near the family dining room. Values for this china were relatively low, so the assumption can be made that most of butler Frank's responsibility was "the blue and white china in common use" mentioned later in Martha Washington's will. Portions of the eight known shipments of blue-and-white china from London (1762, 1763, 1765, 1766, and 1772), New York (1783), and Philadelphia (1790 and 1796) seem to have been used together as a color-coordinated but mixed set decorated with various landscapes and river scenes. Since only twenty-five of the five dozen cups sent from Philadelphia in August 1790 survived, the rate of breakage makes it unlikely that many of these were survivors of the prewar shipments from London. Serving dishes, salad dishes, butter boats, and plates in the closet could have been from the 1783 New York purchase with additional serving dishes and mugs from the March 1796 Philadelphia expenditures "for Mrs. Washington." Blue-and-white custard cups and pickle plates, on the other hand, were possibly from the 1762 and 1765 shipments, since they were not known to have been purchased later.

An "Egyptian China" teapot was stored with the blue-and-white china and other pieces in Frank's closet. "Egyptian black" was an eighteenth-century term for the matte-finished, refined earthenwares or stonewares made black by manganese and iron additives. Black teapots were advertised in New York in 1762 and "Egyptian Tea Pots, Sugar Dishes, and Milk Pots" in 1785.[310] Tea and breakfast sets of the black material, also called basalt, were popular from mid-century through the 1820s, perhaps for the reason given by Josiah Wedgwood to his partner Thomas Bentley in 1772: "Thanks for your discovery in favour of the black teapots. I hope white hands will continue in fashion and then we may continue to make black Teapots."[311] Other manufacturers also produced black tewares. In

140. Chinese porcelain bottle, ca. 1770. A multipurpose, utilitarian shape decorated with a casually painted, underglaze-blue landscape composition. The bottle was probably included with "the blue and white china in common use" which Nelly Custis Lewis inherited from her grandmother, Martha Washington. Height: 6¾ inches. (Lewis Collection, The National Museum of American History, Smithsonian Institution)

141. Chinese porcelain washbowl and "gaglet" or water bottle, made for the English market, ca. 1765–1775. Chinese figures and a colorful landscape setting are painted in the "Mandarin" style within the large reserved areas which are framed by underglaze-blue scrolls and foliage. The smaller reserves contain delicately painted birds on branches. Augmenting the rich, decorative effect desired by the European trade, an enameled Chinese Y-diaper ground pattern fills the spaces between the underglaze-blue borders and scattered flowers. According to Peter family tradition, this bowl and bottle were in Mrs. Washington's bedroom. Thomas Peter bought "3 Jugs and Eason" at the sale of Martha Washington's personal property on July 20, 1802. Height of bottle: 10 inches; diameter of bowl: 10½ inches. (Peter family collection)

142. Chinese porcelain bowl, ca. 1755–1770. The underglaze-blue decorations of peonies and rocks with an inner border of stylized plum blossoms, wheel symbols, and *ju-i* or cloud motifs show no western influence although they are applied to a form, the punch bowl, which was manufactured for the English market. "China" punch bowls were sent to Mount Vernon from Bristol in August 1758 and from London in November 1766. Diameter: 11¼ inches. (Lewis Collection, The National Museum of American History, Smithsonian Institution)

143. Chinese porcelain meat dish, underglaze-blue painted riverscape, made for the English market, ca. 1770–1780. A standard pattern sometimes called "Pavilion on Rocky Peninsula" with borders of various diaper motifs appears on this large dish attributed to ownership by the Washingtons and subsequently by the Lewis family. The inventory taken at Mount Vernon in late 1799 or early 1800 included twenty-four "China Dishes" among the commonly used china pieces in the closet "under Franks direction." Length: 20½ inches. (The Mount Vernon Ladies' Association collections)

144. Chinese porcelain custard cup with cover, underglaze-blue landscape with vase of flowers, ca. 1770. It is traditionally attributed to ownership by the Washingtons. The form of the handle and finial and the decoration indicate that this cup was made later than the "Ribbed Custard Cups" sent from London to Mount Vernon in April 1762. Blue-and-white custard cups found in the closet "under Franks direction" after the death of General Washington could have been from the 1762 shipment or from a later, unrecorded purchase. Height: 3¾ inches. (The Mount Vernon Ladies' Association collections)

CHINA, GLASS, and EARTHEN-
WARE STORE.

WILLIAM WILLIAMS, No. 46,
Maiden-Lane, near the Fly-Mar-
ket, has imported in the Mentor, from
London, the following Articles, which
he has just opened, and is selling on the
lowest Terms:
 BLUE and Burnt China Cups and
Saucers, all sizes, with Sugar Dishes,
Slop Basons, and Milk Pots to match;
Egyptian Tea Pots; Sugar Dishes and
Milk Pots, ditto; Blue and Enameled
Punch Bowls, different sizes; elegant Cut
Glass in setts or otherwise, various fancies;
Quart and Pint Decanters for Taverns;
ditto Gallon and half Gallon, &c. &c.
 Likewise, EARTHEN-WARE of all
kinds, necessary in Families.   7 2 3 m

145. "Egyptian Tea Pots" with matching sugar dishes and milk pots were advertised by William Williams in the *Independent Journal or General Advertiser* in New York on July 23, 1785. "Egyptian" was a popular term for the black basaltic ware made by a number of Staffordshire manufacturers, including Wedgwood and Turner. (Courtesy, The New-York Historical Society, New York City)

146. Fragments of black basaltic teaware found at Mount Vernon. (The Mount Vernon Ladies' Association collections)

1785, Turner and Abbot, retailers and "Potters to his Royal Highness the Prince of Wales, and Manufacturers of Queen's and all other sorts of Staffordshire Ware, No. 82, Fleet Street," advertised that they "manufacture a very general assortment of Egyptian Black, and Bamboo, or Cane Colour Tea-Pots. . . ."[312]

Twenty-seven pickle pots and eight soap jars were found in the cellar at Mount Vernon in 1800 and entered on the inventory. The latter, valued at a remarkable $25, have traditionally been identified as tall, coarse, earthenware jars, thinly glazed on the interior. Lawrence Lewis bought three "soap jars" at the sale of household furnishings in 1802, and two jars were acquired by the Mount Vernon Ladies' Association from the Peter family. Fragments of similar jars, usually called "Spanish oil jars," have been found at several sites in England and Virginia, but the disputed site of their manufacture was probably Spain, Portugal, or Italy.[313]

MRS. WASHINGTON'S WILL AND INVENTORY

Less than a year after the general's death, Martha Washington composed her will, which contained several bequests and the order that the "rest and residue" of her estate be sold by the executors as soon as possible after her death.[314] Porcelains mentioned in her will were the "Cincinnati tea and table China, the bowl that has a ship in it, the fine old China jars which usually stand on the chimney-piece in the new room . . . also, the set of tea china that was given me by Mr. Van Braam, every piece having M.W. on it," all of

147. Chinese porcelain sauceboat stand, made for the English market, ca. 1770. The standard, painted, underglaze-blue pattern sometimes called "two figures before a pavilion" was later copied—with some differences—by the English porcelain factory at Caughley on transfer-printed wares. This piece has a history of ownership by descendants of Eleanor Parke Custis Lewis. Length: 7½ inches. (The Mount Vernon Ladies' Association collections)

148. Earthenware jars, thinly glazed interiors, probably Portuguese or Spanish, ca. 1750–1775. Eight "soap jars" were inventoried in the cellars at Mount Vernon in 1800, and three were sold to Lawrence Lewis in 1802. The soap jars have traditionally been identified with these large oil or storage jars, which were acquired by the Mount Vernon Ladies' Association from the Peter family. The red clay jar at the right bears worn medallions molded below the handles. Height: 31 inches. The green-gray jar at the left has no visible marks or decoration. Height: 25 inches. (The Mount Vernon Ladies' Association collections)

149. Four Chinese porcelain vases from a garniture of five, ca. 1775–1785. Decorated with the same popular river scene found on the washbasin and bottle in fig. 139, the vases were enriched with gilding in either Canton or London. Garniture sets of three, five, or seven vases were shipped to Europe as early as the end of the seventeenth century for the ornamentation of mantels and cabinets, but the beaker and baluster forms of the vases remained markedly Chinese throughout the eighteenth and early nineteenth centuries. Five blue-and-white "Jarrs" were inventoried in the sweetmeat closet after Mrs. Washington's death, and eight china jars with undesignated decorations were found in other rooms. Overall height of covered vases: 13 inches; height of beaker vase: 10 inches. (Lewis Collection, The National Museum of American History, Smithsonian Institution)

150. A small storage room as it appears today at Mount Vernon. This area is believed to be the "Closet under Franks direction" noted in the inventory made after the death of General Washington and the "Sweet Meat Closset" inventoried after the death of Mrs. Washington. In 1799, the closet held the blue-and-white china in common use. Since that china was bequeathed to Nelly Custis Lewis, the closet held miscellaneous articles, including the Custine service and "8 China Bowls," when the next inventory was made in 1802. (The Mount Vernon Ladies' Association collections)

which she left to her grandson, George Washington Parke Custis, whose house, Arlington, was then under construction. To her recently married granddaughter, Eleanor Parke Custis Lewis, she bequeathed "all the blue and white china in common use." Two days after her death, on May 22, 1802, an "inventory of Property that belonged to Mrs. Martha Washington," minus the bequests, was made. The inventory was revised somewhat on July 11, 1802, nine days before the public sale. Sometime before July 11 a private sale, held by the heirs among themselves, had taken place.[315] The history of these sales and the subsequent sharing of objects among descendants is described by Christine Meadows in the Epilogue.

The May 24, 1802, inventory of Mrs. Washington's undevised property reveals that the ceramics in the house had been somewhat rearranged after the death of General Washington. The "Sweet Meat Closset" which is believed to have been the same storage space as "the Closet under Franks direction" in the 1800 inventory now held an assortment of miscellaneous tea services, bowls, and ornamentalwares instead of the blue-and-white table and tea china which had been given to Mrs. Lewis under the terms of her grandmother's will. Eight "china bowls," valued at $5.50 each, were now in the closet with glassware, "Coloured Images," and five "Cornicopias." The closet also held five jars, three flowerpots, a basin and jug, and three pitchers —all of "blue & white." Three sets of tea china were listed, one of which—entered as "G.W."—was probably the Custine china. Two other sets, one green and of comparable value to the Custine china and the other "Common Red & White," have not been identified with existing objects.[316]

A "China flour bottle," valued at a curiously low twelve cents in the 1802 inventory, was also in the sweetmeat closet. The low value could refer to the bottle's small size. In 1898, a miniature Chinese porcelain vase with underglaze blue borders and enameled flowers and with a history traced to Mary Lear Storer, niece of Tobias Lear, was given to Mount Vernon.[317]

In addition to five blue-and-white jars in the closet, eight china jars—three in the New Room and five in the front

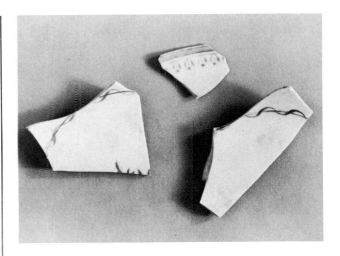

151. Fragments of Chinese porcelain, made for the American market, ca. 1795–1800, found at Mount Vernon. Pieces of teacups and saucers bearing slight decorations in red enamel may correspond to the set of "Common Red & White" tea china inventoried in the sweetmeat closet after the death of Mrs. Washington in 1802. (The Mount Vernon Ladies' Association collections)

parlor—were listed. If George Washington Parke Custis had removed the Worcester vases bequeathed to him by Martha Washington, the three jars on the inventory in the New Room would have been replacements; however, the jar question is confusing at best. One of the jars inventoried may have been a baluster-shape vase decorated with a view of a castle and floral springs in sepia. The jar, now at Mount Vernon, is Chinese export porcelain dating to about 1790. It was purchased for Mount Vernon from the Peter family.

The two large biscuit-porcelain groups which had been on the sideboards in the New Room in 1800 were evidently moved to the front parlor either during the last two years of Mrs. Washington's life or after Eleanor Parke Custis Lewis removed the sideboard table she inherited from her grandmother. Originally appraised at only $4, the "2 Images and glasses" were given a "New Appraisement" of $8 in July just before the private and public sales.

THE SALES

Two of the husbands of Mrs. Washington's three granddaughters were listed among the buyers in the "Account of Sales of the Personal Estate of Martha Washington (not specially devised)," dated July 20, 1802; and Eliza Parke

152. Chinese porcelain vase, made for the English market, ca. 1775–1785. Underglaze-blue borders of Chinese motifs are combined with enameled flowers executed in a style used by the Lowestoft factory from 1775 to 1790. The miniature vase was given by the Washingtons to Mary Lear Storer, the niece of Tobias Lear, according to family tradition. In 1898, it was acquired from the Storer family and returned to Mount Vernon. Height: 5 inches. (The Mount Vernon Ladies' Association collections)

153. Chinese porcelain vase, made for the American market, ca. 1790–1795. A castle in a landscape setting and scattered blossoms are painted in sepia on a covered vase which may have been part of a garniture. A similar covered baluster vase with dragon finial and sepia decorations is known to have been owned by Capt. John Barry, who sailed to Canton from the port of Philadelphia. Washington's vase was probably among the eight china jars found in the "New Room" and the front parlor after the death of Mrs. Washington. Height: 12 inches. (G. Freeland Peter Collection, The Mount Vernon Ladies' Association)

154. Chinese porcelain baluster vases and hat-shape covers with lion of "Fo" finials, ca. 1795. Enameled butterflies and flowers are scattered on a dark blue ground in a style of decoration that is usually associated with the early nineteenth century. The vases were seen at Mount Vernon in 1858 in the possession of John Augustine Washington III, grandnephew and heir of Judge Bushrod Washington, who bought "2 China Jars" for $41 at the sale held after the death of Mrs. Washington in 1802. Overall height: 17½ inches. (The Mount Vernon Ladies' Association collections)

Custis Law, estranged from her husband, was listed under her own name. Each family—Law, Lewis, and Peter—bought "1/3 Set China" for $12.67. With no mention of the French white-and-gold service in Mrs. Washington's will, and with the evidence of numerous surviving pieces having Law, Peter, and Lewis histories, the set of china thus divided is thought to have been the Sèvres service purchased from the Count de Moustier in 1790.[318]

Other ceramics sold that day included two china jars, for $41, to Judge Bushrod Washington, who also bought three "Images" and the Sèvres bust of Necker. Two covered, blue jars—now at Mount Vernon—which Benson Lossing saw there in 1858, were in the possession of John Augustine Washington III, grandnephew and heir of Judge Washington. If the blue jars are those which the judge bought at the sale, they must have been among George and Martha Washington's last acquisitions, for the style of decoration dates to no more than a year or two before 1800. John Augustine Washington III told Lossing that the dark blue jars had been on the mantel during General Washington's lifetime.[319]

With the bequests in Martha Washington's will and the sales following her death, ceramics and other household furnishings accumulated since 1755 left Mount Vernon. Many objects disappeared, but others, with documentation intact, were carefully preserved within the circle of the Washington–Custis families. Of these, a great number have been purchased by or given to the Mount Vernon Ladies' Association of the Union. Some of the china owned by the heirs of Eleanor Parke Custis Lewis was purchased by the United States government in 1878, and, with several other pieces belonging to the heirs of Martha Parke Custis Peter, are now displayed in the First Ladies Hall of the Smithsonian's National Museum of American History. Porcelains originally owned by the Washingtons are also found in the China Room at the White House, at the Henry Francis du Pont Winterthur Museum, and in other private and public collections. A sufficient number of objects and documents survive to permit reconstruction, both factual and conjectural, of the table, tea, and ornamental ceramics—even of the utilitarian kitchen and farm vessels—used by the most prominent American family of the eighteenth century.

EPILOGUE:

DISPERSAL

AND

RETRIEVAL

With Martha Washington's death in 1802 the "golden age" of Mount Vernon ended. The household furnishings were dispersed and all that remained in their original location were those few things acquired by Bushrod Washington at the sales following her demise. For half a century the estate remained in limbo while Bushrod and his successors, all descendants of George's brother, John Augustine, tried to maintain the property. Bushrod was Washington's immediate heir to Mount Vernon and, like his uncle, died childless. His nephew, John Augustine II, inherited after him and then his son, John Augustine III, who sold the mansion, dependencies, and two hundred acres to the Mount Vernon Ladies' Association in 1858. The Association's goal was to rescue Mount Vernon in its incipient decline and preserve it for posterity. Ann Pamela Cunningham, founder and first Regent of the organization, was a woman of intelligence, foresight, charm, and courage whose single-mindedness reversed the depressing decline and impending destruction of Washington's home. Her idea of a total restoration of the property—as it had been under "the great Washington"—was an ambitious plan that required the return of original furnishings, which by then were widely scattered but largely concentrated in the families of Mrs. Washington's descendants.

George Washington had provided generously for his widow. At his death in 1799, she was given "the use, profit and benefit" of his entire estate, other bequests excepted, and received outright the "household and kitchen furniture of every sort and kind, with the liquor and groceries which may be on hand at the time of my decease; to be used and disposed of as she may think proper."[1] Two of Washington's bequests involved major pieces of furniture from his study, the room in the mansion most intimately associated with his daily life at Mount Vernon. To his battlefield companion and "old and intimate friend," Dr. James Craik, Washington gave a handsome tambour secretary, made especially for the study by John Aitken of Philadelphia, and the revolving desk chair—a New York piece by Thomas Burling —that had served him through two presidential terms and his retirement years at Mount Vernon. Dr. David Stuart, another close friend, was given a brass telescope and the dressing table, bought in New York in 1790 from the departing French minister, the Count de Moustier.[2] Stuart had the added distinction of having married Eleanor Calvert Custis, widow of Martha's son, John Parke Custis. With the exception of these few pieces, all of which are now back in their accustomed places, the essential household furnishings remained intact for the two and one-half years that Mrs. Washington survived her husband. During this cheerless interval little changed in the mansion, as Mrs. Washington's health declined and she looked forward to entombment at the general's side.[3]

Washington's will was filed for probate on January 20, 1800, and the court ordered an inventory of his personal estate. Thomson Mason, Tobias Lear, Thomas Peter, and William H. Foote[4] were assigned the task of appraising the contents of the mansion and dependencies on the Mansion House Farm and all the goods and chattels on the four outlying farms. Their fifty-two-page document, completed during 1800, was titled "An Inventory etc. of Articles at Mount Vernon with their appraised value annexed." It and a copy kept by Thomas Peter for his own files are among the original estate papers in the Mount Vernon archives. The appointments of Tobias Lear and Thomas Peter were of particular significance since both had a personal connection with the Mount Vernon household—Thomas Peter as a grandson-in-law of Martha Washington and Lear as a one-time family tutor and private secretary to Washington. The latter's familiarity with his employer's accounts and business records may account for the close correspondence between some of the appraised values and original prices where they can be documented.[5] In the past, the values attached by the appraisers have been underrated[6] as more sentimental than real, but their work had greater contemporary relevance than has been credited.

The appraisers began "In the New Room," a large dining room that was Washington's last structural addition to his house. The men worked their way systematically through twenty-nine rooms and areas of the mansion, including the piazza, where thirty Windsor chairs were listed at ten dollars each. While the widow went into mourning, the appraisers went about their assignment, listing the furniture, identifying portraits by subject, prints and books by title. In all, thirty-eight neatly written pages were used for the objects in the mansion; another eight pages for the dependencies; and the balance for those things on the four other farms that comprised the Mount Vernon tract. Brief as the descriptions are, the overall clarity of the inventory attests to the care with which the appraisers completed their task. Washington's clothes and accessories were omitted, as were the personal possessions of other members of the household, notably Mrs. Washington's grandchildren, George Washington Parke Custis and Eleanor Parke Custis Lewis and her husband, Lawrence Lewis.

In preparation for her own death, Martha Washington drew her will and disposed of the household furnishings inherited from her husband. This document, dated September 22, 1800, is in the handwriting of Mrs. Lewis, whose marriage to George Washington's nephew had further united the two families.[7] Mrs. Washington's principal heirs were her four grandchildren, the offspring of her son, John Parke Custis. The two youngest, Eleanor—known by the family as Nelly—and Washington Custis, had been raised at Mount Vernon by the Washingtons and it was natural for them to receive larger shares of her estate than those allotted their two older sisters, Eliza and Martha, who had remained with their mother.[8] Their marriages to men of property, Eliza Parke Custis to Thomas Law and Martha Parke Custis to Thomas Peter, may have influenced Mrs. Washington's apportionment. Her most liberal bequest was to Washington Custis, the only male member of the family, who received the silver, several plated pieces, "all the family pictures of every sort" and even those "painted by his sister," presumed to be Eleanor. By Mrs. Washington's will, the choice ceramics and the bed on which George Washington had died went to Custis. Eventually, he would enshrine his collection at Arlington House, a handsome Greek revival dwelling overlooking the city of Washington, now known as the Custis–Lee Mansion. It has been rumored that Custis tried to buy Mount Vernon from Bushrod Washington after Martha's death. Had he been successful, its subsequent history might have been different.[9]

Martha Washington died on May 22, 1802, and her will was filed for probate a month later. Following her specific bequests, the will stipulated "that all the rest and residue of my estate of whatever kind and description not herein specifically devised or bequeathed shall be sold by the executors of this my last will for ready money as soon after my decease as the same can be done."[10] She appointed as her executors Washington Custis, her nephews, Julius B. and Bartholomew Dandridge, and her "son in law," Thomas Peter, who now rendered this final service to the Washington family. Within two days of Mrs. Washington's death,[11] a room-by-room inventory of the mansion was prepared with values attached to the contents. The first draft of May 24 was subsequently annotated to reflect her bequests of household furnishings. A second inventory listing the undevised pieces was prepared and is dated July 11. Thomas Peter, in his capacity as an executor, retained copies of both lists, which were purchased by the Association from descendants in 1956.

The "rest and residue" of Martha Washington's estate was then disposed of in separate but related transactions. Public notice was given in the *Alexandria Advertiser and Commercial Intelligencer*, "For sale at Mount Vernon on the 20th day of July, and continue till all is disposed of, for cash, the household and kitchen furniture, consisting of almost every description, some valuable Paintings and Prints, also a pipe of choice old Madeira Wine."[12] This public auction of George and Martha Washington's possessions would have evoked considerable interest and curiosity in the immediate countryside and beyond. Notice of the event was picked up as far away as New England, where the *Courier* of New Hampshire reported on August 5, 1802, a story with an Alexandria dateline.

Virginia

Alexandria, July 15.

We understand that there will be exposed, during the sale at Mount Vernon, some very superb paintings by the first artists, and some very elegant prints; many of these were presents to the late General Washington, and executed in the most masterly style.—This will afford the lovers of the fine arts a rich field for enjoyment, and such an opportunity will probably not again offer where gentlemen may enrich their collections with more valuable works.

The author of these remarks could not foresee future dispersals that would again place Washington memorabilia on the auction block.[13]

As the public sale of July 20 commenced, it became apparent that it would not measure up to the enticing notice that lured potential buyers to Mount Vernon. George Deneale, an Alexandria resident and a pallbearer at General Washington's funeral, attended the sale on commission of a Boston friend who was eager to own a bit of Mount Vernon memorabilia. Deneale learned "on consulting one of the Executors" that the "pipe of choice old Madeira Wine" would not be sold. Apparently Washington Custis had learned that he would inherit whatever pipe of wine was in the house at the time of his grandmother's death, so he had bought a quantity of younger wine for consumption in order to protect his inheritance.[14] Deneale's frustration increased further when he discovered that "all the furniture that was worth moving had been previously divided among the Legatees at Appraisement prices, except 4 large Paintings which they disagreed about dividing."[15] Deneale eventually had the satisfaction of bidding on a landscape, the *Great Falls of the Potomac* by George Beck, who had painted it and a companion view of Harper's Ferry under the specific direction of George Washington. At $101, the painting brought one of the highest prices at the auction. It was returned to Mount Vernon in 1886 and hangs again in its original location in the large dining room.

Almost two hundred lots of household goods and furnishings were sold on July 20, 1802, with Martha's grandchildren the principal buyers. By a curious happenstance a document calling itself an "Account of Sales of the Personal Estate of Martha Washington (not specifically devised) late of Mount Vernon deceased—as rendered to me by Thomas Peter the Executor" turned up among the records of Arlington County, Virginia, in 1959. A collateral descendant of Martha Washington pursuing genealogical interests came upon court papers relative to a suit brought against Mrs. Washington's executors by a nephew whose education "in a useful trade" was guaranteed under the provisions of her will.[16] Her executors and the other legatees held that he had forfeited his inheritance by studying law, a learned profession rather than a useful trade. Despite their efforts, the young lawyer won his case when the court decided that the law was after all a useful trade. In the course of the trial, a full accounting of Mrs. Washington's estate was presented by her executors, and among the papers was the sales list with its invaluable record of objects, their buyers, and the prices.

To date, no record of the private division of Martha Washington's estate has surfaced, although it would be possible to compile an approximate list from the existing documents, minus, of course, the important link of buyer to object. It would be interesting to know the rules established by the heirs for its execution and what produced the disagreement about the paintings mentioned in George Deneale's letter.

With Mrs. Washington's death, the final settlement of her husband's estate could now proceed. Some livestock had been sold publicly in 1800[17] and again the following year, but while Mrs. Washington lived she had the full use of Washington's estate. The remaining livestock and farm equipment were disposed of privately on July 21, 1802, and January 3, 1803.[18] On the earlier date, there also occurred an exclusive sale of Washington's remaining effects. At a meeting of the legatees held in June it was agreed, at the suggestion of Bushrod Washington, himself a lawyer and heir, to hold private sales as a way of dividing the estate among those specified in Washington's will as residuary heirs. Their purchases were to "be deducted from the proportion of the Estate to which we may be entitled at the final Division, without any charge of interest."[19]

On this occasion an intriguing assortment of objects, many evocative of Washington's military career—epaulets, swords, and spurs—were sold and appear on the list of "Private sales, which took place up stairs among the Legatees...."[20] His badge of the Order of the Cincinnati and other medals, among them the one ordered by the Congress in 1776 to commemorate the siege of Boston by the Continental Army, were purchased by Washington's nephews and other family members. Also dispersed were cherished mementoes of the private man, a pair of slippers, shoes and shoe buckles, his spectacles, razors, dental instruments, "plotting instruments," seals, and a simple farmer's lunch box used on his inspection tours of the five farms. The dispersal was now complete, and Bushrod Washington prepared to claim his inheritance. He had acquired little in the way of furniture at the various sales so the mansion was devoid of standing pieces when he moved in. Their own furniture would not fill the empty rooms, and he and his wife must have felt overwhelmed at the prospect of furnishing a large house and providing the equipment necessary to run an extensive estate.

Among Bushrod's purchases were several pieces from his uncle's study, and with his inheritance of Washington's "private papers... and ... library of Books and Pamphlets of every kind,"[21] that room retained something of its original character. Two globes, a table, and a letter press, once used to make copies of Washington's correspondence, stood in their accustomed places. A portrait of George's elder half-brother, Lawrence Washington, survived, as did busts of Jacques Necker and John Paul Jones, as well as one of George Washington by Jean Antoine Houdon.[22] This trio of muted dignitaries is now on brackets above the doors of the study.

The Houdon bust of George Washington was Bushrod's most significant purchase at the sales following Martha Washington's death. This superb portrait of Washington at age fifty-three had been modeled from life at Mount Vernon in 1785 by Europe's foremost sculptor.[23] It is the one from which all of Houdon's later Washington busts derive and was considered by the family one of the two best likenesses of the subject.[24] Houdon captured the qualities of strength and resoluteness that insured Washington's success during the Revolutionary War and inspired his fellow citizens to elect him president of the United States. It is a commanding portrait of an extraordinary man and is one of the few original pieces never to have left the estate. Bushrod's grandnephew, John Augustine Washington III, left it at Mount Vernon when he departed, and it stands today in the museum as a tribute to his generosity and confidence in the Mount Vernon Ladies' Association.

In time, Bushrod converted the study into a dining room, and its appearance and that of the house were further altered by the addition of a two-story porch on the south façade and a railing on the piazza roof. Bushrod and his wife lived at Mount Vernon for twenty-seven years, dying within days of each other in 1829. His household furnishings, including most of his Washington memorabilia, descended to his nephew, John Augustine Washington II. The collection remained substantially intact[25] until Mount Vernon was sold by John Augustine Washington III.

The sale of Mount Vernon in 1858 to the Mount Vernon Ladies' Association revived interest in George Washington's home, although in truth the flow of the faithful to that American mecca had never really ceased. On occasion, Bushrod and his successors were forced to restrict the activities of the more assertive pilgrims. For a time, John Augustine Washington III and his family kept to the second floor of the mansion while strangers satisfied their curiosity wandering through the first-floor rooms.

From 1853, when Miss Cunningham conceived the idea of an association of women to save Washington's home, the newspapers kept the public informed of the progress of this novel idea and its chances of success. The story caught the attention of Benson J. Lossing, a newspaper editor, writer, and wood engraver, who had published a two-volume *Pictorial Field Book of the Revolution* between 1850 and 1852. Lossing was thoroughly familiar with the scenes of General Washington's military life and during the course of his work had met George Washington Parke Custis. Probably through Custis's intercession, he secured permission from John Augustine Washington III to visit Mount Vernon in 1858 while researching Washington's domestic life for an article, "Mount Vernon as it is," for *Harper's New Monthly Magazine*. With the encouragement of the publishers, Lossing expanded the essay into a book-length study, *Mount Vernon and Its Associations*, a popular volume that went into several editions.

As Lossing relates the circumstances, the publishers "conceived the plan of a more extended account of Mount Vernon and desired me to prepare it.—As the possession of that estate was to pass . . . from the Washington family forever, it appeared to be an appropriate time for the preparation of such a memorial. . . ."[26] Lossing dedicated his book to the "Patriotic Countrywomen By Whose Efforts The Home and Tomb of Washington Have Been Rescued From Decay."[27] The author's considerable contribution was his focus on Washington memorabilia. He "visited Arlington House and other places, where . . . there were objects that were once at Mount Vernon, and made sketches of them. Those, and the drawings made for *Harper's Magazine*, and a few . . . in . . . Field-Book of the Revolution, are given in this work."[28] There are 139 illustrations in *Mount Vernon and Its Associations*, more than half of which depict original Mount Vernon pieces. Those that disappeared after 1860 are known only through Lossing's sketches. John Augustine Washington III cooperated fully with the project, identifying the Washington memorabilia inherited in direct line from his great-uncle, Bushrod Washington, and sharing the traditions that formed a rich family archive. Lossing's *Mount Vernon and Its Associations* remains one of the best sources for authenticating Washington memorabilia despite its errors and obvious limitations.

John Augustine Washington III had reserved the right to stay at Mount Vernon until the Association made its final payment. He was still in residence when the first piece of Washington memorabilia came back. Early in 1859, he received a letter from Mrs. Robert E. Lee of Arlington House in which she reported Mrs. Lorenzo Lewis's wish to return the harpsichord that had belonged to her late mother-in-law, Nelly Custis Lewis, when the latter lived at Mount Vernon. Mr. Washington wrote Miss Cunningham to say that he had ". . . taken the liberty of writing to Mrs. Lee, accepting Mrs. Lewis' liberal offering to the Association, and trust to your goodness to confirm my action. As soon as the Harpsichord is received I will inform you of the fact. . . ."[29] It was unlikely that Miss Cunningham would have refused such a prize. Nelly's harpsichord had been a gift in 1793 from George Washington. She used it first in Philadelphia and, after the family's return to Mount Vernon at the close of Washington's second term, the harpsichord stood in the Little Parlor, where Nelly played for the enjoyment of the household. Later she used the instrument at Woodlawn, near Mount Vernon, her home from 1802 until 1839. After the death of her husband, she moved to Berryville, Virginia, where she took up residence with her son, Lorenzo. It was at this time that Nelly left her harpsichord with her brother, Washington Custis, at Arlington House, but retained ownership. There it remained among Custis's Mount Vernon treasures until 1859, when Lorenzo's widow offered the piece to Mount Vernon. Nelly's death in 1852 and Custis's five years later left Mrs. Lee, who had inherited Arlington House from her father, to coordinate the transaction for Mrs. Lorenzo Lewis. Her generous act probably preserved the harpsichord from abuse at the hands of the federal troops that occupied Arlington House during the Civil War.

In the fall of 1859, the Washington family left for Waveland, an estate in Fauquier County, Virginia, about forty-two miles west of Mount Vernon.[30] While attending to his remaining affairs at Mount Vernon, John Augustine Washington III maintained a room in the mansion, conferring on occasion with his kinsman, Upton Herbert, whom the Association had named its first resident superintendent. Herbert's connection to the Washington family was invaluable during the early years of restoration and established a continuity that has characterized the work of the Association throughout its long history.

Before leaving Mount Vernon for the last time in late 1860, John Augustine presented to the Association a small collection of memorabilia which he felt properly belonged to Mount Vernon.[31] Houdon's original clay bust of Washington was the greatest of these treasures, and nothing since then has surpassed it in value to the collection. But lesser objects have attracted greater attention, among them an iron key, weighing little more than a pound, that he left in the first-floor passage where Washington himself placed it. This souvenir of the French Revolution was a gift from the Marquis de Lafayette, whose eloquent message of presentation was worthy of both writer and recipient: ". . . Give me leave, my dear General," he wrote, "to present you with a picture[32] of the Bastille, just as it looked a few days after I had ordered its demolition, with the main key of the fortress of despotism. It is a tribute, which I owe as a son to my adop-

tive father, as an aide-de-camp to my general, as a missionary of liberty its patriarch. . . ."[33] Washington's guests were fascinated by Lafayette's gift, and several contemporary accounts mention the "small crystal lantern"[34] which housed it. The Key to the Bastille falls into a special category of objects, fewer than a dozen, that have never left Mount Vernon, all presented by the last private owner of Washington's home.

The events of John Augustine Washington's life after the family left Mount Vernon are a poignant epilogue to his story. Having successfully resolved the preservation of Mount Vernon, he looked forward to a future at Waveland. In the fall of 1860 his wife died unexpectedly, leaving him with seven children, the last Washingtons born at Mount Vernon, ranging in age from two to sixteen years. His enlistment in the cause of secession proved a fatal decision. Serving as an aide-de-camp to Gen. Robert E. Lee, he was killed on September 13, 1861, at Elkwater in what is now West Virginia. In a prophetic letter, written only two weeks before his death, he seemed to anticipate his fate. "For my own part, I expect to come out of this war, if I get through it at all, as clean shorn as a sheep in June. I want my children to understand, at once, that they are poor, and instead of living as we have done, that they will have to work for their living, and an indifferent one at that. This does not deprive us of, it adds to our self respect. . . ."[35] John Augustine's Washington memorabilia are not specifically mentioned in his will, but they are probably included in the bequest to his son, Lawrence, ". . . of all the Books, Manuscripts, papers, engravings, pictures, Medals and Arms of which I may die possessed. . . ." All other property was divided equally among his children.[36]

In 1891, John Augustine's son, Lawrence, Bushrod Corbin Washington, and Thomas Blackburn Washington authorized "The Final Sale of the Relics of General Washington" in Philadelphia.[37] Bushrod Corbin and Thomas Blackburn were Lawrence's cousins, sons of his father's brother, Thomas Blackburn Washington. Included in the auction was the Sèvres bust of Jacques Necker presented to

President Washington in 1790 by the Count d'Estaing, who had served with the French fleet during the American Revolution. At the auction, the small bust of Necker was sold to the Historical Society of Pennsylvania, whose membership had formed a subscription for the purpose. It remained there until 1969, when the Society and the Association effected a special agreement that permitted M. Necker's return to George Washington's study, where it rests today on a bracket over the east door.

At the "Final Sale," sponsored by Lawrence Washington and his cousins, the Association's representatives were successful bidders on an engraving of Louis XVI from the large dining room of the mansion and a handsome gilt looking glass with a reverse painting of the Washington coat-of-arms, identified in the catalogue as having hung in the West Parlor. The engraving of Louis XVI was in its original frame, an elaborate gilt molding with the French monarch's cipher in one corner and the American president's in the corresponding corner.[38] Over the years other pieces from this landmark sale have been restored to Mount Vernon by gift, loan, and purchase from descendants of the original buyers, including members of the Washington family who saw an opportunity to buy Washington memorabilia that had been inherited by closer kinsmen. Other pieces sold in 1891 have disappeared despite efforts to trace them.

The Civil War that cost John Augustine Washington III his life was devastating to Arlington House, which had by far the largest concentration of Mount Vernon memorabilia within its walls. Martha Washington's only grandson, George Washington Parke Custis, had amassed by inheritance and purchase an impressive collection of family plate, portraits, pocelains, and other furnishings. He devoted a lifetime to immortalizing the life of "The Chief," as he called General Washington, and Benson Lossing's work, devoted to Custis's favorite topic, would have had special appeal for this amateur painter and playwright whose patriotic subject matter was usually drawn from the events of the American Revolution. It must have seemed to Benson Lossing that his eye fell on Washington memorabilia wher-

ever he stood at Arlington. Custis used and enjoyed this wealth of memorabilia. In the summer, General Washington's military marquee was set up to shade his guests, who drank from silver cups, engraved with the Washington crest, set out on trays emblazoned with the full Washington coat-of-arms. Ancestral portraits established Custis's place among Virginia's venerable families. Presidential and Cincinnati porcelains were stacked on pantry shelves beside glassware used during Washington's presidency and later at Mount Vernon. Flatware made for Washington by the best Philadelphia silversmiths was arranged in handsome mahogany knife cases that once had stood on the sideboards at Mount Vernon. An ancient English sideboard table, formerly owned by Lawrence Washington, George's half-brother, was described in considerable detail by Benson Lossing, evidence, perhaps, of the high esteem with which Custis regarded it. The best traditions of Mount Vernon hospitality were perpetuated at Arlington House, dedicated by its master to the memory of George Washington.

George Washington Parke Custis had considerable pride of possession, but was exceedingly generous, sometimes shockingly so, in sharing his treasures with strangers, family, and friends. In the midst of such plenty, it may have seemed ungracious not to share the wealth. In 1857, the year of his death, Custis explained to a correspondent that he was frequently importuned for information and mementoes of General Washington. His time was spent, he said, "cutting up fragments from old letters and accounts some of 1760, or nearly an hundred years ago, to supply the call for Anything . . . of his venerated hands. . . ."[39] A casual dispensation of family mementoes was not an unusual gesture. Custis must have been aware of his grandmother's small presentations to favored recipients, particularly after the death of her illustrious husband. He may also have known of Bushrod Washington's liberal tendencies with Washington manuscripts and signatures cut from George Washington's letters to satisfy souvenir hunters.

Washington Custis was spared the grief visited upon his household by the events of the Civil War. Had he lived,

Arlington House might not have been subjected to the indignity of occupation by Union troops, but that is conjecture since its spectacular site on a prominence overlooking Washington made it attractive to both armies. General Lee recognized its vulnerability and expected an early occupation by northern forces. He also admitted that as the home of the Confederate commander, Arlington House might be subject to plunder by the rabble. He urged Mrs. Lee to have everything in readiness for a sudden departure, if it became necessary.[40] In May 1861, she left with the most important Mount Vernon relics, some of which were deposited with family in nearby Fairfax County; the silver went to Richmond in General Lee's baggage train. Of necessity, many things, including Washington relics, were left at Arlington House behind locked doors, where they were thought to be secure from the Union troops. It proved a delusion. Lee's old friend, Gen. Winfield Scott, issued orders for the protection of the house, but the troops ignored the courtesy extended to Mrs. Lee and broke into the cellars and attic where her treasures were discovered. When it was learned that the soldiers had found the Washington relics, Gen. Irvin McDowell, commanding officer at Arlington House, sought their removal to a safer repository. It was suggested, with the concurrence of the secretary of the interior, that "the cases in the public saloon of the Patent Office . . . [were] the most appropriate resting place for these mementoes of General Washington, which . . . 'the whole country has an interest in preserving.'"[41]

Among the pieces discovered by the troops in the cellars at Arlington House was a superb bowl of ample proportions whose interior was covered with a drawing of a three-masted frigate named *Defender*. Once part of Custis's inheritance from his grandmother, it had seen service in the presidential household, at Mount Vernon, and later at Arlington House. While at Arlington in 1861, a Union soldier from New Bedford, Massachusetts, had "liberated" the bowl with other Washington relics and carried them back to New England. Later, his sister came into their possession and it was she who bequeathed these treasures to a friend. In 1930, the bowl surfaced briefly when it was offered for sale to Mount Vernon, but the high price during the depression precluded purchase. Forty-five years later, on the eve of the Bicentennial, a letter arrived at Mount Vernon requesting assistance in identifying a large bowl which was thought to have belonged to George Washington. There was little doubt from the writer's description that this was the missing "bowl that has a ship in it" and subsequent snapshots confirmed the early identification. Occasionally, the booty of war falls to responsible and caring people who view ownership as a public trust. So it was with Mr. Custis's bowl, which is once again at Mount Vernon.

The removal of the Mount Vernon relics to the Patent Office preserved the Arlington House collection from total dispersal during the Civil War. From the Patent Office the memorabilia were taken to the Smithsonian Institution, where they were held until 1911, when President William McKinley ordered their return to the Lee family. Mrs. Lee's failure to have her possessions returned after the war exemplified the sectionalism that lingered so long. Those who would have made the gesture due Mrs. Lee were continuously overruled by an embittered northern faction within the Congress. Mrs. Lee did not live to recover her Mount Vernon relics, and her last glimpse of Arlington House was a melancholy moment.[42]

Of the four grandchildren of Martha Washington, Nelly Custis Lewis was the only one to remain on land once a part of the Mount Vernon estate. At the time of her marriage, George Washington presented Nelly and Lawrence Lewis —son of his sister, Betty Washington Lewis—with a tract of land about three miles west of Mount Vernon. His will confirmed the gift,[43] which included the mill on Dogue Creek. On a hill overlooking the old grist mill, Nelly and Lawrence built a handsome brick house designed by Dr. William Thornton, a longtime friend of the Washington family. Like her brother, Washington Custis, Nelly would have preferred to remain at Mount Vernon. The pain of leaving the house in which she had been raised was increased by the loss of her grandmother, to whom she was unusually devoted. Nelly received a generous portion of Mount Vernon's furnishings, and this inheritance combined with her husband's purchases at the sales of 1802 formed a large and important assemblage of Washington furniture and household goods. The rooms of Woodlawn filled quickly with furnishings brought from Mount Vernon. A sideboard, looking glass, and twelve chairs from Washington's large dining room[44] nearly furnished Woodlawn's new dining room. Blue-and-white china, silverplate, glassware, Mount Vernon bedsteads to accommodate a growing family, miniatures, textiles, needlework, and dozens of miscellaneous Washington pieces were among Nelly's treasures from her old home. The comfort of familiar objects probably eased her transition, but life changed dramatically for her after 1802, and Nelly's life at Woodlawn never equalled the social activity of Mount Vernon.

Nelly Custis Lewis outlived all but one of her eight children, only three of whom had lived to marry and have children of their own. Her one surviving child, Frances Parke Lewis Butler, was mentioned in her will as were the children of her late son, Lorenzo, and those of another daughter, Mary Eliza Angela Lewis Conrad, who had died in 1835. It seems likely from the content of her will that the major pieces of furniture had been disposed of among the children prior to 1850 when she drew her final testament, which is an interesting catalogue of objects dear to Nelly's heart; but on its own merit is not entirely satisfactory for identifying Washington memorabilia.[45] An occasional reference to something of "Grandmama's" (Martha Washington's) is useful information, but her disposal of a box of china "under Norah's Bed" leaves room for speculation. In 1878, her grandson Lorenzo's son, George Washington Lewis, and other descendants sold a sizeable collection of Mount Vernon furnishings to the United States government.[46] Those pieces are now exhibited in the Smithsonian Institution's National Museum of American History. In 1893, another grandson, H. L. Daingerfield Lewis, ordered the sale of more family memorabilia, some of which had been owned by his grandfather Lawrence Lewis, and other pieces had

belonged to General Washington. Among the pieces acquired by the Association at Daingerfield Lewis's auction was the French mantel clock from Washington's bedroom that had ticked off his last hours.[47] The clock had been sold in 1802 to Charles Carter, husband of Washington's niece, Betty Lewis Carter.

An important item that escaped sale by Nelly's heirs was her Mount Vernon sideboard that had stood with its companion piece on either side of the Palladian window in Mount Vernon's large dining room. She had left it at Arlington House with the harpsichord in 1839 and it probably remained there for the duration of the Civil War, but may have been removed for safety to Alexandria, Virginia, by Mrs. Lee's friends.[48] In any event, Nelly's sideboard landed "at Green's furniture ware rooms in Alex'a" in 1873, and Mrs. Robert E. Lee offered it to the Association at that time with a suggestion that minor repairs would restore it to a condition worthy of "its former position" at Mount Vernon.[49] The restoration envisioned by Mrs. Lee did not occur until 1967, when another sideboard, nearly identical in size and detail to Nelly's original, was found as a suitable substitute for the missing mate that Robert Peter, Jr., brother-in-law of Martha Custis Peter, had bought in 1802. The present whereabouts of the original companion sideboard—if it still exists—is a mystery, but no chapter is ever closed on missing memorabilia.

Many of the porcelains discussed in this book are from the collection of Martha Parke Custis and her husband Thomas Peter, who bought extensively at the sales following Martha Washington's death.[50] His wife's inheritance from her grandmother was small; only her "writing table and the seat to it standing in my chamber, also the print of Genl. Washington that hangs in the passage" were bequeathed by will.[51] Some things in the Peter collection were undoubtedly gifts from Martha Washington, but the documentation is at best fragmentary, as was the case with gifts to her other grandchildren.

The Peters spent most of their married life at Tudor Place, the Georgetown house in Washington City designed for Thomas Peter by Dr. William Thornton. This elegant and interesting home is still owned by a descendant, Armistead Peter III. Martha and Thomas Peter had eight children whose rate of survival was only slightly better than that of their Woodlawn cousins. Those who lived to adulthood received some portion of the total collection, and memorabilia have filtered back to Mount Vernon from their various descendants, but Tudor Place and its collections are most closely associated with Thomas and Martha's youngest daughter, Britannia Wellington Peter, who was born there in 1815 and died there one day short of her ninety-sixth birthday. The untimely death of her husband, Comdr. Beverly Kennon, sent Brittania and her child, Martha Custis Kennon, back to Tudor Place to live. When Martha Peter died in 1854, Brittania Kennon inherited the house and most of its contents. Like Arlington House, Tudor Place was affected by the Civil War, but to a considerably lesser degree. When the war broke out, Mrs. Kennon was preparing to go abroad and had installed a tenant at Tudor Place. Informed that the house might be seized by the federal government for a hospital, she returned to Georgetown and turned Tudor Place into a boardinghouse to protect it from confiscation.[52] Her plan worked and the house stands today a tribute to a remarkable lady. She was a worthy descendant of Martha Washington, for her resourcefulness and longevity insured the continuity of a large portion of the Tudor Place collection of Mount Vernon memorabilia.

After her death in 1911, this collection was divided among the five children of her only daughter, Martha Custis Kennon, who had married a cousin, Dr. Armistead Peter. A grandson died shortly after the division, and his portion was further divided among his three brothers and a sister. In 1956, the Association purchased from another of her grandsons, G. Freeland Peter, "the largest and most varied single accession in the history of the Association." Numbering over one hundred items, it included intimate reminders of the mistress of Mount Vernon: her prayer book and her cookbook; household china, pewter, and glass; cooking utensils; furniture; three splendid miniatures; and documents of rare interest.[53] In the aggregate, the Tudor Place collection was impressive, and Mrs. Kennon a "dedicated custodian of the Mount Vernon mementoes which she had inherited."[54] Her informal "catalogue" of the Mount Vernon relics, drawn from her long association with the collection, is evidence of her concern. All too few owners of historical collections bother to write down provenance, erroneously assuming that someone will always be available to make the necessary identifications, but with such collections the importance of a piece of memorabilia is in direct ratio to what we know about its association.

Eliza Parke Custis Law, eldest of Martha Washington's grandchildren, nearly matched in "curatorial" zeal that of her niece, Mrs. Kennon, but hers was a more personal response that is lacking in Mrs. Kennon's straightforward approach to the task. Eliza's descriptions, often penned, pasted, written upon, or wrapped around the objects, express a deeply sentimental attachment to family and may reflect in part the sadness of her later years. Perhaps because of her divorce from Thomas Law—after which she was known as Mrs. Custis—Eliza seems rootless and is the only one of Martha's grandchildren whose adult life is not associated with a great house wherein centered her collection of Mount Vernon memorabilia.

Her direct inheritance from her grandmother consisted of only three pieces, a "dressing table and glass that stands in the chamber called the yellow room, and Genl. Washington's picture painted by Trumbull,"[55] but carefully selected for their importance to Mrs. Washington. The small equestrian portrait of Washington is a fine study and had the special significance of being a gift from the artist.[56] The "dressing table," a substantial piece of English manufacture, was in fact a four-drawer mahogany chest with an interior looking glass and fitted compartments for toilet accessories. It was an early piece purchased by Colonel Washington in 1757, two years before his marriage to Martha Dandridge Custis. Highly prized by Eliza's descendants, the chest remained in the family until its recent return to Mount Vernon, where it stands again in the Yellow Bedroom, one of the few pieces of furniture whose exact location is supported by documentation other than the inventory prepared after George Washington's death.

The Association's purchase of memorabilia from descendants of Eliza's daughter, Eliza Law Rogers, brought to Mount Vernon in 1945 a large leather trunk filled with clothing and textile fragments that had once belonged to the Washingtons. It was typical of Eliza that the note she pasted to the inside trunk lid glowed with sentiments of familial affection. She has left us a delightful glimpse of Mount Vernon domestic life that would be lost except for her tender remembrances.

Washington July 4th 1830

My dear Brother who I love much George Washington Parke Custis has made me a present of this trunk. I write these lines to tell my dear grand children I prize it most dearly. It was that in which the cloaths of my Sainted Grandmother Mrs. Washington were always pack'd by her own hands when she went to visit, & spend some time with the General, whenever the Army were in quarters. I have stood by it as she put in her cloaths sadly distress'd at her going away—& oh how joyfully when she returned did I look on to see her cloaths taken out, & the many gifts she always brought for her grandchildren!—no words can express how I loved her—she, & all else most fondly beloved are gone to their proper home among the Angels—my darling Grand children, three yet live, I leave this trunk to my Rosebud—it is fill'd with sacred Relics for my children—may God bless them!

Eliza P. Custis

A variety of small possessions of the Washingtons has survived among Eliza's descendants, fragile pieces that add a personal dimension and give a sense of Martha Washington's private life. Her sewing chair, a simple upholstered piece whose legs were shortened for her accommodation, was presented by the family. Her needlework tools, slippers, and a brown satin dress in a style favored in her later years bring Mrs. Washington to life in her role as mistress of Mount Vernon.

The concentration of Mount Vernon memorabilia within the families of George and Martha Washington has greatly simplified the task of tracing the original furnishings from the moment of their dispersal in 1802. To their care was committed the major portion of the contents of Washington's home and through the years they have preserved and assured the authentication of innumerable objects without which the mansion might be simply another historic house. Those outside the family have made no small contribution to the present high state of Mount Vernon's restoration. Washington became a legend in his own time and everything about him commanded interest. He has inspired the "spontaneous generation" of Washingtoniana, and there are those who would believe that every "W" on a piece of eighteenth-century silver commemorated the great Washington. We are asked to believe that he left a trail of possessions from New England to Savannah and west to the Ohio, but General Washington would have been appalled by such careless waste.

The nation's fascination with George Washington has never abated, though he seems to be the least understood of the Founding Fathers. He has been the object of continuous veneration in spite of attempts to impugn his character, discredit his abilities, and cast him in the role of autocrat. Private collectors and public institutions vie for the privilege of owning Washingtoniana, though many of his furnishings would be considered less than "museum quality." A French army chaplain who saw him in 1781 expressed most clearly the compelling figure of Washington:

. . . I gazed at him earnestly with the eagerness that is always aroused by the presence of great men. It seems that one may find in their features the marks of the genius which sets them apart and places them above their fellow men. More than any other man Washington can vindicate this opinion: a tall, noble and well proportioned figure, an open, kind and calm expression, an appearance simple and modest, he strikes, he interests Frenchmen, Americans and even his enemies.[57]

Christine Meadows, curator
The Mount Vernon Ladies'
Association of the Union

NOTES

References to ceramics in Washington's correspondence, invoices, inventories, and account books have not been cited in the text. Transcriptions of excerpts from the originals have been arranged chronologically in the Appendix. The notes are in a short form. For the complete citation, *see* the Bibliography.

Abbreviations and Short Titles for frequently cited works:

LC	Library of Congress, Manuscript Division, George Washington Papers. Number following (for example, LC 101) refers to the reel number in the microfilm edition. See *Index to the George Washington Papers*, Library of Congress, Presidents' Papers Index Series, Washington, D.C., 1964, for the division of the documents into eight series.
W	John C. Fitzpatrick, ed., *The Writings of George Washington.* 39 vols. Washington, D.C.: United States Government Printing Office, 1931–1944. Numbers following (for example, W 31:152) refer to the volume and page.
Freeman	Douglas Southall Freeman, *George Washington. A Biography.* 6 vols. New York: Charles Scribner's Sons, 1948.
Diaries	Donald Jackson and Dorothy Twohig, eds., *The Diaries of George Washington.* 6 vols. Charlottesville: University Press of Virginia, 1976.
Ledgers A, B, and C	Washington's account books for the Mount Vernon Mansion House and other farms. Ledgers A and B are in the George Washington Papers at the Library of Congress, and Ledger C is in the Lloyd W. Smith Collection, Morristown National Historical Park.

PROLOGUE

1. The two older children of Custis, Eliza Parke and Martha Parke Custis, remained with their mother, Eleanor Calvert Custis, but were frequent visitors in the Mount Vernon household.

2. Lossing, ed., *Recollections and Private Memoirs*, p. 406.

3. W 29: 160–61.

4. W 29: 159.

5. W 28: 470.

6. *Diaries*, vol. 6, p. 307.

7. Martha Washington to Mercy Otis Warren, November 26, 1789. Copy in the Henry E. Huntington Library; location of original unknown.

8. Freeman, vol. 3, pp. 22–23.

9. *Diaries*, vol. 4, pp. 277–78.

10. "Arlington and Mount Vernon 1856 As Described in a Letter of Blanche Berard" (from a description of Mount Vernon by George Washington Parke Custis as related to Blanche Berard), *The Virginia Magazine of History and Biography* 57, no. 2 (1949): 162.

11. W 35: 80.

12. Martha Washington to Frances Bassett Washington, July 1, 1792, from a typescript published in *The Washington Post*, December 12, 1943.

13. Vail, ed., pp. 72–85.

14. *Diary of Amariah Frost*, American Antiquarian Society Proceedings, 1879, pp. 71–79.

15. Ibid.

16. Budka, ed., p. 106.

17. W 36: 118.

18. *Diary of Amariah Frost*, pp. 71–79.

19. Cutler, ed., vol. 2, pp. 56 ff.

20. Wansey, pp. 108 and 112.

21. W 35: 455.

22. Chastellux, vol. 2, p. 595.

23. W 29: 287.

CHAPTERS I–VIII

1. Robert Orme, aide-de-camp to General Braddock, to GW, Williamsburg, March 2, 1755. Freeman, vol. 2, p. 13.

2. Journal of 1748, "Memorandum to have my Coat made by the Following Directions," LC 1.

3. Colony of Virginia. King George County Inventories, 1721–1744, pp. 285–91. In George H.S. King, pp. 269 and 270. Mary Ball Washington left her blue-and-white tea china to Fielding Lewis and her "red-and-white tea china" to Betty Carter. Her will, dated May 20, 1788, is registered in the Clerk's Office at Fredericksburg and has been reprinted by the Home of Mary Washington, Fredericksburg, Virginia.

4. George Washington to George William Fairfax, February 27, 1785, W 28: 83.

5. Belvoir was destroyed by fire during the Revolution. *See* Miller for photographs of Gunston Hall, designed by William Buckland.

6. Inventory in Conway, pp. 217–19. Washington was Fairfax's agent for the rental of Belvoir, according to an advertisement in the *Philadelphia Gazette*, October 19, 1774. He also purchased £ 200 worth of furnishings at two sales held at Belvoir in 1774. *See* text, pp. 63, 65.

7. Ledger A, LC 115.

8. GW to Richard Washington, December 6, 1755, LC 116. George Washington thought he was distantly related to Richard Washington. The latter visited Mount Vernon from December 24, 1774, to January 2, 1775. *See Diaries*, vol. 3, pp. 297–98 and 302.

9. "Invoice of goods shipped by Anthony Bacon on board the Ruby, Cap Edward Ogle pr Maryland on Acct and by order of Jno Carlyle Esq—," LC 116. Carlyle's manor house, built in 1742 and recently restored, is at 121 North Fairfax Street, Alexandria, Virginia. His wife was Sara Fairfax, a daughter of Col. William Fairfax; another Fairfax daughter, Anne, was married to Lawrence Washington. Carlyle was an executor of the estate of Lawrence Washington.

10. GW to Richard Washington, December 6, 1755, LC 116.

11. Rosenblatt, pp. 385–86. *See also Diaries*, vol. 1, p. 251: "Saturday Mar. 8 [1760] Gave Captn. Cawseys Skipper namely William Vicars—1 Tobo. Note and an Order on Hunting Creek Warehouses [in Alexandria] for 7 Hhds. of my Mountain Tobo."

12. GW to Richard Washington from Fort Loudon, April 15, 1757, LC 116. Washington served as an aide to General Braddock. Recapture of Fort Duquesne was the objective of the expedition.

13. GW to Richard Washington, Fort Loudon, Sept. 10, 1757, W 2:124. Encloses copy of his April 15 letter which "I find has mistaken her Rout and got to France." This letter also mentions "the Invoice Mr. Carlyle sent you for me."

14. GW to Richard Washington from Mount Vernon, December 26, 1757, W 2:160.

15. Ibid. Washington instructed Knox to pay the proceeds of the sale of this tobacco and that of a previous shipment to Richard Washington, whom he directed to draw upon Knox for payment for the expensive furnishings ordered from the former.

16. GW to Thomas Knox, January 8, 1758, W 2:161.

17. Ibid.

18. February 1755, Ledger A, Washington Papers, LC 115. Washington's diary and ledger occasionally note purchases in Alexandria of "necessaries," some of which may have been items of tableware. *See Diaries*, vol. 1, p. 130 (November 1, 1753) and p. 216 (January 7, 1760).

19. The famous "King of Prussia" plates were made after November 1757. *See* Noël Hume, *A Guide to Artifacts*, p. 115.

20. Berling, figs. 23 and 27.

21. For an account of the development of salt-glazed stoneware in England, *see* Barber and also Blacker.

22. The complex processes are described clearly in Mountford, *The Illustrated Guide*, pp. 29–30. He also points out that mass production of tableware was possible because of a new trade, that of model or block cutter, added to the roles of the traditional Staffordshire thrower and turner. One popular block cutter or mold maker who worked for several factories was Aaron Wood, father of Enoch Wood. *See* reprint of Shaw, pp. 150 and 156.

23. Molded wares were placed in a kiln and fired in a reducing atmosphere to about 2000 F., at which point salt was thrown into the kiln. The sodium oxide and hydrochloric acid of the decomposed salt then combined with the alumina and silica of the clay to produce a hard, transparent glaze. *See* Godden, *An Illustrated Encyclopedia*, p. xiv.

24. In Mountford, *The Illustrated Guide*, pp. 11 and 12.

25. Overglaze decoration requires greater skill and, therefore, labor costs are greater than those for the underglaze decoration possible with lead glazes.

26. Letter from A.R. Mountford to the author, December 3, 1980.

27. Evening tea was served an hour or more after dinner. *See* Roth, p. 67.

28. John Augustine Washington managed the plantation at that time in his brother's absence.

29. GW to Richard Washington, December 6, 1755, and GW to Richard Washington, January 8, 1758, LC 116.

30. *See* p. 23 in text.

31. March 16, 1758, "to Mrs. Custis's Servants," Ledger A, LC 115.

32. Richard Washington to GW, August 20, 1757, LC 116. The total expenditure of £ 274.2. indicates that Washington had begun to furnish Mount Vernon in earnest. The invoice is one of the most interesting in the Washington Papers. Six mahogany chairs with "Gothick arch'd Backs" are listed as well as bedroom furniture bought "at an auction" and a Wilton carpet.

33. *See* Godden, *Caughley*, p. 59. Other patterns in 1789 included "Common Nankin" and "New Landscape."

34. Scheurleer, fig. 336.

35. Ibid., p. 175. "Mandarin" was evidently a term used in the mid-eighteenth century in The Netherlands for this decoration. *See* Fisher, pl. 21.

36. Scheurleer, pp. 92, 106, and pl. 104.

37. Beurdeley, cat. no. 197, p. 196.

38. Cushion, p. 194. The Liverpool, Chelsea, and Worcester factories made teapots of similar form.

39. Large bowls were also made at Ch'ing-tê Chên for Chinese consumption. The word "punch" itself is of Eastern origin from the Hindu "panch," meaning five for the five ingredients: arrack, tea, sugar, water, and lemon juice. *See* Johnson.

40. Capt. Augustine Washington left a blue-and-white punch bowl and a gilt one in 1743. King George County Inventories, 1721–1744, p. 285. Inventories of the period often list punch bowls and tea sets on parlor tables.

41. "Account of Sundrys taken and used by Mrs Custis out of the Inventories . . . James City," Virginia Historical Society, Custis family papers, n.d. *See* Appendix for ca. 1757–1759.

42. Freeman, vol. 3, pp. 20–21.

43. Custis family papers.

44. Freeman, vol. 2, p. 300.

45. *See* Appendix for ca. 1757–1759.

46. Custis family papers. There are columns for appraised value and "sold for." The personal property at the Williamsburg residence was sold October 25, 1759. Freeman, vol. 3, p. 29.

47. *See* Appendix for ca. 1757–1759. Compare this terminology and the relative values to George Washington's "Compleat sett fine Image china," Appendix, August 20, 1757.

48. Handwritten card. The Historical Society of Pennsylvania, Manuscript Department. The Washingtons attended the wedding of William Jackson to Elizabeth Willing in Philadelphia on November 11, 1795. The wedding was one of the brilliant social occasions during Washington's second administration. *See* Joseph Jackson, p. 152. *See also* Griswold, p. 306. Ann Willing Jackson was still alive when Griswold wrote his account.

49. Scheurleer, p. 80. Hobson, vol. 2, pl. 119, fig. 3; Williamson, chap. 5, pl. 7, and p. 38. *See also* Barrett, p. 14.

50. Opinion of Stephen Little, curator of Chinese Art, Asian Art Museum of San Francisco. Letter to author, January 7, 1981. Mr. Little noted the Han robes of the rider amidst the Ch'ing costumes of the other figures.

51. The Campbell Museum, *Selections from the Campbell Museum Collection*, no. 95. *See also* Beurdeley, no. 77, p. 166.

52. The Chinese term for these opaque enamels in use by 1722 was "Yang ts'ai" (foreign colors) or "Youang ts'ai" (soft colors). *See* Williamson, p. 61.

53. *See* Honey, *The Ceramic Art of China*, p. 187 and pl. 186a for an example of Nabeshima porcelain.

54. Mackenna, *Chelsea Porcelain, the Gold Anchor Period*, p. 12.

55. A salter is a seller of salt. Jacob M. Price, pp. 401–2. Other members of the Cary family were Virginia merchants in Bristol. Members of both branches of the Cary family actually lived in Virginia.

56. Joseph Ball to his sister, Mary Ball Washington, May 19, 1747. Joseph Ball Letter-Book, Library of Congress. Freeman, vol. 3,

chap. 3, gives a vivid account of tobacco growing, use of slaves, and shipping, which at this period often involved protective convoys. *See also Diaries*, vol. 1 (1760 diary), pp. 228, 229, and 251, for Washington's account of his tobacco in the Alexandria warehouses.

57. Toppin, p. 53.

58. Haggar and Adams, p. 22.

59. Mackenna, *Chelsea Porcelain, the Red Anchor Wares*, p. 97. The Chelsea factory produced figures with open bases to attach to ormolu candelabra.

60. Noël Hume, *Pottery and Porcelain*, p. 10. Hood, p. 218.

61. *Colonial Williamsburg Today*, p. 7. A Bow sweetmeat dish was found at the Prentis House in Williamsburg.

62. William King, p. 47.

63. Read, ed., p. 17, item no. 38; p. 30, item no. 50. *See also* p. 36, item no. 50: "A pair of exceeding fine table candlesticks representing the seasons."

64. Mackenna, *Chelsea Porcelain, the Gold Anchor Period*, pl. 52, fig. 100, p. 74. Rackham, vol. 1, no. 291.

65. Honey, Rackham, and Read, pp. 292–302.

66. Barber, p. 29. *See also* Noël Hume, *A Guide to Artifacts*, pp. 113–14. Sherds of Nottingham ware exhibit a white line between glaze and body.

67. Fleming and Honour, "Westerwald Potteries," in *Dictionary of the Decorative Arts*, p. 856.

68. Noël Hume, *Here Lies Virginia*, pp. 220–21.

69. These mugs, however, were less expensive than four heavily decorated mugs (£2) sent in November 1766.

70. Scheurleer, pl. 339. A mug of European shape in Te-hua ware with relief blossoms is preserved at Winterthur. *See* Palmer, fig. 13.

71. *See* Palmer, fig. 29, for ceramic-handle knives and forks.

72. Document reproduced in Morse, vol. 5, p. 34. The table services from Sweetia were valued at 15 taels each. The "tael" was a monetary unit used in the East Indian trade. It was worth between five and seven shillings. *See* Scheuerleer, p. 66.

73. Morse, vol. 2, p. 3

74. Mrs. Washington's will is reproduced in Lossing, *George Washington's Mount Vernon.*

75. Fleming and Honour, p. 855. Brears, p. 241. Noël Hume, *Here Lies Virginia,* pp. 283–84.

76. A china basket is preserved at the Adams National Historic Site, Quincy, Massachusetts.

77. GW to Daniel Parker, September 12, 1783, W 27: 151.

78. Scheurleer, p. 194.

79. Freeman, vol. 3, p. 207.

80. GW to Capel, Osgood, Hanbury (the firm to which tobacco belonging to John Parke Custis was consigned), July 25, 1769, W 2:515.

81. GW to Robert Cary, November 10, 1773, W 3: 165.

82. Meteyard, *The Life of Josiah Wedgwood,* pp. 382–83.

83. GW to Robert Cary, July 25, 1769, W 2: 512.

84. Freeman, vol. 3, p. 223.

85. Morison, p. 198.

86. Meteyard, *The Wedgwood Handbook,* p. 318. There are no known pre-1774 catalogues in existence. Letter to author from Gaye Blake Roberts, curator, The Wedgwood Museum, June 18, 1981.

87. Mankowitz, pp. 63–67, pls. 1–13. A memorandum dated May 29, 1764, in the Wedgwood Museum Archives, Barlaston, Stoke-on-Trent (reference no. 6-5003), refers to the firm of Farrer and Garrett and "samples for a foreign market."

88. Shaw, p. 185. *See also* Noël Hume, "The What, Who and When of English Creamware Plate Design," pp. 350–55.

89. Meteyard, *The Life of Josiah Wedgwood,* p. 56.

90. Inventory in Noël Hume, *Here Lies Virginia,* pp. 296–97.

91. Walton, p. 75.

92. *See* Lawrence.

93. Towner, p. 21.

94. Letter from Arnold Mountford, director of museums, City of Stoke-on-Trent, to author, December 3, 1980.

95. Godden, *Caughley,* fig. 222.

96. September 4, 1774, Ledger B, p. 121, LC 115. There were no identifiable ceramics. See also Ledger B, p. 90, May 1773. Washington bought a horse and "phaeten" in Philadelphia after he took John Parke Custis to "the College" in New York.

97. Inventory in Conway, pp. 217–19. That there were two sales is revealed in Washington's account with George William Fairfax, August 15, 1775, Ledger B, p. 66: "By Sundries bought at Sale on the 15 Augˢ 1774, at 12 Mᵒ Credit . . . £ 169/12/6" and "By Ditto Dᵒ at the Subseq one . . . £ 31/11/9." Washington made a few purchases for others at the August sale, and in turn he purchased a card table from the successful bidder the day after the sale. Ledger B, p. 121, Cash Accounts, August 16, 1774.

98. Freeman, vol. 4, p. 471. Knight, p. 52.

99. Knight, p. 51. Separate accounts of Austin, Gibbs, and Colfax are on LC 117.

100. July 12, 1789, in Mitchell, ed., pp. 17–18.

101. *New York Packet,* April 17, 1786, in Gottesman, ed., vol. 2, p. 102. Golden Hill was the former name of John Street between William and Pearl streets. Burling Slip or Burling's Slip extended into the East River. *See* "Plan of the City" in Franks, ed., and "A Directory of Forgotten Streets," in Dunshee, unpaged appendix.

102. Breton, ed., vol. 1, pp. 96–97. Arlene Palmer Schwind is preparing a study of these papers to be published in the *American Ceramic Circle Bulletin.*

103. Shaw, p. 18.

104. *The New-York Journal or General Advertiser,* August 3, 1775, in Gottesman, ed., p. 87.

105. Inventory of James Pemberton, Boston, 1747, in Roth, p. 80.

106. Meteyard, *The Life of Josiah Wedgwood,* vol. 1, p. 372.

107. Noël Hume, *A Guide to Artifacts,* p. 259.

108. Freeman, vol. 5, p. 411.

109. Morgan, p. 137.

110. GW to Samuel Miles, July 8, 1782, W 24: 404.

111. On June 14, 1781, Rendon sent Washington a list of produce available from Havana, including limes, pineapples, chocolate, sugar, snuff, and "segars." LC 78.

112. Martha Dangerfield Bland to Frances Bland Tucker, Philadelphia, 1781, in "Randolph and Tucker Letters," p. 44. *See also* Chastellux, vol. 1, p. 234: [1780] ". . . our minister maintains a considerable State, and gives frequently great dinners. . . ."

113. Armes, ed., p. 156. Lady Kitty Duer and her sister, Lady Mary Watts, were later belles of New York society in the period of the so-called Republican Court.

114. *New York Gazette,* March 11, 1772, reprinted in Gottesman, ed., vol. 1, p. 88; *Pennsylvania Packet,* April 13, 1771, and *Freeman's Journal,* May 5, 1784, are reprinted in Prime, vol. 1, pp. 113 and 132. The long "Assortment of goods" given in the *Pennsylvania Packet* includes red "China" teapots under "Earthen Ware." In 1771, "China" usually meant wares of Chinese origin or Chinese-type wares.

115. Scheurleer, p. 167.

116. R. Price, pp. 1–9.

117. Balch, ed., p. 16. Much of the material

on pages 67 through 73 and additional information about the French presence in America by the author is in the *American Ceramic Circle Bulletin*, no. 3 (in press).

118. January 24, 1781, W 21: 138. Custine had visited Washington's headquarters.

119. Heuser-Speier, p. 54. He mentions a catalogue of forms and a "Geheimbuch" of 700 recipes for faience, pipe clay, porcelain, biscuit, glazes, and colors. Unfortunately, these records have not survived, but a form and price list for ornamentalwares is known from the copy made in 1868 by Tainturier, p. 84.

120. Balch, ed., pp. 166–67. Actually, Washington had raised Mount Vernon to two-and-one-half stories in 1758.

121. Acomb, ed., p. 214. There were no "arms" in the design.

122. Bonsal, p. 235.

123. Gauthier, p. 267.

124. The Mount Vernon Ladies' Association of the Union, *Mount Vernon China*, pp. 25–28.

125. GW to Custine, August 7, 1782, W 24: 485.

126. David Howell to William Greene, Princeton, September 1783, in Burnett, vol. 7, p. 292.

127. *The New York Gazette or the Weekly Post-Boy*, February 14, 1757, in Gottesman, ed., vol. 1, pp. 90–91.

128. October 30, 1783, W 27: 216–17. Washington, however, did acquire English silver in 1784 through Daniel Parker. *See* Buhler, p. 42.

129. GW to James Milligan, February 18, 1784, W 27:334.

130. GW to Baron von Steuben, December 23, 1783, W 27: 283. For purchases in New York (six pairs of plated candlesticks, for example) and Philadelphia (such items as a silver coffee pot, tea waiter, and umbrella), *see* Ledger B, p. 196, LC 115. *See also* p. 177 for freight charges on twenty-two boxes and other packages of goods from Philadelphia. These charges, however, probably followed his later trip to Philadelphia in May 1784.

131. "Notes of a Tour through Holland the Rhine Valley," in Boyd, ed., vol. 13, p. 1 .

132. Bigelow, ed., vol. 8, p. 439.

133. Gottschalk and Bill, eds., p. 273.

134. In France, Count d'Estaing, leader of the French naval forces in America, was first president of the French Society of the Cincinnati, which then admitted only colonels and generals to membership.

135. A description of the fête is given in a long letter written by Dr. Benjamin Rush, July 16, 1782. See *The Pennsylvania Magazine of History and Biography* 21 (1897): 257 ff. The banquet pavilion is illustrated in Kouwenhoven, p. 81.

136. Musée de Rennes. *Les Français dans La Guerre d'Indépendance Américaine*, no. 295, p. 112.

137. Gottschalk and Bill, eds., p. 273.

138. Bigelow, ed., p. 439.

139. *Diaries*, vol. 4, p. 89; Acomb, ed., p. 232.

140. Ledger B, pp. 177 and 198, LC 115.

141. *See* Appendix, pp 208–9.

142. "First Voyage to Canton," in Quincy, ed., pp. 198–99.

143. *See* Franks, ed. Parker was the same merchant who had sent blue-and-white china to Mount Vernon in 1783.

144. "On the First American Ship That Explored the Route to CHINA, and the EAST-INDIES, After the Revolution," in Freneau, p. 32.

145. Woodhouse, "The Voyage of the Empress of China " pp. 24–36.

146. Ibid., pp. 30–36. Green also purchased wallpaper and special articles for Robert Morris. Molineaux's receipt book for the 1784 and 1786 voyages of the *Empress of China* is in the University of Pennsylvania Library, Rare Book Department.

147. Ibid., p. 32.

148. Quincy, ed., pp. 198–99.

149. W. Stephen Thomas, pp. 176–79. Feller, pp. 760–68. Shaw's own service seems to have been much more extensive than the tea services he gave or sold to his comrades.

150. *Antiques* 23 (October 1936), frontispiece.

151. Lossing, *George Washington's Mount Vernon*, p. 254.

152. Templeman, pp. 758–59. This article insists that Henry Lee, who procured Washington's service in New York, also purchased one for himself. Convincing documentation for the descent of the china at Stratford, the Lee home, to Charles Lee from Henry Lee is not presented in the article, but recent examination of Constable and Rucker's "Ledger B" for 1786 did reveal that two sales of £60 each were made to Henry Lee, one in June and the other in August. The ledger and other business papers of the firm are in the Constable-Pierrepont Collection, Manuscript Department, New York Public Library. The papers contain important documentation for the earliest years of the China trade from New York with references to the first two voyages made by the *Empress of China* and to the cargos of several other ships owned by Constable. Unfortunately, the ledger for 1785—the year the *Empress* returned from her first voyage to Canton —is not among the papers in the collection. A note in one folder states, "Old commercial papers sent to A.A. Low, a modern India merchant to compare trade." The author wishes to thank the staff of the New York Public Library for their help in gaining access to these papers.

153. The *Experiment* sailed from New York in 1785, but did not return until December 1786. *See* Latourette, p. 240.

154. *Independent Journal*, New York, May 25, 1785, in Henderson, p. 19. Maria Morton also advertised china from the *Empress* on June 1–, 1785, in the *New York Gazetteer*, in Gottesman, ed., vol. 2, p. 101.

155. *See* Henderson, p. 22, for the subsequent history of Capt. John O'Donnell, who continued to sail out of Baltimore. In 1790, he sent an "Indian apparatus for smoking called 'a Hooka'" to George Washington. September 9, 1790, LC 99.

156. Thomas Tilghman to GW, April 22, 1786, LC 96. Encloses unitemized bill of Washington's account with the Tilghman firm.

157. Kline, p. 288.

158. Ibid., pp. 297–98. Tench Tilghman papers (MSS 1445), Maryland Historical Society.

159. Woodhouse, "The Voyage of the Empress of China," pp. 35–36.

160. Quincy, ed., p. 217. Those complexities included the bankruptcy of Daniel Parker, Washington's supplier of blue-and-white china in 1783.

161. Constable-Pierrepont Collection, New York Public Library. William Constable's business establishment was on South William Street, between Broad and Mill Lane (see Franks, ed.). Mill Street was the former name of that section of South William Street. "A Directory of Forgotten Streets," in Dunshee, unpaged appendix. Scoville [Barrett], vol. 2, p. 250: "William and James Constable lived at the corner of Wall and William Streets."

162. *See* the *New Webster Encyclopedic Dictionary*, p. 659, and Johnson's 1785 *Dictionary* for the definition of "prime cost" as "original cost." The cost to Washington of 60 New York pounds for 302 pieces (.199 per piece) was little more than that of the ordinary blue-and-white service of 1783 at 36 guineas or £39.6. for 205 pieces (.193 per piece).

163. Quincy, ed., pp. 115–20. Shaw died at sea in 1794.

164. The punch bowl is at the Historical Society of Pennsylvania, the tea caddy in the Diplomatic Reception Rooms of the Department of State. Both are illustrated in Feller, pp. 765–66.

165. Abby Gunn Baker, p. 322.

166. Copy of the letter in the Mount Vernon archives.

167. Earle, p. 232.

168. Brissot de Warville, pp. 342–43.

169. Hadfield, pp. vi and 13.

170. GW to Samuel Vaughan, April 8, 1784, W 27: 390.

171. "An English Admirer of Washington," The Mount Vernon Ladies' Association, *Annual Report*, 1959, p. 16.

172. GW to Bushrod Washington, January 15, 1784, W 27: 304. GW to Samuel Vaughan, January 14, 1784, W 27: 298.

173. Stetson. Vaughan headed the building committee for Philosophical Hall and designed the grounds of the State-House Yard and other gardens in Philadelphia. He drew a plan of the grounds at Mount Vernon during his 1787 visit to Virginia.

174. GW to Samuel Vaughan, February 5, 1785, W 28: 63.

175. The Mount Vernon Ladies' Association, *Annual Report*, 1959, p. 16, and GW to Benjamin Vaughan, February 5, 1785, W 28: 63.

176. GW to Samuel Vaughan, June 20, 1784, W 27: 425. The Mount Vernon Ladies' Association, *Annual Report*, 1959, p. 16. The records of Dr. Wall's Worcester factory do not survive. Letter of January 8, 1981, to author from Henry Sandon.

177. *See* Tapp.

178. Sandon, pp. 51–52.

179. Hodnett, p. 102. Tapp, p. 26.

180. Tapp, p. 7.

181. Sandon, pl. 83. A comparable covered vase with landscapes and a boar hunt by O'Neale is in the British Museum. The Dyson Perrins Museum at Worcester has a vase with a reserve composition of Aeneas and Anchises signed and dated (1769) by O'Neale. Mazarine-blue grounds were used at Chelsea in imitation of the *gros-bleu* underglaze grounds used at Sèvres after about 1749.

182. Hunt, pp. 110 and 112.

183. GW to Edmund Randolph, April 9, 1787, W 29: 198.

184. The Powel house is preserved and open to the public. Woodwork, wallpaper, and furnishings from two of its rooms are now in the Philadelphia Museum of Art and the Metropolitan Museum of Art.

185. *Diaries*, vol. 5, p. 159.

186. Anne Bingham to Thomas Jefferson, February 7, 1787, in Alberts, p. 465.

187. *United States Gazette*, November 16, 1805, advertisement of auction, in Alberts, pp. 467–73.

188. GW to Dr. David Stuart, June 15, 1790, W 31: 53.

189. Letter from a Mrs. Bowman describing a reception held by the president and Mrs. Washington in New York in 1790. Henry Francis du Pont Winterthur Museum, Joseph Downs Manuscript Collection, no. 3424.

190. Abigail Adams to Mary Cranch, August 9, 1789, in Mitchell, ed., p. 19.

191. Maclay, ed., pp. 137–38.

192. *See* Hodge, Allen, and Campbell. There are two Thomas Burlings listed in the directory. The one on Beekman Street was a chair- and cabinetmaker who also supplied furnishings for the residence.

193. Hoffmann, pp. 90–99. Wharton, "Washington's New York Residence," pp. 741–45.

194. Martha Washington to Fanny Bassett, June 8, 1789, in Decatur, *Private Affairs of George Washington*, p. 21.

195. Tobias Lear to GW, October 24, 1790, LC 99.

196. Ibid.

197. Klapthor, p. 24.

198. Alberts, p. 471.

199. Much of the material in the following section also appears in an article by the author in the *American Ceramic Circle Bulletin*, no. 3 (in press).

200. Ibid. *See also* Boyd, ed., vol. 18, pp. 34–38.

201. Schmidt, p. 294. *See also* Watson, pp. 20–26, and Gruber, pp. 285–300.

202. Davenport, ed., vol. 1, pp. 277, 291, and 363.

203. Ibid., p. 366. Morris himself bought tableware at the Manufacture of Angoulême. For an account of his many French purchases, see Schreider, pp. 470–83.

204. Davenport, ed., p. 24.

205. Guillebon, pp. 200 ff.

206. Ibid., p. 205. In 1785, the factory employed twelve modelers; ibid., p. 150.

207. Dauterman, p. 42.

208. Bourgeois and Lechevallier-Chevignard, vol. 1.

209. ". . . l'on peut apprendre la mythologie sans sortir de table." Reynière, p. 79. *See also* Bellaigue, p. 99.

210. Davenport, ed., p. 369. A Louis equaled twenty francs or livres.

211. "An Act for laying a Duty on Goods, Wares & Merchandizes imported into the United States," in Hodge, Allen, and Campbell, pp. 138 ff.

212. "Household furniture," end of February 1797, LC 110. *See also* Buhler, fig. 38.

213. In Wharton, pp. 233–34. Congressman Bradbury revealed the general form of the central group, "Apollo Instructing the Shepherds," as that of a pedestal with figures on it. "Apollon instruisant les bergers" was entered as one of the large biscuit-porcelain groups in the inventory made after the death of Dihl in February 1830. The inventory has recently been found by Régine de Plinval de Guillebon. Letter to author, June 22, 1981. Mme de Guillebon also mentioned a 28-inch-high biscuit group by Guérhard and Dihl in the Museo Arqueológico Nacional in Madrid. Washington's central group may well have been of similar dimensions.

214. The New York pound was worth about $2.50 at this time of conversion to the dollar. The account books were kept in United States currency after the transfer to Philadelphia in the fall of 1790.

215. Decatur, *Private Affairs of George Washington*, pp. 40 and 115. *See also* Account Book, 1793–1797, kept by Tobias Lear and

Bartholomew Dandridge, The Historical Society of Pennsylvania, Manuscript Department.

216. *See* Tainturier, pp. 90–95, for a price list (1789) of nearly 300 figures, groups, and vases "peints et en biscuit qui se fabriquent dans la manufacture de porcelaine et terre de pipe de Niderwiller, arrondissement de Sarrebourg, département de la Meurthe."

217. New York, Wednesday, May 13, to Saturday, May 16, 1789, no. 10, p. 39.

218. In Griswold, p. 158.

219. Gottschalk and Bill, eds., p. 332. Rice, p. 96. Moustier was also a friend of the American artist John Trumbull, who noted a visit from the French diplomat in Paris or August 17, 1786. *See* Sizer, ed., pp. 119–20.

220. *Diaries*, vol. 5 (November 2, 1788), p. 418. Vol. 5 (October 3, 1789), p. 451 The Mount Vernon Ladies' Association, *Annual Report*, 1968, pp. 20–25.

221. In Stokes, vol. 5, p. 1241.

222. Verplanck, Bryant, and Sands, eds., pp. 333–41.

223. Monaghan and Lowenthal, p. 34. On November 25, Gouverneur Morris in Paris wrote in his diary (Davenport, ed., p. 312), "Go hence to visit Monsᵣ de Moustiers and Madame de Bréhan who arrived yesterday."

224. *Diaries*, vol. 5 (October 14, 1789) p. 460. Washington had decided to pay no calls as a presidential policy, so the farewell was remarkable.

225. Ibid., vol. 6, p. 27.

226. Henry Francis du Pont Winterthur Museum, Joseph Downs Manuscript Collection.

227. Maclay, ed., p. 201. *Diaries*, vol. 6, p. 40.

228. W 31: 15. After the arrival of the seven *plateaux*, Washington tried to countermand the request of March 1, 1790. Upon trial, however, it was observed that seven *plateaux* were too small for the table and "too short to receive the ornaments which accompanied, and were designed for them without being crowded."

GW to Gouverneur Morris, July 7, 1790, W 31: 69.

229. The American Presidential China Index survey of collections provided information about the extant Washington pieces. The repository of the Index is the Division of Political History, National Museum of American History, Smithsonian Institution.

230. Several of the Sèvres models are illustrated in Brunet and Préaud. Tamara Préaud identified many of the Sèvres models for pieces at Mount Vernon. Letter to author, June 26, 1979.

231. Copied for the author by Mme Préaud, archivist, Manufacture Nationale de Sèvres. *Registre de vente, Vy 7, fol. 15: Du 9 may 1778*

Livré à Mr. le comte de Moutier	[livres]
60 Assiettes	6/360
4 Compotiers	18/72
4 id.	15/60
4 id.	15/60
4 id.	12/48
4 Sucriers	24/96
2 Saladiers	24/48
36 Tasses à thé	4/144
24 Pots à jus	4/96
18 Gobelets	4/72
12 id.	5/60
2 Pots à sucre	6/12
4 Plateaus à deux pots	18/72
1 Ecuelle	30
4 Beurriers	18/72
24 Coquetiers	3/72
24 Tasses à glaces	4/96
12 Coquelles	4/48
12 Plateaux Bourette	10/120
12 Assiettes de dessert	5/60
1 Coquelle	4
1 Pot à lait	12
1 Buillotte	120
1 Groupe Girandole	192
1 id. La Nourice	132
2 Mercure Pigal et pendant	72/144
8 Divinitez	24/192

232. Inventory of Château de Montgeofroy, August 1775, in Verlet, p. 264.

233. Guillebon, p. 73. *See also* Hunt, p. 110, for a description of the gilding process at Sèvres.

234. Identification for the known gilders from Brunet and Préaud and from Dauterman. Hard-paste porcelain began to be produced on

a commercial basis in 1772 at Sèvres. Soft-paste porcelain continued to be made there until 1804.

235. Maclay, ed., p. 374.

236. *See* text, p. 107.

237. Budka, ed., p. 106.

238. "A Sale and a Suit," The Mount Vernon Ladies' Association, *Annual Report*, 1959, pp. 26–27. Belote, p. 12.

239. The Washington entourage included the two grandchildren (Nelly and George Washington Parke Custis), four black and four white servants, two maids, Major Jackson, and Mr. Nelson. Tobias Lear to Clement Biddle, August 26, 1790, W 31: 100. Lear remained in New York to supervise the move to Philadelphia.

240. "Burnt China": *see* text, p. 66.

241. In Godden, *Caughley*, p. 153.

242. Opinion of Geoffrey A. Godden in letter to author, September 12, 1973. The pattern, later so common on Chinese export porcelains called "Canton," is not known on Caughley wares. The configuration of the cup handle is also unlike that of comparable Caughley pieces.

243. The 1791 purchase of queensware was also made in anticipation of a visit from the Washingtons to Mount Vernon in September. GW to Anthony Whiting, August 29, 1791, W 31: 351.

244. GW to Thomas Paine, August 10, 1790, W 31: 80, and GW to Lafayette, August 11, 1790, W 31: 85.

245. Hart and Biddle, p. 251. At that time, the bust of Necker was at the Historical Society of Pennsylvania.

246. Bourgeois and Lechevallier-Chevignard, unpaged introduction, and pl. 55, no. 452. The incised mark on the base of the Necker bust, however, appears to be that of Josse-François-Joseph Le Riche, who was active at Sèvres as a modeler and sculptor from 1757 until 1801. Although he was head of sculptors from 1757 until 1768, in this case he executed the designs of Boizot.

247. Prudhomme, vol. 1, p. 215.

248. "In the French Manner," The Mount Vernon Ladies' Association, *Annual Report*, 1969, pp. 26–29.

249. For an account of the house *see* Eberlein, pp. 161–77. Morris built a new house next door at 192 High Street. Henry Sheaff, wine merchant, was on the east side of the president's house at number 180. Bailey, p. 11.

250. W 31:110.

251. *Pennsylvania Packet*, December 8, 1790, in Eberlein, p. 168.

252. In William Spohn Baker, p. 203.

253. Abigail Adams to Mary Cranch, February 5, 1792, in Mitchell, ed., p. 77.

254. Eberlein, p. 163. The state drawing room on the second floor was also enlarged by the new bow window. According to William Sullivan, however, Washington's formal Tuesday levees were held in the large dining room on the ground floor.

255. December 15, 1790 (contingency expense): "p.^{d} for 2 pcs. of Crimson Persian for enlarging the Window Curtains of the dining Room, 10 yds ea @ 7/ $18.66." Entry in account book for first administration. Decatur, *Private Affairs of George Washington*, p. 175. Washington's list of public and private Household Furniture made in February 1797 (LC 110) included "Crimson Sattin W. Curt.^{ns} large Dining Room" and a "sett la. dining tables" with "2 end Tables for d.^{o}" The sideboards purchased from Moustier were noted as "fixed" and were valued at only £9.10. while two other sideboards purchased from public funds were "circular" and cost £38.

256. Tobias Lear to GW, November 14, 1790, LC 99.

257. *See* Prologue by Christine Meadows, text pp. 14–15.

258. *See* Bailey.

259. Descendants of Samuel and Elizabeth Powel believed that Washington gave a large service of gilt Nanking porcelain to the Powels in the 1790s. Pieces of an exceptionally fine service traditionally ascribed to that source, but with no known documentation, are pre-

served at Mount Vernon and at the Powel house in Philadelphia.

260. Manuscript in the Germantown Historical Society Library, Philadelphia. *See also* Fanelli. The house is administered by Independence National Historical Park.

261. There is a corner cupboard in the "Back room adjoining" the "First Left hand room."

262. February 4, 1797. Adams, vol. 2, p. 235. *See also* Klapthor, p. 27.

263. *See* text, p. 118.

264. William Wilson Corcoran (1798–1888) was a wealthy banker and art collector, but from 1817 until 1823 he headed a dry-goods and auction firm in Washington, D.C. Another piece, now in a private collection, bears an old label, "No. 1 General Washington." *See* Earle, p. 246.

265. *Diaries*, vol. 6, p. 147.

266. May 24, 1791, LC 100.

267. GW to Richard Champion, July 19, 1791, W 31: 314–15. The original of this letter was found among the papers of Edmund Burke at Wentworth House, Yorkshire. Wecter, pp. 151–56.

268. Minchinton, pp. 87–97. *See also* Owen, pp. 316–19.

269. Original documents, including patents, petitions, and correspondence pertaining to Champion and the Bristol "china works," are reproduced in Owen's complete account of Champion's enterprise. They are also given in Jewitt, vol. 1, pp. 356–97. The "Report of Committee," House of Commons, upon the application of Richard Champion for the renewal of Cookworthy's patent is in Jewitt, pp. 360–61.

270. Cooper, p. 692.

271. Ibid., p. 102. *See* Owen, pp. 87 and 289, and Jewitt, p. 397, for a list of Bristol porcelain craftsmen including several from Derby and at least two from the Continent. Elliot, p. 24.

272. Jewitt, p. 390.

273. *Bristol Porcelain Bicentenary Exhibition*,

nos. 57 and 58. *See* Elliott, p. 27, for a list of fourteen Bristol portrait plaques thought to have been in English collections between 1775 and 1933.

274. Sellers, pl. 12 and p. 369. Sellers labels the plain, circular medallion profile of Franklin as Sèvres, but Owen, p. 93, wrote of a similar or matching medallion in the collection of Mr. Edkins: "For some years, this medallion had been accepted as Sèvres until the label was washed off and the Bristol mark exposed." The Bristol mark was an incised cross or X.

275. Information about early portraits of Washington available in Europe in 1778 from Wendy Wick, curator of prints, National Portrait Gallery. An undated portrait of Washington engraved by Justus Chevillet resembles both the Peale 1776 portrait and the Bristol plaque in pose and features.

276. Jewitt, pp. 365–70.

277. Ibid.

278. Ibid., p. 380.

279. Vail, ed., p. 80. Reprinted in the Mount Vernon Ladies' Association, *Annual Report*, 1947, pp. 19–25.

280. Sellers, p. 364. *See also* Thomas Birch's Sons, Catalogue no. 657, December 10, 11, 12, 1890, lot no. 141: "Oval Porcelain plaque, with bust of Benj. Franklin in relief, surrounded by a wreath of roses and lilies in high relief. Presented to Genl. Geo. Washington by some of his admirers. size of plaque 8½ by 8¼ in." The copy of the catalogue in the library of the University of Pennsylvania belonged to a Dr. Lamborn, who noted prices and buyers in the margins. The Franklin plaque was sold to a Mr. Murphy for $90.

281. Franklin left the portrait to his daughter, Sarah Franklin Bache. In 1820, Mrs. Bache deposited a "China Bas relief of Dr. Franklin" temporarily at the Pennsylvania Academy of the Fine Arts. *See* Sellers, p. 274. Casper Wister Hodge, a Franklin descendant, lent it to the *Loan Collection of Portraits, Relics, and Silverware*, exhibited at the Metropolitan Opera House, New York, April 17–May 8, 1889, no. 285.

282. Fitzhugh lived until 1798. Information

about Fitzhugh in "The Fitzhugh Family," pp. 91–92.

283. *See* Davis.

284. Lossing, *George Washington's Mount Vernon*, p. 317. *See also* the Mount Vernon Ladies' Association, *Annual Report*, 1975, pp. 18–23.

285. Palmer, p. 37.

286. Hutchinson, frontispiece. There were also earlier editions. The ship depicted in the famous Grand Turk punch bowl at the Peabody Museum, Salem, Massachusetts, is from Hutchinson, as are the ships in Capt. John Green's and Cmdr. Richard Dale's bowls of 1785–1788. Green's bowl is in the New Jersey State Museum and Dale's bowl and a copy of the fourth edition of *Naval Architecture* are in the Philadelphia Maritime Museum. *See* Dorman, p. 179, and *Antiques* 107 (1975):270. The information about Thomas Truxtun's bowl was received just before this text went to press. The following references to Truxtun are grouped in this note although they apply to several statements: Latourette, p. 241; Quincy, ed., pp. 295–96; W 32:40; *Diaries*, vol. 6, p. 364.

287. Will of Martha Washington, 1800, The Mount Vernon Ladies' Association Archives. Mrs. Washington's will is in the handwriting of Nelly Custis Lewis. The original manifest of the *Lady Louisa* and van Braam's supplement listing his personal property are in the National Archives, custody of the Judicial and Fiscal Branch. *See also* Carpenter, p. 344.

288. Moreau de Saint-Méry, p. 321. Van Braam dedicated his journal to George Washington.

289. *See* Barnsley. Mr. Barnsley is a descendant of van Braam's eldest daughter. The house was demolished in May 1960. *See also* "China's Retreat," pp. 16–17.

290. Budka, ed., pp. 62–63.

291. Van Braam's eldest daughter married Capt. Richard Brooke Roberts, an American officer. Their first child was named Lucius Quintus Cincinnatus Roberts.

292. Budka, ed., p. 62.

293. A copy of the sales catalogue is preserved

at Christie's auction house in London. *See* Loehr, p. 189.

294. Christie's sales catalogue, pp. xi and xiv.

295. The chain of states without the medallion and sunburst was used in an engraving by Amos Doolittle, *A Display of the United States*, in 1788, and on queensware made by Wedgwood for Robert Morris in 1781–1785. The latter is illustrated in *Antiques* 118 (May 1980):1004. Brass buttons decorated with "GW" and surrounded by the initials of the thirteen states in oval links were struck in 1789; one is at the Metropolitan Museum of Art. The chain of states also occurs in a French engraving of 1778 by J.C. LeVasseur after Antoine Borel called *L'Amérique Indépendante*; a copy is at the Philadelphia Museum of Art.

296. Alciatus, p. 94. *See also* Camerarius.

297. Book V, line 262. H. Rushton Fairclough, Loeb Library translation, London, 1929. Robert E.A. Palmer, Department of Classical Studies, University of Pennsylvania, found the reference.

298. The sugar bowl is at the White House, its cover at the National Museum of American History, Smithsonian Institution. The large plate is at Winterthur.

299. John Cushion also believes that two-handle, covered cups of the late eighteenth century were "on the whole made for display, not use." *See* Cushion, p. 159.

300. Woodhouse, "Martha Washington's China," p. 186.

301. The decorating firm, Warren and Bryan, of New York, copied a plate from the original service on Haviland blanks in early 1876 for R.H. Macy and Company. At first they made cups and saucers, then plates, covered dishes, compotes, and fruit baskets. The cups and saucers were often used at "Martha Washington Receptions" or tea parties where the hostess and her guests wore appropriate costumes. Information from files in the Division of Political History, National Museum of American History, Smithsonian Institution, courtesy of Margaret B. Klapthor, curator.

302. *Diaries*, vol. 6, pp. 231, 234, 235. *See also* GW to Henry Knox, March 2, 1797, W 35:410. A "sett of china" at $22.33 and, therefore, probably a tea or coffee service, was

purchased from John Inskeep on February 13, perhaps in anticipation of the crowd.

303. Lancour, p. 16. Footman is listed in Philadelphia directories from 1785 until 1800. He was called "vendue-master" at 47 North Third Street in 1791. In 1792, Footman sold Benjamin Franklin's house and some of his personal property, including silver.

304. Washington's Household Account Book, 1793–1797. Second Administration Account Book, March 25, 1797. The desk by "T.B." cost £ 98, according to Washington's House-hold Inventory of February 1797 (LC 110). In a letter from Tobias Lear to Elizabeth Powel, March 9, 1797 (The Historical Society of Pennsylvania, Manuscript Depart-ment), he mentioned that the desk originally cost £ 98 and added, "Mrs. Powell will also receive a pair of Oval Mirrors, Brackets & Lamps, which the General begs she will accept as a token of his respectful & affectionate remembrance."

305. Vail, ed., pp. 72–81.

306. Ibid. Words in brackets were supplied by Dr. Vail. "Mr. Craig" was Dr. James Craik, Washington's friend and physician.

307. Ibid.

308. *See* text, p. 126.

309. "All the Images": *see* text, p. 118.

310. Gottesman, ed., vol. 1, p. 90; vol. 2, p. 103. Edward Nicoll in New York offered "Crates of black" in 1757.

311. In Godden, *An Illustrated Encyclopedia*, p. xix.

312. Ibid. *See also* Hillier.

313. Noël Hume, *Here Lies Virginia*, p. 306.

314. Martha Washington's will of September 22, 1800, is reprinted in Lossing, *George Washington's Mount Vernon*, pp. 420–25.

315. A memorandum mentioning the private sale is in the Mount Vernon archives. *See* The Mount Vernon Ladies' Association, *Annual Report*, 1959, p. 24.

316. Fragments of poor-quality Chinese export porcelain, decorated with red penciled wavy-line borders and floral centers, have been found near the laundry yard and wash house at Mount Vernon.

317. Mary Lear Storer, who was sixteen in 1802, left her china figures to her niece, the daughter of her younger brother, George Washington Storer. *See* Decatur, "A Gift from Washington." Decatur thought that Washington had sent the figures to Mary Lear Storer after his trip through New England in 1790, but there is no known documentation for this supposition. The Storer family also had Washington manuscript material given by the widow of Tobias Lear to George Washington Storer. Stephen Decatur, Jr., was the great-grandson of the latter. *See* Decatur, *Private Affairs of George Washington*, p. vi. Lear's second mar-riage was to Frances Bassett Washington, niece of Martha Washington and widow of George Washington's nephew and manager, George Augustine Washington. After her death, Lear married Frances Dandridge Henley, another niece of Mrs. Washington.

318. Thomas P. Law and Eliza Parke Custis Law were divorced in 1811. After the divorce, Eliza called herself Mrs. Custis. Their grand-son, Edmund Law Rogers of Baltimore (1818–1896), had Washington memorabilia. *See* "From the Collection of Edmund Law Rogers, Esq.," *Century Magazine* 18 (May 1890): 10–13.

319. Lossing, "Mount Vernon as it is," p. 450.

EPILOGUE

1. Fitzpatrick, ed., *The Last Will*, pp. 1–2.

2. Ibid., p. 17. Articles purchased by the president of the United States from Monsr. Le Prince, Agent for the Count de Moustier, March 4, 1790. The Mount Vernon Ladies' Association archives.

3. Harrison, ed., pp. 111–13. Cope gives an excellent description of Martha Washington in the last days of her life.

4. "An Inventory &c. of Articles at Mount Vernon with their appraised value annexed," folio 25. The Mount Vernon Ladies' Associa-tion archives.

5. Lear had access to George Washington's ledger and accounts, invoices, etc., in which many of his household purchases are listed with the prices paid. As an intimate member of the Mount Vernon and presidential house-holds, Tobias Lear was personally familiar with the individual prices as well as the rec-ords relating to them.

6. Ford, ed., p. vi. The 1810 date in the title of Ford's book is misleading since it refers to the presentation of the inventory to the court at Fairfax on August 20, 1810. The inventory itself was completed sometime during 1800.

7. Fitzpatrick, ed., *The Last Will*, p. 56. Eleanor Parke Custis and Lawrence Lewis, son of George Washington's sister, Betty Wash-ington Lewis, were married at Mount Vernon on February 22, 1799.

8. There was no formal adoption of Nelly and Washington Custis by the Washingtons. On the eve of her marriage Nelly chose George Washington as her guardian "to authorize a license" for her marriage to Lawrence Lewis. *See Diaries*, vol. 6, p. 331. The division for the children seems to have evolved from the fact that the two youngest had spent much of their life at Mount Vernon due to their moth-er's ill health after Nelly's birth. *See Diaries*, vol. 4, p. 109.

9. George Washington Parke Custis's daugh-ter married Robert Edward Lee, later com-manding general of the Army of the Confeder-acy. Mrs. Lee and her husband lived at Arlington House, which was occupied by the Union Army during the Civil War. The house and grounds and dependencies were taken over by the federal government to prevent their return to the Lee family. A similar fate might have befallen Mount Vernon.

10. Fitzpatrick, ed., *The Last Will*, p. 60.

11. "Inventory of Property that belonged to Mrs Martha Washington Taken the 24.th of May and Eleventh of July 1802." Original manuscript in the Mount Vernon Ladies' Association archives.

12. "A Sale and a Suit," The Mount Vernon Ladies' Association, *Annual Report*, 1959, p. 21.

13. *Courier* of New Hampshire, August 5, 1802, p. 2, col. 3. The Mount Vernon Ladies' Association archives.

14. George Deneale to Colonel May, July 21,

1802. The Mount Vernon Ladies' Association archives.

15. Ibid.

16. The Mount Vernon Ladies' Association, *Annual Report*, 1959, p. 25.

17. Book of Sales and of Mount Vernon Property, March 5, 1800; October 15, 1800; November 12, 1801. The Mount Vernon Ladies' Association archives.

18. Prussing, p. 109.

19. Book of Sales, statement follows the entry for "Private Sale. 21ˢ July 1802."

20. "Private sales, which took place up stairs among the Legatees, to be settled on the final adjustment without interest—22.ᵈ July 1802." Washington Papers, Library of Congress.

21. Fitzpatrick, ed., *The Last Will*, p. 14.

22. The list of busts appears in "In the Study," folio 6, of "Inventory of Property that belonged to M.ʳˢ Martha Washington Taken the 24.ᵗʰ of May and Eleventh of July 1802." Original manuscript in the Mount Vernon Ladies' Association archives.

23. Washington noted the arrival of Houdon in his diary on October 2, 1785. *See Diaries*, vol. 4, p. 200. Houdon's mission was to execute a full-length statue of Washington for the Capitol at Richmond, Virginia. He preferred to work from life, which explains his decision to make the voyage to Virginia.

24. The second portrait favored by the family is the pastel by James Sharples done in 1796 in Philadelphia. *See* Lossing, ed., *Recollections and Private Memoirs*, p. 517.

25. After the death of John Augustine Washington II in 1832, his wife, Jane Blackburn Washington, continued to live at Mount Vernon and manage the estate until her son, John Augustine Washington III, attained his majority.

26. Lossing, *George Washington's Mount Vernon*, pp. 7–8.

27. Ibid., dedication page.

28. Ibid., p. 8.

29. John Augustine Washington III to Ann

Pamela Cunningham, February 11, 1859. Early records of the Mount Vernon Ladies' Association.

30. Wayland, p. 299.

31. Harrison Howell Dodge to Mrs. J. Scott Laughton, Regent of the Mount Vernon Ladies' Association, June 27, 1889. Early records of the Mount Vernon Ladies' Association. Dodge's letter recounts an interview with Upton Herbert, who recalled the memorabilia left at Mount Vernon by John Augustine Washington III.

32. *The Final Sale*, Catalogue no. 663, item 268, p. 38 and illustrations. The sketch was bought by Walter Benjamin, a well-known manuscript dealer, but has since disappeared. The sketch now at Mount Vernon is a copy based on the illustration in this catalogue.

33. Gottschalk and Bill, eds., p. 348 of 1944 ed.

34. Budka, ed., p. 96.

35. John Augustine Washington III to Mrs. Gustavus B. Alexander, August 31 1861, as extracted by Betty Carter Smoot in *Days In An Old Town* (Alexandria, Va.: 1934), pp. 79–80.

36. Will of John A. Washington III, August 5, 1861, in Wayland, p. 305.

37. *The Final Sale*, p. ii.

38. Ibid., item 266, p. 36 and illustration.

39. George Washington Parke Custis to J Pickett, Esq., April 17, 1857. The Mount Vernon Ladies' Association archives.

40. Nelligan, p. 455.

41. Ibid, pp. 457–58. Assistant Adj. Gen. Seth Williams to Secretary of the Interior C.B. Smith, January 17, 1862. From a typescript at Mount Vernon. Original in the National Archives, Washington, D.C.

42. Ibid., p. 498.

43. Fitzpatrick, ed., *The Last Will*. pp. 22–23.

44. Ibid., p. 58.

45. Wayland, pp. 205 and 207.

46. Belote, p. 2.

47. Thomas Birch's Sons, Catalogue no. 657, December 10, 11, 12, 1890, item 115, p. 14.

48. Nelligan, p. 480.

49. Mrs. Robert E. Lee, April 27, 1873, as quoted in the *American Autograph Journal*, April 1939.

50. The Mount Vernon Ladies' Association, *Annual Report*, 1959, p. 27.

51. Fitzpatrick, ed., *The Last Will*, p. 58.

52. Peter, pp. xi–xii.

53. "The G. Freeland Peter Collection," The Mount Vernon Ladies' Association, *Annual Report*, 1956, p. 30.

54. Ibid., p. 31.

55. Fitzpatrick, ed., *The Last Will*, p. 58.

56. This painting is now in the collection of the Henry Francis du Pont Winterthur Museum.

57. Chinard, ed., p. 68.

APPENDIX:

THE

DOCUMENTS

Excerpts from correspondence, invoices, inventories, ledgers, and cash memoranda. The arrangement is generally chronological.

ABBREVIATIONS AND SHORT TITLES:

LC
Library of Congress, Manuscript Division, George Washington Papers. Number following (for example, LC 101) refers to the reel number in the microfilm edition. See *Index to the George Washington Papers*, Library of Congress, Presidents' Papers Index Series, Washington, D.C., 1964, for the division of the documents into eight series.

W
John C. Fitzpatrick, ed., *The Writings of George Washington*. 39 vols. Washington, D.C.: United States Government Printing Office, 1931–1944. Numbers following (for example, W 31:152) refer to the volume and page.

Freeman
Douglas Southall Freeman, *George Washington. A Biography*. 6 vols. New York: Charles Scribner's Sons, 1948.

Diaries
Donald Jackson and Dorothy Twohig, eds., *The Diaries of George Washington*. 6 vols. Charlottesville: University Press of Virginia, 1976.

Cash Memoranda—Mount Vernon
Pocket daybooks for Mount Vernon expenditures paid by Washington's managers, March 25, 1788–October 7, 1792. Lloyd W. Smith Collection, Morristown National Historical Park.

First Administration Accounts
A Cash Memorandum of Monies received and paid by Tobias Lear for, and on Account of the President of the United States, April 24, 1789–December 31, 1792. Privately owned. Excerpts published in Stephen Decatur, Jr., *Private Affairs of George Washington*. Boston: Houghton Mifflin, 1933.

Second Administration Accounts
Washington's Household Account Book, 1793–1797. Kept by Tobias Lear through August 31, 1793. The remaining pages are in the handwriting of Bartholomew Dandridge, another secretary to President Washington. The Historical Society of Pennsylvania, Manuscript Department.

Ledgers A, B, C, and G
Washington's account books for the Mount Vernon Mansion House and other farms. Ledgers A and B are in the George Washington Papers at the Library of Congress, and Ledgers C and G are in the Lloyd W. Smith Collection, Morristown National Historical Park.

July 1, 1743

An Inventory of the Estate of Capn. Augustine Washington in King George County, Virginia[1]

	£	s.	d.
China Ware[2]			
9 Gilt Sawcers			
6 Do Cups[3]			
1 Do Tea pot Milk Do			
1 Slop bowl[4] & Butter Dish			
1 Tea pot Stand & spoon Boat[5]			
	1		
8 blew Cups and Sawsers			
1 Slop Bowl & Tea Pot			
1 Milk Pot & Stand & Sugar Dish			
	1		
1 Large Blew and White Bowl		7	
1 Do Gilt		10	
2 Dishes		5	
9 Custard Cups		9	
4 Coffee Cups		4	
11 Plates		11	

1. In George H.S. King, "Washington's Boyhood Home," *William and Mary Quarterly*, 2d ser., 17 (1933): 265.
2. China Ware: until about 1770 usually used specifically for Chinese porcelains.
3. Do: ditto, same as above.
4. Slop bowl: a small basin for tea dregs and for rinsing teacups.
5. Tea pot Stand: a plate or shallow bowl used under the teapot to protect the table; spoon Boat: a small tray to receive wet spoons before the teacup on its saucer was raised to the drinker's mouth.

February 1, 1755

LC 115

Ledger A

	£	s.	d.
By two salts		1	3
By 1 Mustard Pot[1]		1	11
By a Beer glass and Pepper box[2]		1	9

1. Mustard Pot: there were two forms, one of baluster shape with holes pierced in the dome cover—for dry mustard; the other of barrel shape with a handle and cover, often notched for a small spoon—for prepared mustard.
2. Pepper box: a caster similar in form to the dry-mustard pot.

December 6, 1755

LC 116

GW to Richard Washington

Inclosed is an Invoice of Sundries which I entreat you to buy and send me by the first Ship in the Spring either to the head of Potomack or Rappahannock; the cost of these things will amount to more than the Tob.[o] &.[ct] for which Reason I shall take the earliest oppertunity of remitting you a Bill of Exchange. I have left many of the Articles with blank prices leaving it discretionary in you to fix them with this only desire, that you will choose agreable to the present taste, and send things good of their kind. . . .[1]

1. The invoice is unknown.

August 20, 1757

LC 116

Invoice of goods shipped by Richd Washington to George Washington from London, per the *Sally*, Capt. Dick [arrived Mount Vernon, March 1758]

	£	s.	d.
11 fine oblong china dishes /11/[1]	6	1	
1 Tureen to match Ditto		14	
2 doz[n] fine plates a/4/	1	8	
1 doz Ditto soop do		11	
a Compleat sett fine Image china	3	10	

1. Dishes: platters, serving pieces.

September 28, 1757

LC 116

Shipped by Thomas knox of Bristol per Capt[n] Callihall [arrived Mount Vernon, December 1757]

	£	s.	d.
6 doz[n] finest white stone plates[1]	1	4	
1 doz[n] ditto Dishes 6 sizes		18	
4 doz[n] Patti pans 4 sizes[2]		5	4
6 Quart mugs		2	
6 pint ditto		1	
6 Tea pots		1	
6 Slop Basons		1	
12 smaller ditto			
12 Butter dishes		1	
12 Mustard pots		1	
all in a crate			

1. White stone: white saltglazed stoneware.
2. Patti pans: tart pans of a small size. The spelling could also be "petty," and the pans could also function as dessert or sweetmeat plates.

January 8, 1758

LC 116

GW to Richard Washington

I have had an opportunity of seeing the great damage china is apt to come to in its transportation to this Country unless much care is used in the package which has determined me to desire you . . . to send me instead of what was directed in a former invoice, 2 doz[n] Dishes, properly sorted, 2 doz[n] deep Plates, and 4 doz[n] Shallow Ditto that allowance may be made for breakage, pray let them be neat and fashionable or send none. . . .

January 8, 1758

W 2:161–62

GW to Thomas Knox

. . . I have also receiv'd my Goods from the Recovery, and cant help again complaining of the little care taken in the purchase: Besides leaving out one half, and the most material half too! of the Articles I sent for, I find the Sein is without Leads, Corks and Ropes . . . the Crate of Stone ware dont contain a third of the Pieces I am charg'd with, and only two things broke, and every thing very high Charg'd . . . and to the things wrote for in my last add these following viz. . . .

> ½ doz'n dep white stone Dishes sortd.
> ½ Doz'n fashiol. China Bowls from a large to a Midlg. Size
> 3 doz'n Plates deep and Shallow . . .

Your sending these things together with those wrote for in my last by the first Vessel will very much Oblige. . . .

March 18, 1758

LC 116

GW to Richard Washington

Since My last of 8 January I have received your favour of the 9th of September together with an invoice and Acct. Currt. but the carelessness of the Captn prevented their coming to my hand til near six weeks after his arrival and the Goods got home but a few days ago . . . unaccountably indolent is Capt[n] Dick! . . . The China came without breakage for which Reason I must counter order the addition to it desir'd in my last. . . .

———————

April 5, 1758
LC 116
GW to Richard Washington

. . . You will perhaps think me a crazy fellow to be ordering and counter ordering Goods almost in a breath. . . .

———————

May 1, 1758
W 2:190
GW to David Franks in Philadelphia[1]

. . . you would provide for me . . . the following articles . . . Half a dozen *china* cups and saucers. . . .

1. David Franks was a prominent Jewish merchant in Philadelphia from about 1743 through the Revolutionary War. At the time of Washington's order, Franks was official contractor for the British Army in North America. He sold army supplies as well as general merchandise imported from London. See Edwin Wolf II and Maxwell Whiteman, *The History of the Jews of Philadelphia* (Philadelphia: The Jewish Publication Society of America, 1956), p. 38.

———————

August 18, 1758
LC 116
Shipped by Thomas Knox of Bristol to George Washington per the *Nugent*

	£	s.	d.
6 White stone soop Dishes[1]		15	
3 doz[n] plates ½ soop		10	6
3 punch bowls	1	11	6
2 two Quart ditto		17	
1 two Quart ditto coloured		7	6
4 three pint ditto enameld	1	1	4
2 large quart ditto		9	
Box		2	

1. White stone soop Dishes: not soup plates, but tureens. Six of them cost fifteen shillings—which was more than the thirty-six plates.

———————

ca. 1757–1759
Account of Sundrys taken and used by M[rs] Custis out of the Inventories, *Estate of Daniel*

Parke Custis, Custis Papers, Virginia Historical Society.[1]

New Kent[2]

	£	s.	d.
1 Set gilt China etc.	4		
2 Muggs etc.		6	9
Earthenware	1	5	
China Plates & Dishes	10		
Teacups etc.	5		
1 Crate Earthen Ware		14	
5¾ doz pewter plates	5	10	
41 Dishes (pewter) etc.	11	10	

James City[3]

	£	s.	d.
20 Plates	1		
8 Dishes & (?) 30/ 2 Scallop Shells 1/	1	11	
A set fruit peices 5/ a set of flower peices 5/[4]	10		
8 China Bowls etc.	1	10	
China and Earthenware	1	10	

Goods Mrs. Custis had out of those Shipped by Cary & Company

	£	s.	d.
Glass ware & China of Richard Farrar & Co.	10	2	8

1. The document is undated, but the items listed for "Miss Paty" and "Mr. Jackey" indicate that they were about two to four years old. Daniel Parke Custis died July 8, 1757. The first sales of personal property occurred October 20, 1759 (Freeman, vol. 3, p. 3). An order for appraisal of the personal estate of Daniel Parke Custis, dated August 11, 1757, is in the Etting Collection, vol. 8, p. 51, Historical Society of Pennsylvania, Manuscript Department.
2. New Kent: White House Plantation on the Pamunkey River in Virginia.
3. James City: Six Chimneys at Williamsburg, Virginia, the Custis town house.
4. Listed with the ceramics. Probably ornamental porcelains of a relatively high value.

———————

April 17, 1759
LC 115
Ledger A, Summary of accounts with Jn[o] Aug[e] Washington[1]

	£	s.	d.
Cash to Mr. Seymour for 6 China Cups & Saucers		9	1

Cash for 2 Butter Plates	1	3

1. John Augustine Washington (1736–1787) managed Mount Vernon in the absence of his older brother.

———————

May 1, 1759
W 2:320
GW to Rob[t] Cary Esq[r] & Comp[a] Merchts London

On the other side is an Invoice of some Goods which I beg of you to send me . . . direct for me at Mount Vernon Potomack River Virginia; the former is the name of my Seat the other of the River on which 'tis Situated. . . .

4 Fashionable China Branches, & Stands, for Candles . . .
1 Fashionable Sett of Desert Glasses, and Stands for Sweet Meats Jellys etc together with Wash Glasses and a proper stand for these also. . . .

———————

August 1759
LC 116
Invoice of goods shipped by R. Cary on acct of Col. George Washington[1]
Richard Farrer
[5 salvers & assorted glasses and]

	£	s.	d.
1 pair Branches and Candlesticks with flowers	1	10	
1 pair ditto ditto	1	12	
1 pair Seasons, & 1 pair Music's figures for Ditto[2]	1	1	
1 sweet meat stand[3]		10	
Box		3	

1. The invoices from Cary were itemized under the name of the shopkeeper or supplier.
2. See "Price List of Groups and Single Figures" in John Haslem, *The Old Derby China Factory* (London: George Bell, 1876), p. 172, no. 61: "Sitting Seasons," four for £1.1.0.
3. Sweet meat stand probably glass.

———————

September 1760
LC 116
GW to Robert Cary

[beer, cider, punch and wine glasses, "all of y[e] newest Fash." and]
½ doz[t] glass Milk Pots
6 China Mugs, two of a sort
6 ditto potting pots[1] 2 of a size, none large

288   THE ART OF COOKERY

To pot a Lobster.

TAKE a live lobster, boil it in salt and water, and peg it that no water gets in; when it is cold, pick out all the flesh and body, take out the gut, beat it fine in a mortar, and season it with beaten mace, grated nutmeg, pepper, and salt; mix all together; melt a piece of butter as big as a large walnut, and mix it with the lobster as you are beating it; when it is beat to a paste, put it into your potting pot, and put it down as close and hard as you can; then set some fresh butter in a deep broad pan before the fire, and when it is all melted, take off the scum at the top (if any), and pour the clear butter over the meat as thick as a crown piece; the whey and churn-milk will settle at the bottom of the pan, but take care none of that goes in, and always let your butter be very good, or you will spoil all; or only put the meat whole, with the body mixed among it, laying them as close together as you can, and pour the butter over them. You must be sure to let the lobster be well boiled. A middling one will take half an hour boiling.

155. Potting pots were used to preserve meats such as lobster and calves' tongues with clarified butter. This recipe is in Hannah Glasse, *The Art of Cookery*, London, 1796. Martha Washington owned a copy of the 1765 edition, now at Mount Vernon, which contains the identical recipe. (Courtesy, The Library Company of Philadelphia)

---

2 large stone churns each to hold 10 Gall.
6 doz[n] earthen Milk Pans[2]
1 doz[n] strong Mugs different sizes
½ doz[n] ditto Pipkins[3] 2 of them to hold a gall[n] each
   2 a pottle[4] & 2 a quart
12 white stone butter plates
1 doz[n] Stone Chamber Pots
1 doz[n] ditto wash Basons

1. Potting pots: containers for potted meat or fish.
2. Milk Pans: large, redware basins with flat bottoms and straight, sloping sides. Used for setting milk and other utilitarian purposes. Usually glazed only on the interior surfaces.
3. Pipkin: an earthenware vessel used for heating liquids. From Johnson's 1785 *Dictionary*, "a small earthen boiler."
4. Pottle: from Johnson's 1785 *Dictionary*, "Liquid measure containing four pints. It is sometimes used licentiously for a tankard, or pot out of which glasses are filled."

September 1760
LC 115
Ledger A
to George W[m] Fairfax[1]

	£	s.	d.
By 1 Dozen white Earthen Chamber Pots		15	

1. Washington's neighbor at Belvoir.

March 1761
LC 116
Invoice from Robert Cary to GW
Richard Farrer, Glass, etc.

	£	s.	d.
6 Milk pots on Feet		2	6
6 Emboss'd China Mugs 3 sizes[1]	1	10	
2 Oval potting pots		7	
2 smaller ditto with covers and 2 stands		8	
2 smaller ditto do do		6	
12 white stone sweetmeat plates		2	6
4 Qt mugs brown stone[2]		1	8
4 pints Ditto 1/ and 4½ pints			
do 6/		1	6
2 Gallon Pipkins		6	

---

1 2 Quart Do 2/3 & Qt Ditto	4	3
1 doz blew & white stone Chamber Pots[3]	8	
8 large red Milk pans	9	4
8 next size 6/8 & 8 next size 5/4	12	
6 next size 2/6 18 smaller 6/ & 12 smaller 3/	11	16
4 white stone hand Basons 2/ 2 larger 1/6 6 la 6/	9	6
1 Glass Pyramid in 8 arms & 1 Salver 6/6	6	6
Packing and case		

1. See text, p. 50.
2. See text, p. 49.
3. Blew & white stone Chamber Pots: probably English "scratch-blue" products. However, note "Dutch Chamber Potts" in December 1771 invoice of same price. See text, p. 49.

October 1761
LC 116
GW to Robert Cary

1 doz breakfast cups & as many saucers of china[1]
1 doz China custard cups
1 doz[n] China tart Pans

1. Breakfast cups: large tea bowls and saucers.

April 1762
LC 116
Invoice, Robert Cary to GW
Rich[d] Farrer & Co China

	£	s.	d.
1 Doz[n] China Patty Pans		8	
1 Doz[n] Ribbed Custard Cups		5	
12 Breakfast Cups 12 Saucers B & W China[1]		15	
Box			6

1. B & W China: blue-and-white Chinese porcelain.

May 1, 1762
LC 115
Ledger A
Under accounts with "M[r] Benj[a] Grayson"

	£	s.	d.
1 Sett Tea China—cost Sterl[g]		64	
a Tea Tabl and Appurt[s] from Belvoir	7	15	
By 1 Tea Board from Ditto	2	10	

November 15, 1762

LC 116

GW to Robert Cary

. . . one very fine and compl[t] sett of Table China 2 doz[n] Table knives & 2 doz[n] Forks with China handles to suit ditto 2 doz.[n] small desert Knives, & 2 doz.[n] Forks to Ditto

---

April 1763

LC 116

Invoice, Robert Cary to GW

Rich[d] Farrer & Co China

1 Compleat sett Table China fine blue & white consisting of

	£	s.	d.
11 long dishes			
24 plates——12 soop plates			
1 Tureen Cov & Dish			
4 Sauce boats 4 salts		12	
2 Largest red Milk Pans		2	6
12 next size do 10/18 next size 9/		19	
12 next size do 4/ 18 next size 4/6		8	6
12 Welch[1] Do 5/ 2 Wh[t] Stone do 4/		9	
[glassware]			
packing			

Richard Neale, Cut[y]

2 doz.[n] p[n] of neat China handle knives & forks with [illegible] silver Ferrels[2]	5		
2 doz.[n] p.[n] Do Do Desart Do		4	4

1. See text, p. 51.
2. Ferrels: ferrules, metal rings joining the handles and blades.

September 27, 1763

LC 116

GW to Robert Cary

1 China Plate Basket——or Basket proper for China in[1]

1 doz white stone wash basins & bottles to Ditto

1 doz[n] white stone chamber pots

1. China Plate Basket: a hamper for storing and shipping china.

February 1764

LC 116

Invoice, Robert Cary to GW

Jas Maidment Earth[wre]

	£	s.	d.
6 p[n] white stone bottles & Basons		13	
6 p[n] Do Do Do Do lesser	0	9	
12 Chamberpots		8	6

Thomas Johnston Turnery[1]

1 China plate Basket		3	

1. He also supplied hair brooms, coarse sieves, shoe brushes, and a large matt.

August 10, 1764

LC 116

GW to Robert Cary

2 Stone Water Jugs large

2 pint China Mugs

2 Quart Do Do

2 English China TeaPots la that will pour such

6 China pickle Shells blue & w.[1]

1. Pickle Shells: small dishes shaped like shells. These were also made as "pickle leaves."

February 1765

LC 116

Invoice, Robert Cary to GW

Farrer & Company China

	£	s.	d.
2 6-Quart Stone Jugs		2	8
2 large English Teapots[1]		5	
2 blue & white China Qt Mugs		8	
2 pts Nankeen Ditto[2]		8	
6 blue & white Pickle Shells		5	
Box		2	

1. English Teapots: earthen or stoneware, judging from the price.
2. Nankeen: see text, p. 53.

September 1765

LC 116

GW to Robert Cary

12 china cups & 12 saucers for breakfasting

8 doz[n] welch Milk pans a 5/

6 Stone Quart Mugs

12 White Stone Butter pots

2 doz[n] large stone Butter pots of a size to hold 40 and 50 lbs.

1 doz[n] large stone jugs to hold 5 gallons each

December 1765

LC 116

Invoice, Robert Cary to GW

Rich[d] Farrer & Co[o] Earth W

	£	s.	d.
5 large stone butter pots 3/6		17	6
7 Ditto smaller Do 2/6		17	6
6 Quart mugs 5 d.		2	6
8 White Stone Chamber pots 8 d.		5	4
Hogshead		6	
1 large stone Bottle		3	6
11 Butter potts 2/6	1	7	6
4 White stone Chamber pots 8 d.		2	8
[glassware]			
1 doz large welch dishes		6	
5 dozn Do 4/	1		
7 large stone bottles 3/6	1	4	6
12 breakfast cups and Saucers China		14	
Hogshead			
2 Stone Butter Potts 2/6		5	
6 large stone bottles 3/6	1	1	
1 smaller Ditto			
2 dozn welch Dishes 4/		8	
[wine glasses]			
Hogshead			

June 1766

LC 116

GW to Robert Cary

2 blew & white China sugar dishes & covers

2 blew & white milk pots

4 China mugs

4 blew & white Do slop bowls

1 large China Do to hold a Gal

1 Do Do to hold a Gal

November 1766

LC 116

Invoice, Robert Cary to GW

Rich[d] Farrer & C[o] China

	£	s.	d.
2 bleu & white China Milk pots		4	
4 slop basens Do		7	
1 Gall[n] Punch Bowl		14	6
1 Two Qt Do Nank[n] bord[r]		6	6
2 Sug[r] Dishes & Covers		4	6
4 fine painted Image Quart Mugs	2		
Box		1	6

October 1767

LC 116

Invoice, Robert Cary to GW

Rich[d] Farrer E. Ware

	£	s.	d.
9 pint Stone Mugs			7½
6 Quart Ditto		2	6
3 Pottle Do		3	
6 Blew & W stone Chamber Pots[1]		4	
Cask		2	6

1. Blew & W stone Chamber Pots: probably white, saltglazed stoneware decorated with incised flowers, animals, or geometric patterns filled in with an impure oxide of cobalt called zaffer.

July 25, 1769

LC 116

GW to Robert Cary

The following Assortment of ye most fash[e] kind of Queen's Ware—to wit—

6 doz[n] shall[w] Plates

3 doz[n] Soup Do

1 doz Dessert Ditto

16 Oval Dishes of 4 Sizes

4 Round Ditto of 2 Sizes

4 Scallopd Ditto of 2 Sizes

4 Oval baking dishes

2 large Fish drainers

2 large Tureens & Covers

4 Sauce bowls with stands & covers

4 Sauce Boats

2 sallid Dishes

---

6 Fruit dishes

12 fluted egg cups

2 sugar dishes & Ladles[1]

2 Porringers with stands[2]

6 Potting Pots of Diff size

12 Leaves or shells for Pickles

1 Pottle Mug 2 Quart Do

4 Pint Ditto 4 ½-Pint Do

a Sett of breakfast cups, saucers and coffee cups of a large kind (1 doz each) with wash bowl, Tea Pot & etc of ye above

1. Sugar dishes & Ladles: covered tureens, usually oval, often with a notch in the cover for the ladle.
2. Porringers: shallow bowls with one or two handles. From Johnson's 1785 *Dictionary*, "a vessel in which broth is eaten."

January 1770

LC 116

Invoice, Robert Cary to GW

Farrer & Garrett Earth W

	£	s.	d.
6 doz[n] fine Cream col[d] Plates a 4/	1	4	
3 doz[n] Soup Ditto 4/		12	
1 doz[n] Dsert Do		3	
4 large Dishes		14	
4 Ditto less		10	
4 Ditto		6	
4 Ditto		4	
4 Round Ditto		10	
4 Ditto		5	
2 Oval Baking Dishes		5	
2 Ditto		4	
2 large Oval Fish strainers[1]		4	6
1 Round Ditto		1	6
1 Large Tureen, Cover & Dish	1		
4 Sauce Boats & Stands		4	8
4 Ditto covers & spoons		10	
2 Sallid Dishes or Nappys[2]		1	6
2 Fruit Dishes and stands cut[3]		9	
2 Do Oval		5	
2 Do Oval		5	
2 Do smaller		4	
1 doz[n] Egg Cups pierced		3	6
2 sugar dishes & stands oblong octagon		5	
4 round Potting pots covers & plates		4	8
4 Ditto less		3	8

---

1 doz[n] pickle leaves		3	6
1 Pottle Mug		1	9
2 Quart Ditto		1	8
4 Pint Do		2	
4 ½-pint mugs		1	
12 large Breakfast cups, 12 saucers		1	
12 coffee cups handled, 12 saucers		3	
1 slop Bason		1	
Tea Pott		1	6
Milk Pott			8
2 Sugar Dishes		1	
1 Coffee Pott		1	9
2 Mustard Potts			6
2 Pepper boxes			8
2 Butter dishes, stands		2	4
a Hgd		5	

1. Oval Fish strainers: pierced inserts used with serving or baking dishes.
2. Sallid Dishes or Nappys: shallow bowls about 10 inches in diameter to be used either for salad or under a glass of strong ale (nappy) to catch the overflow of foam.
3. Fruit Dishes: oval or round open dishes, often cut or molded to resemble baskets.

August 1770

LC 116

GW to Robert Cary

. . . of Queen's China

1 doz[n] sml tea cups with Handles

1 doz[n] saucers for Do

1 Middle sized Tea & Milk Pott

6 salts

1 1½-gall[n] Bowl

1-2 Gall[n] Bowl

2 3-Qt   Do

1 Gallon   Do

2 2-Qt   Do

2 5-pint   Do

3 Quart   Do

2 3-pint   Do

3 ½-pint   Do

November 1770

LC 116

Invoice, Robert Cary to GW

Farrer & Garrett Earth W

Cream Coulour	£	s.	d.
1 Doz^n handle Teas & Saucers		2	6
1 Tea Pott 6 d. 1 Milk 6 d.		1	
6 salts & spoons		2	6
1 la. bowl		5	
1 smaller Do		3	6
2 Ditto		2	6
2 Ditto		4	
4 Bowls		5	
2 Ditto		2	
3 Do 2/ 3 Do 1/6		10	6
Box		3	

July 1771

LC 116

GW to Robert Cary

Queen's Ware

6 ½-pint Mugs
6 Pint Do
3 Pottle Do
6 Quart Do
6 Strng Wash Basons & Bottles
2 stone Jugs strong
6 Stone Chamberpots

December 1771

LC 116

Invoice, Robert Cary to GW

Farrer & Parrett [*sic*]

	£	s.	d.
a Case		4	6
6 ½-pint cream Col^d Mugs		1	
6 Pint Do 2/ 6 Quarts 4/		6	
3 2 Qts		4	
6 Bottles and 6 Basons		12	
6 Dutch Chamber Potts		4	
2 2-Gallon Stone Jugs		4	
3 doz^n Enamel wine Glasses		13	6
6 Ale Glasses enameld		3	6

July 1772

W 3: 92

GW to Robert Carey & Company

. . . 1 Doz'n large Breakfast Tea Cups and 1 doz'n

Saucers, with 8 Coffee Cups and 8 Saucers, Also 1 doz'n smaller Tea Cups and the like number of saucers, together with 8 coffee cups and Saucers to them, with a Tea Pot, Milk Pot, Sugar Dish, and slop Bowl to each Set, the whole to be of the same kind of China, of a fash'e but not of a costly sort. . . .

September 1772

LC 116

invoice, Robert Cary to GW

Farrer & Garrett, China

	£
1 Comp^l Sett Tea Equipage with 8 Coffee Cups & 8 Saucers, fine Lands^c	
1 Comp^l Sett Breakfast D^o w. 8 coffee cups & 8 Saucers	£5

August 21, 1774

LC 115

Ledger B, p. 121

	£	s	d.
By Butter Boats . . . 2/6			
Water Melons 1/3		3	9

Ledger B, p. 131

	£	s	d.
By 2 Doz^t Wine Glasses & 1 D^o Coffee Cupps 7/6	1	2	6

LC 117

Mr. Austin's Accounts for Cash Expended for the Commander-in-Chief's Household [mainly for food]

	£	s	d.
December 19, 1775			
Paid for 2 mugs		2	
& 1 pair Salts		1	4
December 22, 1775			
Paid Mr Lucas for 1 Doz^n cups & saucers etc.		16	6
January 24, 1776			
Paid for 12 Cups & 12 Saucers		1	4
January 26, 1776			
Paid for six Chamber Pots		2	
Paid for 1 Earthen Platter			6
Paid for 6 D^o Mugs		2	4¾

January 30, 1776		
Paid for a Wash Bason	2	8
Paid for a Sugar Pot	3	
February 29, 1776		
Paid for 1 Doz^n Stone Plates	8	

April 16, and May 14, 1776

LC 117

An Acct of the furniture Bot for His Exc^l Genl Washington

Bot of Mr. Rhinelander

	£	s.	d.
1 2 gall. pitcher		4	
2 Oval Dishes 5/3		10	6
4 Do 3/9		15	
4 Do 2/6		10	
4 Do 1/6		6	
2 Pudg Dishes 2/		4	
5½ Doz of Plates 7/6	2	1	
2 Earthen Dishes		1	6
2 Sauce boats		2	
1 Doz cream small plates		5	6
1 Bowl		2	
2 Chab potts		5	
3 Bowls		2	
2 China bowls		16	
1 Doz of plates		8	
2 sauce boats		2	
2 pudg Dishes		3	6
1 doz of small plates[1]		5	6
3 Washbasons		6	
3 pitchers		9	6
2 half P mugs & 2 pudg dishes		5	10
2 Washbasons, 1 brown mug		5	
2 Earthen dishes, 2 jelly cups and saucers		7	6
2 Oval Dishes		3	
2 Oval Dishes, 1 Fruit basket		8	6
1 China Bowl		5	6
2 Oval Dishes, 1 pudg Dish		7	6
1 doz of plates at 5/6 dozen small		11	6
Chambr potts & soop dish		6	9
3 fluted bowls & 2 wash basons		6	9
1 milk Jug			9

1. The price is the same as that of the "cream" small plates. Unless otherwise specified ("earthen" or "China," for example), all pieces were probably creamware.

April 20, 1776

LC 117

An Acct of the furniture Bot for His Exc[l] Gen[l] Washington

Bot of James Deas

	£	s.	d.
1 Turene	2		
3 China Mugs		1	17
2 dozen of plates		2	2

————————

May 14, 1776

Bot of George Ball

	£	s.	d.
2 china mugs		6	
1 China Teapot		5	
2 setts large burnt china cups & saucers[1]		1	12
1 Quart burnt china bowl		9	
2 China mugs 3 wash basons		15	
1 Sett large china		16	
2 Chamberpots		5	6
2 Water guglets[2]		16	
2½ setts large china cups & saucers		1	15
2 Quart mugs		2	8
3 cups & Saucers		8	
1 China Tea pott		14	
1 Sugar Dish & milk pot		3	
1 Teapot		5	
1 Sugar dish & milk pot		3	
1 China bowl		9	
2 Teapots 2 mugs		7	4

[glassware including print tumblers, cut salts, "neat" wine glasses and decanters as well as cookware]

1. Burnt china: gilt. See text, p. 66.
2. Guglet: a ceramic water bottle, often used with a washbasin.

————————

May 30, 1776

Bot at Sundry Places

	£	s.	d.
3 fruit Basketts at 5/6		16	6
4 plates for the Basketts		4	
6 Earthen Pots, 2 wash hand Basons		12	6
1 Japan Sugar Canister		6	

July 11, 1776

LC 117

Memorandum of articles taken out of Mr. Mortiers Garrett, the property Gen[l] Haldman[1] for the Use of His Excellency General Washingtons Family. . . .

Viz 2 Fruit Baskets
    2 Pudding dishes

1. Perhaps Frederick Haldimand, later British commander in Canada. See Freeman, vol. 5, p. 448.

————————

February 17, 1779

W 14: 127

GW (from camp at Middlebrook) to John Mitchell (deputy quartermaster general in Philadelphia)

My plates and dishes, once of Tinn, now little better than rusty iron, are rather too much worn for delicate stomachs in fixed and peacable quarters. . . . I therefore desire that you will send me a sett of Queens China if to be had; not less I conceive than what follows of each article will do:

2 large Turennes
3 dozn. Dishes, sized
8 dozn. Shallow Plates
3 dozn. Soup Ditto
8 Table drinking Mugs
8 Ditto Salts, and some pickle plates
The whole to be very carefully packed. I also desire you will send me Six tolerably genteel but not expensive Candlesticks all of a kind. . . .

————————

February 23, 1779 [enclosed with March 6 letter]

LC 56

Mr. John Mitchell Deputy Quarter Master General For his Excell[y] Gen[l] Washington Bought of Henry Pratt[1]

	£	s.	d.
11 Dishes Queens Ware	47	12	6
6 Doz of d.[o] Plates a £ 15 pr doz	90		
6 Pint Mugs a 15/ piece	4	10	
2 Quarts d.[o] a 5 Dollars a piece	3	15	
8 salts a 3/9 a piece	1	10	
4 Dishes	15	15	

1. Henry Pratt (1761–1838) was the son of Matthew Pratt, the painter. "Before his majority Mr. Pratt was engaged in the china and crockery trade." In 1799, he built Lemon Hill, now in Philadelphia's Fairmount Park. See J. Thomas Scharf and Thompson Westcott, *History of Philadelphia* (Philadelphia: L.H. Evarts, 1884), vol. 3, p. 2212.

————————

March 4, 1779 [enclosed with March 6 letter]

LC 56

Bought of Henry Pratt

14 Queens Ware Dishes Differ.[t] Sizes

	£	s.	d.
2 d.[o] 14 Dollars each	10	10	
2 d.[o] at 13 ½ d.[o] d.[o]	10	2	6
2 d.[o] at 12 ½ d.[o] d.[o]	9	7	6
2 d.[o] at 11 ½ d.[o] d.[o]	8	12	6
2 d.[o] at 10 ½ d.[o] d.[o]	7	17	6
2 d.[o] at 9 ½ d.[o] d.[o]	7	2	6
2 d.[o] at 8 ½ d.[o] d.[o]	6	7	6

Bot of Deborah & Hanah Mitchel

	£	s.
5 Dozen plates a 15 p[r] doz	75	
2 Tureens a £ 12 each	24	
4 Dishes a £ 4/10 d.[o]	18	
2 D.[o] 4 d.[o]	8	
2 d.[o] 22/6 d.[o]	2	5

————————

March 6, 1779

LC 56

John Mitchell (Philadelphia), to GW

. . . I have sent the Queensware, Candlesticks & snuffers by a Waggon who setts off this day. they are as carefully packed as I cou'd get them . . . the extravagent price of the Articles will no doubt astonish you, but there was no alternative. . . .

Inventory of China ware &c.
6 large round dishes
6 d.[o] plain
6 d.[o] oval
18 small d.[o] of various kinds
7 doz. of plates
4 d.[o] of soup plates
2 large tureens
8 salt sellers
3 dekanters
4 small pans

6 Candlesticks, brass

3 p.ʳ snuffers

March 8, 1779

W 14: 211

GW (Middlebrook) to Maj. Gen. Nathanael
Greene (quartermaster general)

I wrote to Mitchell for a sett of Queens Ware . . . to
which he gave the following answr on the 21st
Ulto. viz . . . 'I have made enquiry . . . but am
afraid it will be difficult if not impossible to
procure them.' I therefore apply to you to procure
them as Lady Stirling informed me a few days
ago that they were to be had at Brunswick.

April 4, 1780

LC 65

John Mitchell (Philadelphia) to GW

. . . have sent you the Mop, two Stone jars & a
large stone Jug, by a Waggon that sett off three
days ago . . . to Headquarters. . . . I can not get a
Punch Bowl under 180 Dollars, & 50 Dollars for
a Wash hand Bason if you aprove of those prices
they shall be sent immediately—the Chamber
Pott goes by the Bearer, who will return with your
answer. . . .

April 8, 1780

W 18:234

GW (Morristown) to John Mitchell

[Directs Mitchell to purchase a carriage and to
have it painted "in a tasty stile" with "a light
airy gilding."]
. . . The Several Articles from Don Juan[1] came
safe. the Mop, Jug, and Jarrs are, it seems, left
somewhere on the road. If it is for an Earthen, or
Queens ware bowl the 180 Dollars is asked, I
shall decline the purchase for I think it is high
time to check such extravagance. . . .

1. Don Juan de Miralles, Spanish agent in Philadelphia, died at
Washington's headquarters in Morristown within a month after
this letter was written. See Dennis C. Kurjack, "St. Joseph's
and St. Mary's Churches," *Historic Philadelphia* (Philadelphia: Transactions of the American Philosophical Society) 43
(1953): 205.

December 1781 through June 1782

LC 117

Captⁿ Colfax Accᵗˢ being Vouchers for the money
charged to him.
Cash Expended in Furnishing the Commander-
in-Chief's Table & Household [daily accounts,
mainly for food]

	£	s.	d.
December 28, 1781			
4 dishes Queen's Ware		2	5
June 12, 1782			
1 Earthen Mugg		2	6
June 13, 1782			
2 Earthen dishes			6

March 31, 1782

LC 117

Account—Provision, Stores received of the
Contractors for the Commander in Chief

	£	s.	d.
2 China Bowls			
1 Large China Tea Pott (red)			
November 2, 1782			
Mending two C. Bowls		30	
February 26, 1783			
6 Sauce Tureenes		72	
2 Bowls		5	8
May 5, 1783			
2 Wash bowls & Pitcher		8	

July 8, 1782

W 24:404

GW (Newburgh) to Col. Samuel Miles (deputy
quartermaster general in Philadelphia)

By the receipt of a Mr. White your Assistant
2 Tureens
2 Sallid Dishes
29 Dishes of difft. Sizes
5 dozn. and 7 Plates: shallow
2 doz. and 10 Soup Do., and 8 Salts
Were left in his care to be sent to me when
ordered . . . but in lieu thereof, I have received the
following:
2 Turenes
8 Dishes
2 Doz. and 10 Shallow Plates

---

3 Doz and 7 Soup Do.   9 more than were left and
6 salts
The deficiency I expect to receive by the first opportunity, if they are not already on their way. . . .

July 1782

Evelyn M. Acomb, ed., The Revolutionary Journal of Baron von Closen *(Chapel Hill: University*
of North Carolina Press, 1958), p. 214.

July 19 . . . Mme Washington begged me to write
for her to M. le Comte de Custine, whose
regiment was at Colchester that day, to invite
him and all the officers of his corps to do her the
honor to dine with her the next day, the 20th.
July 20 . . . Subsequently, M. de Custine arrived
with about 10 of his officers from the *Saintonge*
and with several from the engineers. M. de
Bellegarde preceded him, to bring on behalf of
the Count, a very beautiful porcelain service
from the latter's own factory at Niderviller (near
Phalsbourg). It was designed in the latest style,
with General Washington's arms and mono-
gram under a crown of laurels. Mme Washington was delighted with M. de Custine's attentions,
and expressed her appreciation to him in the
most gracious manner.

August 7, 1782

W 24: 485

GW (Newburgh) to the Count de Custine-Sarreck

Mrs. Washington . . . informs me also of the
obligation you have laid me under, in a present
of eligant China—which as the product of your
own Estate, I shall consider of inestimable
value. . . .

August 19, 1782

LC 86

Samuel Miles (Philadelphia) to GW (Newburgh)

Reudon[1] gave an entertainment a day or two
after you had left the City, and . . . his Stewart
had made use of those dishes, plates etc and had
also lent part of them to the Minister of France's
Stewart, they are, however, I am informed, all
return'd and forwarded, except one dozn. plates.

1. Francisco Rendon was the Spanish agent, replacing Don Juan de Miralles. The French minister was the Chevalier de la Luzerne. Luzerne gave a fête on July 15, 1782, to celebrate the birth of the French dauphin. A thousand guests, including Washington, enjoyed fireworks, dancing, and "a cold collation: simple, frugal and elegant, and handsomely set off with a dessert consisting of cakes and all the fruits of the season." Benjamin Rush to Elizabeth Graeme Ferguson, July 16, 1782, *The Pennsylvania Magazine of History and Biography* 21 (1897): 261.

October 22, 1782
LC 88
Custine to GW [translation accompanying French original]

. . . the extreme pleasure that I experienced at Mrs W—accepting, with that goodness which is natural to her, the production of my Country. . . .

May 1783
LC 117
Cash Expended in Furnishing the Commander in Chief's Table
Account 16

Rec'd of Daniel Parker . . .
4 doz'n Plates Queen's Ware
1 do China Cups & Saucers

September 12, 1783
W 27:151
GW (Rocky Hill) to Daniel Parker (New York)

If a neat and compleat sett of blue and White Table China could be had upon pretty good terms, be pleased to inform me of it, and the price. Not less than 6 or 8 dozn. Shallow and a proportionable number of Deep and other Plates, Butter Boats, Dishes and Tureens, will suffice. They some times come in compleat setts ready packed; shou'd this be the case, altho' there may be a greater number of Pieces than I have mentioned, I should have no objection to a case on that acct. . . . Will you be so good as to inform me what Goods, for family use, are very low in New York, and if they are to be had cheaper, than Goods of the same kind and quality, at Philadelphia.

September 18, 1783
LC 93
Saml Fraunces^1 [New York] to GW

Bot of Edward Nicoll Junr for Genl Washington
[6 dozen cut wine goblets, 2 dozen claret goblets, 1 pair cut rummers, etc.] . . .

	£	s.	d.
1 pr. butter Tubs /2/	42	10	

1. Samuel Fraunces was proprietor of the Queen's Head Tavern. Later, he served for two periods as steward during Washington's presidency.

September 18, 1783
LC 93
Daniel Parker (New York) to GW

. . . I requested Mr. Fraunces to obtain the lowest price that a neat and compleat set of Table China could be obtained for, he has made particular enquiry and can find none on better terms than the inclosed which I think is higher than they can be bought for in Philadelphia. We can find no compleat setts that are ready packed in this city. West India goods in general are 10 per cent cheaper here than in Philadelphia`. . . British goods in general differ very little in price. . . .

27 Dishes
2 Tureens
2 Dishes for Do
2 Sallad Dishes
4 Butter Boats
4 Dishes for Do
6 small Turreens
6 Dishes for Do
43 Flatt Plates
43 Soop Do
42 Dessert Do
24 Froot Do

---

205 pc^s for 36 Guineas Blue and White China

September 22, 1783
LC 93
Daniel Parker to GW^1 [shipping receipt]

. . . Two Barrels of Earthen Ware and a Pipe of wine. . . .

1. The barrels and wine were sent to Mount Vernon.

September 22, 1783
W 27: 160
GW (Rocky Hill) to Bushrod Washington (Philadelphia)

. . . if there is any blue and white table china, to be had in settes and the price. Table china frequently comes packed up in compleat setts, amounting to a gross, or gross and a half of pieces, all kinds included. . . .

December 14, 1783
LC 115
Ledger B, p. 175
GW Account with Lund Washington^1

	£	s.	d.
By Daw & McIver 6 Chamber Potts	12		

1. Lund Washington, a relative and friend, managed Mount Vernon during the war.

August 12, 1785
Maryland Gazette and Baltimore Advertiser

To be sold by Public Vendue, at Baltimore, on the 1st of October next, in Lots, the following Goods, just imported in the Ship Pallas, direct from China.—
Hyson Teas of the first quality, in quarter chests;
Hyson Tea, in canisters of 2½ lb. each;
Hyson Ditto, of the second quality in chests;
Confu Ditto, Ditto, in Ditto;
Hyson Skin, Ditto, Ditto;
Gunpowder, Ditto, Ditto;
Table Sets of the best Nankeen, blue and white stone China;
Ditto of the second quality, Ditto;
Ditto, painted Ditto, Ditto;
Dishes of blue and white stone China, 5 and 3 in a Set;
Flat and Soup Plates, Ditto,
Breakfast Cups and Saucers of the best blue and white stone China, in Sets;
Evening Ditto, Ditto, Ditto;
Painted Ditto, Ditto, Ditto;
Ditto, with the Arms of the Order of the Cincinnati;
Bowls, best blue and white Stone China in sets;

Pint Sneakers,[1] Ditto;

Mugs, best Stone China in sets;

Small Tureens with covers;

Wash-Hand Guglits and Basons;

Brown Nankeens of the first and second quality;

Plain, flowered and spotted Lustrings of all colours;

Sattins, the greatest part black;

Pelongs of different colours in whole and half pieces;

Sarsnet Ditto;

Embroidered Waistcoat Pieces of Silk and Sattin;

Silk Handkerchiefs very fine, 20 in a piece;

Spotted and flowered Velvets;

Painted Gauzes;

Bengal Piece Goods and Muslins, plain, flowered and corded;

Silk Umbrellas of all sizes;

Elegant Paper Hangings;

Japanned Tea-Chests;

Ditto Fish and Counter-Boxes;

Sago, Cinnamon and Cinnamon Flowers;

Rhubarb, Opium, Gambouge and Borax;

Very old Batavia Arrack in leagures, with sundry other articles, the enumeration of which would take up too much room in a public paper.

1. Sneakers: small punch bowls. From Johnson's 1785 *Dictionary*, "small vessels of drink."

August 17, 1785

Historical Society of Pennsylvania, Manuscript Department, Dreer Collection[1]

GW (Mount Vernon) to Tench Tilghman[2] *(Baltimore)*

The Baltimore Advertiser of the 12th. Inst.[t] announces the arrival of a Ship at that Port, immediately from China; and by an advertisement in the same paper, I perceive that the Cargo is to be sold at public Vendue, on the first of Oct.[r] next.

At what prices the enumerated articles will sell, on the terms proposed, can only be known from the experiment, but if the quantity at Market is great, and they should sell as goods have sold at Vendue, bargains may be expected. I therefore take the liberty of requesting the favor of you, in that case, to purchase the several things contained in the inclosed list.

You will readily perceive, My dear Sir, my purchasing, or not, depends entirely upon the prices. If *great bargains* are to be had, I would supply myself agreeably to the list——if the prices do not fall *below* a cheap *retail* sale, I would decline them altogether, or take such articles only (if cheaper than common) as are marked [by asterisks] in the Margin of the Invoice.

Invoice of Goods to be purchased, by Tench Tilghman Esq.[r] on Acc.[t] of George Washington, agreeably to the letter accompanying this, of equal date——

A sett of the best Nankin Table China

Ditto—best Evening China Cups & Saucers

*A set of *large* blue & White China Dishes— say half a doz[n]—more or less

*1 Doz.[n] *small* bowls— blue & white

*6 Wash hand Guglets & Basons

6 Large Mugs—or 3 Mugs & 3 Jugs

With the badge of the Society of the Cincinnati—if to be had

1. Also in W 28: 223. The original was examined to determine the placement of Washington's asterisks and bracket. His craft or copy, which differs slightly, is in the Washington Papers, LC 5.
2. Tench Tilghman (d. 1786): Baltimore merchant associated with Robert Morris and Gouverneur Morris in the tobacco trade. During the Revolution, Tilghman served as secretary and staff officer to Washington.

August 25, 1785

LC 95

Tench Tilghman (Baltimore) to GW

. . . Altho' the greater part of the Cargo of the Ship Pallas is advertised for public Sale on the 1st of October next, it is not a matter of certainty that it will be disposed of in that manner—at least the whole of it. At any rate, I expect it will fall in great degree under my management, as Mr. O'Donnell the Owner, who is a perfect Stranger in this Country, finds himself obliged to seek the assistance of a person acquainted with Characters here and

with our mode of Business. Before he left India, he was recommended to Mr. Morris,[1] and it is thro' my Connection with him that I have to do in the matter. A large parcel of Teas on Board were the property of Major Shaw and Capt Randall who went out Super Cargoes of the Empress of China—Those Teas have all gone to Philadel[a].

Whether those Goods are sold at public or private sale, your Commission shall be punctually attended to. If at public—the several Articles shall not be purchased for you except they go at such Rates as are much below the usual Retail prices—the few marked thus in your letter * [asterisks] excepted—which shall be bought if they are as cheap as goods usually sell for Cash—if a private sale should be determined on, you shall be made acquainted with the lowest prices, and then you may judge for yourself. . . .

Mr. O'Donnell . . . is a Gentleman of large fortune—polished manners, and from 16 years residence in the different parts of India very capable of giving satisfactory accounts of that Country.

The Crew of this Ship are all Natives of India—most of them from the Coasts of Malabar and Coromandel, and are much of the Countenance and Complexion of your old Groom Womely—There are four Chinese on Board, who are exactly the Indians of North America. in Color, Feature—Hair and every external Mark . . . assure [Mrs. Washington] that every care shall be taken to have such Goods as may be purchased the most fashionable and perfect of their kinds. . . .

1. Robert Morris.

August 29, 1785

W 28: 238

GW (Mount Vernon) to Tench Tilghman

. . . I had in contemplation *Bargains*, which, from the quantity of Goods at Market, scarcity of cash according to newspaper Accounts, distress of the Trade, and the mode of selling, I thought might probably be obtained; but if I am mistaken herein, I shall content myself with the few *marked* articles, or such of them as can be had cheap. . . .

_____

August 31, 1785
LC 95
Tench Tilghman to GW

. . . I shall attend to your orders for India Goods—If Mr. O'Donnell adheres to his intent of selling at public sale, you cannot come in there, because the Lots will be larger than your Wants. I do not think a public sale will answer his purpose and so he begins to think now when his goods are assorted and priced. I can easily let you know how he holds them, and then you may purchase or not at your pleasure. . . .

The Chinese of the Northern provinces are fairer than those of the South, but none of them are of the European Complexion. . . .

_____

September 14, 1785
W 28: 264
GW to Tench Tilghman

. . . When Mr. ODonnal has determin'd on his plan, I shall expect to hear from you. . . .

_____

October 13, 1785
LC 95
Tench Tilghman to GW

. . . Mr. O'Donnells sale, or rather no sale, is over. He held his goods so extravagantly high, that you might have bought them cheaper out of any store in Town. He has an Idea they will be in great demand in the Spring, and therefore holds them up. . . .

_____

November 10, 1785
LC 115
Ledger B, p. 205

By 2 China Bowls 10/ 1 Gall Bason 6/8
By ½ gall^n Bason 4/6[1]

1. Entered with expenses "at Lyles's." William Lyles of Charles County, Maryland, had a distillery, dry-goods store, and tavern in Alexandria, Virginia, from about 1782. Washington recorded

that he and Mrs. Washington "went up to Alexandria" on November 10, and that they dined at Lyles' "New Tavern," which was at the corner of Fairfax and Cameron streets. The store was also on Fairfax near King Street; *Diaries*, vol. 4, pp. 198 and 236.

_____

February 22, 1786
LC 115
Ledger B, p. 212

	£	s.	d.
By 4 Wash Basons 4/ 1 Water			
Jugg 2/ 2 Pint Muggs	1		
3 Pint Bowls 1/6 2 Pint Muggs 1/[1]	2	8	6

1. "Mr. Lawe. Washington went up to Alexandria after breakfast." *Diaries*, vol. 4 (February 22, 1786), p. 284.

_____

July 3, 1786
LC 96
Henry Lee (New York)[1] to GW

. . . If you should be in want of a new set of china it is in my power to procure a very gentele set, table & tea—What renders this china doubly valuable & handsome is the order of the eagle engraved on it, in honor of the Cincinnati—It has upwards of 306 pieces, and is offered at the prime Cost, 150 dollars. . . .[2]

1. Henry Lee, also called "Light-Horse Harry Lee" (1756–1818), was in the Continental Congress from 1785 to 1788. Later, he was governor of Virginia and, at the time of Washington's death, was in the United States Congress. It was Lee who uttered the famous "first in war, first in peace, and first in the hearts of his countrymen" eulogy at the memorial service in Philadelphia on December 26, 1799. He was the father of Robert E. Lee.
2. Dollars: Spanish-milled dollars (pieces of eight) won popular acceptance as a world monetary unit in the late eighteenth century. The later United States monetary system was based on a dollar exactly equivalent to the Spanish-milled dollar.

_____

July 26, 1786
W 28: 483
GW to Henry Lee

. . . I am much obliged to you for the information respecting the China which is for sale in New York, with the order of the Cincinnati engraved on it; if it should not be disposed of before this letter reaches you, and you think a ready and safe conveyance can be had for it to Alexandria or this place, I would thank you for buying it for me. In this case, pray let me know

the exchange between New York and London at 60 days sight, and I will by return of the post, give you a good Bill for the sterlg. amount of the 150 Dollars: or, by means of some of the merchts. in Alexandria who have connexions in New York, I will forward an order on that place to that amot. . . .

_____

August 7, 1786
LC 96
Henry Lee to GW

I had the pleasure of hearing from you last week, and have complied with your wishes respecting the china. No conveyance at present offers for Alexandria, but every day presents one to Norfolk, from which place the correspondence up your river is frequent. I intend unless I should meet with a vessel for Potomac, to send the box to Col. Parker, naval officer at Norfolk, and ask his special attention to forwarding it to Alexandria or Mount Vernon . . . the cost of the China is 150 dollars besides the incidental charge of freight to Norfolk, which cannot be much. . . .

_____

August 7, 1786
LC 96
Constable, Rucker & Co (New York) to Henry Lee[1]

Colo Henry Lee
1786 Bot of Constable, Rucker & Co. Aug 7th
1 Sett of Cincinnati China Cont^g
  1 Breakfast ⎫
  1 Table   ⎬ Service of 302 p^s £ 60
  1 Tea   ⎭
Rd New York the 7 Aug. 1786 the Amount/Constable, Rucker & Co.

1. Enclosed in the August 7, 1786, letter from Lee to GW.

_____

August 12, 1786
LC 96
Henry Lee to GW

. . . It is probable that the China will leave New York for Norfolk next week. . . .

August 23, 1786
LC 115
Ledger B, p. 231

Aug. 23 By 32 Guineas & ¼ of Moidore[1] sent to Colo Henry Lee at New York, by Colo Humphreys to pay for a set of China bot. for me there . . . £ 45/5/0

1. Moidore: Portuguese currency.

September 8, 1786
LC 96
Henry Lee to GW

. . . By Col. Humphrey I had the pleasure to receive your letter acknowledging the receipt of the China account paid here by me, and at the same time got one hundred and fifty dollars payment in full for the money advanced. . . . I hope your China has also got to hand—It had left this for Norfolk addressed to Col° Parker before your letter respecting the mode of conveyance got to me. . . .

September 23, 1786
LC 115
Ledger B, p. 235

	£	s.	d.
Sept 23 1786 By freight of China from Norfolk		6	

October 31, 1786
W 29:35
GW to Henry Lee

. . . The China came to hand without much damage. . . .

November 18, 1786
W 29:70
GW to Samuel Vaughan (Philadelphia)

. . . The picture of a battle in Germany, and the Jarrs came very safe. The first is fine: the latter is also fine and exceedingly handsome, they shall occupy the place you have named for them . . .

August 8, 1787
LC 115
Ledger B, p. 248

	£	s	d.
Aug 8 By a Cucumber dish[1]		2	

1. Cucumber dish: perhaps a pickle dish.

June 8, 1789
Historical Society of Pennsylvania, Manuscript Department
Tobias Lear (New York) to Clement Biddle (Philadelphia)

. . . The President is desireous of getting a sett of those waiters, salvers, or whatever they are called, which are set in the middle of a dining table to ornament it—and to occupy the place which must otherwise be filled with dishes of meat, which are seldom or never touched. Mr. Morris & Mr. Bingham have them, and the French & Spanish Ministers here, but I know of no one else who has—I am informed that they are most likely to be got at French Stores as they are made in France; we can find none in this place, and the Presid[t] will thank you to enquire if a sett can be procured in Philad[a] and if it can, to procure it for him. . . .

June 15, 1789
Historical Society of Pennsylvania, Manuscript Department
Tobias Lear to Clement Biddle

. . . if the large & small Glasses of M. De la Croix[1] are of the same set, he will thank you to procure them for him. . . . The President has a French man with him who is said to be a compleat confectioner, & professes to understand everything relative to those ornaments, so that the Glasses only are wanting. . . .

1. Joseph de la Croix was listed as "confectioner" at 533 Second Street (between Arch and Race) in Francis White, *Philadelphia Directory for 1785*, and in Macpherson's *Directory* (Philadelphia, 1785).

July 7, 1789
First Administration Accounts

	£	s.	d.
By House Exp[s] p[d] M[r] Burling[1] for Table Ornaments	43	0	0

1. The 1789 *New York Directory* lists Thomas and William Burling, china and glass shop, 70 Water Street. Thomas Burling, cabinetmaker, 36 Beekman Street, is also listed. The latter supplied mahogany furniture for the Cherry Street house and a writing desk and table for Mrs. Washington in November 1789.

October 13, 1789
W 30: 443–45
GW to Gouverneur Morris

. . . Will you then, my good Sir, permit me to ask the favor of you to provide and send to me by the first Ship, bound to this place, or Philadelphia, mirrors for a table, with neat and fashionable but not expensive ornaments for them; such as will do credit to your taste . . . If I am defective recur to what you have seen on Mr. Robert Morris's table for my ideas *generally*. . . .

December 29, 1789
Abstract of Accounts of sundry persons for Goods furnished and Repairs done to the House occupied by the President of the United States, Auditors Office, Geo. Nixon, Clk.[1]

For Furniture, Furnishings, Wines, and Groceries . . .

	£	s.	d.
J. & N. Roosevelt; China, plated ware, &c.	204	6	10
James Chrystie; Glass & Queens Ware	281	0	3
H. Hawkshurst; Earthen Ware	10	19	1
Samuel Dunlap; Looking Glass, China, &c.	18	4	0

[Undated]
National Archives, Washington, D.C., *Records of the Office of the Register of the Treasury*, Record Group 53, vol. 138, pp. 316–24.[2]

	£	s.	d.
4 sets of Breakfast china J. & N. Roosevelt	14	0	0
Looking Glass, china &c. Samuel Dunlap	18	4	0

Glass and Queen's Ware James Christie[3]	281	0	3

1. Manuscript in the New-York Historical Society, Samuel Osgood Papers. Published in Henry B. Hoffmann, "President Washington's Cherry Street Residence," *The New-York Historical Society Quarterly Bulletin* 23 (July 1939): 95–98.

2. In Margaret Brown Klapthor, *Official White House China: 1789 to the Present* (Washington, D.C.: Smithsonian Institution Press, 1975), p. 21.

3. James Christie, China and Glass Shop, 17 Maiden Lane; Samuel Dunlap, storekeeper, 13 Queen Street; Hannah Hawxhurst, earthenware shop, 2 Cherry Street; John & Nicholas J. Roosevelt, merchants, 33 Maiden Lane. Robert Hodge, Thomas Allen, and Samuel Campbell, *New York Directory & Register for 1789* (New York: 1789).

January 11, 1790

LC, Manuscript Division, Gouverneur Morris Papers, vols. 1–13, Diary of Gouverneur Morris[1]

Madame takes me to the *Porcelaine* to see a Kind of Ornament cemented on Glass, being Birds formed by their Feathers and other natural Objects in the same Way. . . . The Maker is there and we enquire the Price of a Surtout for a Table ten feet long and two feet wide. It is 2000 # [shillings] and cannot be finished before October next. . . .[2]

1. Published in Beatrix Cary Davenport, ed., *A Diary of the French Revolution, 1789–1793* (Boston: Houghton Mifflin, 1939), vol. I. The Morris papers are available on microfilm.

2. On October 30, 1789, Morris and Mme de Flahaut had visited "Sève"; Morris commented, "This Manufactory is superb and far exceeds my Idea."

January 15, 1790 (Morris diary)

I call on Madame de Flahaut and we go to look for a Surtout. Afterwards to the Manufacture of Angoulême. We agree that the Porcelaine here is handsomer and cheaper than that of Sève. I think I shall purchase for General Washington here. We are to go on Monday to see the Person whom we first visited. . . .

January 18, 1790 (Morris diary)

At one go to the Louvre and take Mesdames de Flahaut and de La Tour with me to look for a Surtout for Genl Washington. I make a Purchase at the Manufacture of Angoulême which will cost him ab.[t] 100 Louis. . . .

January 20, 1790 (Morris diary)

I dress and go to Mr Grand's. Leave Directions respecting the Porcelaine for Genl Washington.

January 21, 1790 (Morris diary)

This morning I go to the Manufacture of Angoulême to give some Directions in Consequence of a Letter received from the Director.[1]

1. The letter from Director Dihl was not found in the Gouverneur Morris papers in the Library of Congress microfilm edition.

January 24, 1790 (Morris diary)

LC, Gouverneur Morris Papers, vol. 22 (Commercial Letters)
Gouverneur Morris (Paris) to GW

I expect that this Letter will accompany three cases containing a Surtout of seven Plateaus and the ornaments in Biscuit; also three large glass covers for the three Groups which may serve both for ornaments to the Chimney Piece of a drawing Room (in which Case the Glasses will preserve them from the Dust and Flies) or for the Surtout.[1] The Cases must be knocked to Pieces very carefully after taking off the Top first and then the sides and Ends. The Manufacturers promised me that instructions for unpacking should accompany the Cases. Enclosed is his Note of the Contents of the several Cases. There are in all three Groups two Vases and twelve figures. The Vases may be used as they are or when occasion serves, the Tops may be laid aside and the Vases filled with natural flowers. When the whole Surtout is to be used for large Companies the large Group will be in the middle the two smaller ones at the two Ends—the Vases in the Spaces between the three and the figures distributed along the Edges or rather along the Sides. I shall send you the Amount by another opportunity and the other Articles I shall procure in England.

P.S.   I have directed the Charges of Transportation to be paid by Messrs Wm Constable and for to Whom you will be so kind as to replace the Amount. To clean the *Biscuit* warm water is to be used and for any things in the Corners a Brush such as is used for painting in Water Colours.

1. Sèvres figure groups were also displayed on mantels and console tables under glass domes or covers. See 1799 Palais de Bourbon inventory in Pierre Verlet, *The Eighteenth Century in France* (Rutland, Vt.: Charles E. Tuttle, 1967), pp. 268 and 279.

January 24, 1790

LC, Gouverneur Morris Papers, vol. 22 (Commercial Letters)
Gouverneur Morris (Paris) to GW

I have received your kind letter of the thirteenth of October and immediately set about procuring the Articles you there mention. . . . They are already on their Way to Havre and you will find here enclosed the Amount of the Cost (including the Packages) £ 23 & 4 # [shillings]. The transportation to Havre will cost 46 #. For the cost at the present Exchange of 27½ I charge you £ 91. Sterling. You will perhaps exclaim that I have not complied with your Directions as to Economy, but you will be of a different Opinion when you see the Articles. I could have sent you a Number of pretty Trifles for very little Cost, but the Transportation and the freight would have been more, and you must have had an annual Supply, and your Table would have been in the Style of a petite Maitresse of this City, which most assuredly is not the Style you wish. Those now sent are of a noble Simplicity, and as they have been fashionable above two thousand years, they stand a fair chance to continue so during our time. If well kept they will always be worth the cost. By the bye, you must be thankful that I did not run you to farther Expence, for I was violently tempted to send out two dozen Cups and Saucers with the needful Accompanyments for Mrs. Washington, to whom I pray you to present my Compliments with the Assurance that I am always at her Orders. 100 to 150 Guineas will procure a very handsome Set of Tea China and a very large and neat Table Set. This last by no means in the great style which is from one to two Guineas a plate, but of Plates at about 3 # each. . . .

I think it of very great importance to fix the taste of our Country properly, and I think your Example will go so very far in that respect. It is therefore my Wish that every Thing about you should be substantially good and majestically plain; made to endure. Nothing is so extravagant in the Event as those Buildings and Carriages and Furnitures Where a Taste of this Kind prevails, each Generation has to provide for itself. Whereas in the other there is a vast

Accumulation of real Wealth in the Space of half a Century. Something too much of this perhaps. . . .

March 1, 1790
W 31:15
GW to Gouverneur Morris

. . . Since my last to you . . . I have removed to a larger house (the one lately occupied by the Count de Moustier), enlarged my table, and of course my Guests; let me therefore request the favor of you to add two pieces to the number of plateaux required in the above letter, and ornaments equivalent, for it will take these *in addition* to what I before asked, to decorate the present Table. . . .

March 4, 1790
Invoice of "Save" China Bought from the C.t de Moustier, original manuscript in the Mount Vernon Ladies' Association archives.

	£	s.
2 Iceries compleat	4	12
1 Porringer & Cover	2	4
2 Sallad dishes	1	16
4 square stew dishes	3	12
4 shells	4	12
15 Round dishes [partly illegible]	10	3
4 saucers	4	10
4 butter boats	4	12
4 Confection dishes	5	4
4 mustard pots	4	10
4 sugar dishes	4	12
12 Ice plates	9	
36 Ice pots	9	
23 Pl . . . [illegible]	9	
21 Egg dishes	4	6
8 Cocottes	1	12
20 small pots	6	0
12 Chocolate cups & saucers	3	12
15 Coffee do & do	4	10
17 Tea do & do	4	19
3 Sugar dishes	3	4
2 Cream Pots	1	7
2 flower Pots	2	5
7½ doz.n plates	27	0

156. Fragment of unglazed earthenware flowerpot. found at Mount Vernon. Flowerpots are not mentioned in the cash memoranda and ledgers for Mount Vernon until April 790, when James Lownes, probably a local potter, was paid £3.6.5. for making seventy-four "Flour Pots." In September 1798, "Earthen flour pots for the Gardener" were purchased from Robert Gordon, who also supplied milk pans and stoneware mugs. Length of fragment: 6½ inches. (The Mount Vernon Ladies' Association collections)

March 8, 1790
First Administration Accounts

By Cont.gt Exp.s p.d Mons.r Le Prince for furniture and china bot. of the C.t de Moustier as per bill [New York currency] £665. 15. 6.[1]

1. Le Prince was probably a member of the French legation, but he has not been identified. He is not listed in the 1789 or 1790 New York directories. For the diplomatic career of Moustier, see *Dictionnaire Diplomatique* (Paris: Académie Diplomatique Internationale, n.d.), vol. 5, pp. 740–41.

March 20, 1790
LC 99 [translation follows French original]
Charles Henri Hector, Count d'Estaing (Paris) to GW

. . . the small token which I take the liberty to send you begging your acceptance of the Bust of M. Necker, and the engravings which accompany it. . . .

April 7, 1790
Cash Memoranda—Mount Vernon

By John Lownes p[d] him for his
Father James Lownes for making
74 Flour Pots   £3. 6. 5.

———————

April 15, 1790
W 31:38
GW (New York) to Gouverneur Morris

Since my last to you, dated March 1st. I have
been favored with your letter of the 24 of January
accompanied by the surtout of Plateaux & ca.
These came very safe, are very elegant,
much admired, and do great justice to your
taste. Accept my thanks for the attention.

Upon trial it appears that they need no addition,
the intention therefore of this letter is to counter-
act, if it should arrive in time, my request of the
first of March of two Plateaux more and ornaments equivalent thereto. . . .

———————

May 27, 1790
First Administration Accounts
By Contgt Exp[s] p[d] W[m] Constable
& Co. freight & ch'gs of the Table
Ornaments from France   £20. 4. 9.

———————

June 20, 1790
W 31:58
*Tobias Lear (New York) to Clement Biddle
(Philadelphia)*

. . . Mrs. Washington requests you to be so kind as
to inform me if any handsome blue and white
china Tea and Coffee Cups and Saucers can be
had in Philadelphia and the price per Dozn. She
does not want a sett of china but Cups and
saucers only to match some which she has at
Mount Vernon. . . .[1]

1. Biddle's replies in this series of letters to and from Tobias
Lear are not in the Washington Papers in the Library of
Congress. Clement Biddle (1740–1814), Philadelphia merchant, had been appointed marshall of the District of Pennsylvania by President Washington. He often acted as agent for the
president in matters of buying and selling furnishings and
agricultural supplies for Mount Vernon. Most of Biddle's known
papers are at the Historical Society of Pennsylvania, where a
recently acquired group awaits cataloguing.

July 7, 1790
W 31:58
*Tobias Lear (New York) to Clement Biddle
(Philadelphia)*

If the Artizan in France can recollect the form of
the surtout which you sent to me, it will be
convenient for me, notwithstanding my late
countermand, to be furnished with two more
plateaux. Those I already have are found upon
trial insufficient for my present table, and are
besides too short to receive the ornaments which
accompanied, and were designed for them without being crowded. That he may have some data
for his government I will add that the Plateaux
which have been sent me are two feet in
dimensions across way the table and eighteen
inches in the other direction from edge to edge,
where they join, English measure. . . .

———————

July 10, 1790
Cash Memoranda—Mount Vernon

	£	s.	d.
By Rogerson and Dabney for 3			
Sifters & 4 Chamber Potts[1]		12	
By 4 Basons		6	

1. On December 23, 1790, Rogerson and Dabney advertised
lime, "Country Linen," cider, and beef in the *Virginia Gazette
and Alexandria Advertiser.*

———————

July 18, 1790
W 31:70
Tobias Lear to Clement Biddle

. . . Your attention to this matter, Dear Sir, is
highly obliging and deserves our best thanks, as
well as your information respecting the China
and Muslin. Of the former Mrs. Washington
wishes to get 2 dozn. Tea Cups and Saucers and
a dozn. Coffee Cups and saucers with 3 or 4 Slop
bowles to match them; all of blue and white
China, handsome, but not of the highest price, as
they are for common use, and send them to
Mount Vernon by the first Vessel. . . .

———————

July 25, 1790
W 31:73
Tobias Lear to Clement Biddle

I have before me your favors of the 21st and 23rd

Inst. If blue and white China cups and Saucers
can be procured (as you observed in your last was
probable) and agreeably to my former letter you
will please to get three dozen of Tea cups and
Saucers and 2 dozn. of Coffee ditto with the
bowls. Should these not be found you will get the
same number of the enameld which you mentioned in your letter of the 21st. . . .

———————

August 7, 1790
Cash Memoranda—Mount Vernon

By Thomas Poultney p[d] him for 2
Burnt China Sugar dishes[1]   £0. 4. 4.

1. Poultney later sold padlocks and files to Mount Vernon.

———————

August 8, 1790
W 31:77
Tobias Lear to Clement Biddle

I have received your favor of the 5th Inst.
inclosing a bill of the China sent to Mount
Vernon. . . .[1]

1. Washington's account with Clement Biddle was kept as an
"account current" and not itemized. On November 10, 1790,
Biddle was paid £ 277/10/1 or $740 to cover the February 10–
November 10, 1790, period. See Ledger C (1787–1799), Lloyd
W. Smith Collection, Morristown National Historical Park, p. 14.

———————

September 12, 1790
LC 99
Tobias Lear (New York) to GW (Mount Vernon)

. . . and so far as relates to the furniture, Linen,
china etc under [Hyde the steward's] care, he
seems to have been very careful of it, and on a
late inspection everything appears to be in good
order, and much less china and glass destroyed
than one could expect in so large a quantity; and
the pieces of those broken are all produced[1] . . .
and we shall next pack up the Table ornaments
in the same manner in which they came. By or
before the first of October we shall be ready to
remove. . . .

1. Produced: presented as proof.

———————

September 17, 1790
W 31:116
GW (Mount Vernon) to Tobias Lear

. . . The motive for writing to you at this time, is, that upon unpacking the china ornaments which accompanied the Mirrors for the Tables; it was found (notwithstanding they were in Bran) that many of the delicate and tender parts were broken; occasioned I believe by the Bran not being put in and settled down by little at a time.[1] To press the Bran around the images (you have to remove with the Plateaux) will not answer; still, it must be so compact as to prevent friction, in moving; and this can only be done by putting each image or figure in a seperate box, with Bran by little and little, shaking and settling it by degrees, as it is added. . . .

1. Washington is referring to the original unpacking in New York in April 1790.

September 26, 1790
LC 99
Tobias Lear (New York) to GW

. . . The Table Images had been packed up some days before your letter of the 17th came to hand; but precisely in the mode which you there recommended—viz. each Image in a separate box made amply large, with bran put in and shook down (not pressed) by degrees. The small Images were put into two boxes, six in each (as they came) with bran as the others. If anything will preserve them I think it must be this mode of packing, and particular attention paid to their removal. . . .

September 27, 1790
W 31: 126
GW (Mount Vernon) to Tobias Lear

. . . How have you disposed (for safety) of the Pagoda? It is a delicate piece of stuff, and will require to be tenderly handled. . . .[1]

1. The "Pagoda" was probably not porcelain. A white nephrite pagoda with gilt wooden bells was given to the East India Marine Society by Nathaniel Ingersoll in 1801. That pagoda is now in the Peabody Museum, Salem, Massachusetts. Samuel Shaw brought a five-foot pagoda of ivory from Canton for Mrs. Josiah Quincy. See Carl L. Crossman, *The China Trade* (Princeton: The Pyne Press, 1972), fig. 157 and p. 202.

October 1, 1790
Cash Memoranda—Mount Vernon

By Col° Marsteller[1] for 1 p. doz. Queens China plates 5/77
4 Mugs & 1 Jugg 4/10

1. *Diaries*, vol. 5, p. 70. Marsteller was an Alexandria merchant who also obtained the services of a German redemptioner for Mount Vernon.

October 3, 1790
W 31: 130
GW (Mount Vernon) to Tobias Lear

. . . When you can get at the last letter, or letters of the Count de Estaing to me, I wish you would send me a transcript of what he says, or whether anything, of a Bust he has sent me of Mr. Necker, together with a number of prints of that Gentleman and the Marquis de la Fayette which are come to my hands in a package from Baltimore. . . .

October 3, 1790
LC 99
Tobias Lear (New York) to GW

. . . The Pagoda is put up with soft cotton in the same case in which Mrs. Washington received it. As I was present when it was opened and saw the manner in which it was then packed up, I have put it up in the same way, and have no doubt (without some extraordinary accident) of its getting safe to Philad for it shall be carried carefully on board the vessel. . . . The Glass Case is well provided for in another box. . . .

October 17, 1790
LC 99
Tobias Lear (Philadelphia) to GW (Mount Vernon)

. . . The want of a closet in the large dining room for the Images, save [Sèvres] China etc will be a serious inconvenience. . . .

October 24, 1790
LC 99
Tobias Lear (Philadelphia) to GW

. . . The Images for the table . . . have not received the smallest injury—they are unpacked, cleaned, and I think, look much whiter and more delicate

than they did after their first cleaning. One of the large glasses that cover the Images was cracked in unpacking; but it is mended and made as useful as ever in preserving them from the dust—I have not yet opened the Pagoda, as I do not know where you would wish to have it put. . . . We have not opened the Save [Sèvres] and Cincinnati China, as the closets in which they are to be put have been lately painted and are not yet dry; but the Common China which we have unpacked is preserved beyond expectation, not a single piece is broken. . . .

October 27, 1790
W 31: 136
GW (Mount Vernon) to Tobias Lear

. . . there is a small room adjoining the Kitchen (by the Pump) that might if it is not essential for other purposes be appropriated for the Images, Save [Sèvres] China, and other things of this sort which are not in common use. Mrs. Morris who is a notable lady in family arrangements, can give you much information in all the conveniences about the House and buildings. . . .

October 31, 1790
LC 99
Tobias Lear (Philadelphia) to GW

. . . The closets in the Steward's room, opposite to the large dining room, will be very convenient for the Save [Sèvres] and Cincinnati China, the plate and other things which are not used common. But neither those Closets, nor that adjoining the kitchen would . . . be proper for the Images. . . . It has therefore struck me that it might not be improper to let the large Images stand on the Side Boards in the Dining Room. The Glasses which cover will preserve them from the dust, and prevent delicate parts from being touched. They will likewise be an ornament to the Room. . . . The small Images can be put in the closets with the China, without any rusque in removing them. . . . I have unpacked, cleaned, and put up the Pagoda in the front drawing room. We found it perfectly safe, and cleaned it without any injury. As the side Boards which you bought of the C.te de Moustiers were found very convenient in New York, we shall put them up here, if it can be done without injuring the room or hurting the appearance. . . .

October 31, 1790
W 31:139
GW (Mount Vernon) to Tobias Lear

. . . As the Pagoda can be put up in half an hour, at any time, it may (if not already disposed of) remain unfixed until we arrive. . . .

November 7, 1790
W 31:148
GW (Mount Vernon) to Tobias Lear

. . . I approve, at least till inconvenience or danger shall appear, of the large table ornaments (images) remaining on the Side boards; and of the Pagoda's standing in the smallest drawing Room as you may have fixed it. . . .

May 20, 1791
First Administration Accounts

Cont^g Exp^s p^d for 2 doz^n Cups & Saucers—12 bowles, 24 teaspoons for Serv^{ts} $4.70[1]

1. After the move to Philadelphia, Lear kept the president's accounts in Pennsylvania pounds and United States currency (7½ shillings to the dollar).

May 25, 1791
LC 101

Richard Champion (Camden, South Carolina) to William Jackson[1]

Mr. Champion presents his Compliments to Major Jackson, and requests the favour of him to present the Letters, Book and parcel which accompanies this to the President. Mr. Champion has taken the Liberty to entreat the Honour of the President's acceptance of a Book, and a Manuscript enclosed. And he will tresspass on the Indulgence of Major Jackson to beg him to procure the President's acceptance of the Parcel. It contains two Reliefs in a very fine porcelain exquisitely wrought round with flowers. The one of Dr. Franklin. The other taken from a Relief, (a good likeness, as he was informed of the

President when young,) which Mr. Champion directed a Statuary to make. But in the likeness Mr. Champion finds himself disappointed. He therefore merely presents it as a Curiosity, made from a beautiful native Porcelain, which is to be found in America. Mr. Champion took a similar Liberty during the War, in sending these Reliefs to the President, by way of Paris, but he never knew whether they arrived safe. These were finished, the ornaments having been enamelled with Gold, which he laments is not the Case with these. But being two which he had by him, he brought them out England with him, and through forgetfulness or accident omitted it.

Mr. Champion begs Major Jackson with [illegible] the Trouble he has given him, and will do him the Honour to accept one of the C [illegible] himself, which accompanies the other. Mr. Champion meant to have [illegible] Major Jackson's Indulgence in requesting to know whether the President had a Levee, but he finds that his Stay will be short, and therefore he is too unwilling to break in upon the hour before Dinner, as the President must necessarily be [illegible] to have the Honour of being presented to him.

Wednesday 2 o'clock

1. William Jackson was one of President Washington's secretaries. He accompanied the president on his tours of New England in 1790 and the Southern states in 1791. Champion's note is not dated. It is placed at the end of 1791 in series 4 of the Washington Papers in the Library of Congress, but it was written on May 25, 1791, at two o'clock in the afternoon before the public dinner given for Washington in Camden.

Cash Memoranda—Mount Vernon
July 1, 1791

	£	s.	d.
By Korn & Wisemiller for 6 course ½ pint mugs		2	

August 12, 1791

	£	s.	d.
By Mr Geo Hunter p^d him for 4 Queens China Dishes & 1 doz^n deep Plates & 1000 10^d nails		2	7
By Mr Philip Marsteller p^d him for 2 doz Queens China Shallow plates			7
By a Box to pack up Plates & Dishes		1	4

September 20, 1791

	£	s.	d.
By Buchan & Patton p^d them for . . . [blankets, nails, etc.] . . . 4 Wash Basons	6	7	6
By Jonah Thompson for 4 Chamber Potts			6

First Administration Accounts
June 5, 1792

Cont^{gt} Exp^s for mending a Tureen $ .72

June 11, 1792

Cont^{gt} Exp^s p^d for mending China dishes $ .72

LC 115
Ledger B
July 16, 1792

By Geo. Hunter p^d him for Chamber pots		£0.	9.
By Matthew Robinson for Lemons 8/ and Earthenware 2/			

August 14, 1792

By Mathew Robinson p^d him for 4 water juggs[1]		£0.	9.

September 3, 1792

By Mat.^{w} Robinson p^d him for . . . [36 gallons rum] . . . & ten half-pint mugs	£8.	19.	4

September 11, 1792

By M^w Robinson p^d him for china   £0. 3. 7½.

1. Robinson, Sanderson and Company advertised madeira, sherry, and ''Queen's and Stone Ware in Crates'' at their warehouse on Prince Street, in the November 19, 1789, *Virginia Gazette and Alexandria Advertiser.*

First Administration Accounts
November 10, 1792

Cont^{gt} Exp^s p^d Gallagher[1] for Glass & China $34.66

December 31, 1792

Cont^{gt} Exp^s p^d J^s Gallagher for glass &c $27.91

1. James Gallagher, china and glass merchant, 5 South Second Street (1793, 1796, and 1797 Philadelphia directories). He advertised china and queensware in the *Pennsylvania Packet*

as early as November 20, 1781. See Alfred Coxe Prime, *The Arts and Crafts in Philadelphia, Maryland and South Carolina, 1786–1800* (The Walpole Society, 1932), vol. 1, p. 131. James Gallagher and Sons continued in business into the nineteenth century. Invoice for a set of china from James Gallagher and Sons to Mrs. Hall, 1803. Historical Society of Pennsylvania, Manuscript Department.

May 24, 1793

LC 103

William Frisbie Fitzhugh (Baltimore) to GW[1]

. . . My Father desires me to present you his most respectful & affectionate wishes—He begs your acceptance of a China Bowl which may possibly be novel from its size & antiquity—it being much older than himself—it has been very carefully packed up & he hopes it will reach you safe. . . .

1. The son wrote the letter because the father was blind.

June 16, 1793

W 32:504

GW (Philadelphia) to William Frisbie Fitzhugh

The China Bowl with which your good father was so obliging as to present me came safe and I beg you to assure him that I shall esteem it more as a memento of his friendship than for its antiquity or size. . . .

June 18, 1793

Second Administration Accounts

contingency exp.[s] p.[d] I. Bringhurst[1] for a sett of China $211.00

1. John Bringhurst, fancy-goods merchant, 12 South Third Street, is listed in James Hardie's 1793 Philadelphia Directory, but not in later directories. He was presumably not the John Bringhurst who made carriages in Philadelphia and Germantown. Washington's Ledger B, p. 198, listed £ 22/4/9 to "Mr. Bringhurst's Acct" on May 18, 1784, when Washington was in Philadelphia for the first general meeting of the Society of the Cincinnati. On June 30, 1792, Mrs. Washington bought "Sund[s]" (sundries) from Bringhurst and on July 3, 1792, she bought "2 Breast pins & 2 pearl knitting Shuttle" from him. *See First Administration Accounts* in Decatur, pp. 276 and 278.

July 3, 1793

Reel 115, Ledger B

By p.[d] M.[w] Robinson for 27
    gallons of rum & 2 bowls   £4. 2.

August 31, 1793

Second Administration Accounts

contingency exp.[s] p.[d] B. Gallagher
    for china & glass   335.50

September 9, 1793

LC 115, Ledger B

By p[d] for 2 doz plates & ½ doz.
    pint bowles   £0. 10. 6

Second Administration Accounts

December 30, 1793

House Exp.[s] p.[d] for 3 sets, tea china
    & 6 chocolate cups $102.00

March 29, 1794

Contg.[s] Exp.[s] p.[d] for a p[r] gloves for

Kennedy to wear when putting on
    table ornaments   .50

September 29, 1794

contingency exp.[s] p.[d] Gallagher in full
    for China   158.15

July 14, 1795

Ledger C, p. 5

(contra Tobias Lear)

By Cash p[d] for 2 stone pitchers 6/ and
    6 tumblers 6/ (Va.)   £ 2

Second Administration Accounts

December 21, 1795

House expence p.[d] J[s] Gallagher for
    Glass & China ware in full $13.42

PETER BENSON, auctioneer.

Just Imported in the ship Pigou,

Richard Dale, master, from Canton, and for sale
ARCHIBALD McCALL;
No. 187, south Second street,

A general assortment of china
Imperial tea in boxes
Young hyson do. in chests and boxes
Hyson skin and souchong do.
Black and coloured sattins
Black and coloured lutestrings
Bogglampores
Short and long white and yellow nankeens
Black and coloured sewing silks
Hair ribbon, &c. &c.   March 14

Coffee at auction.

On Thursday the 16th instant, at 10 o'clock in

157. Archibald McCall (1727–1799), a prominent merchant in Philadelphia's China trade, sold china worth $92.96 to the presidential household on April 1, 1796. A year later, on March 14, 1797, he advertised a new shipment of merchandise in *Claypoole's American Daily Advertiser.* (The Historical Society of Pennsylvania)

	£	s.	d.

February 15, 1796
House expence P.[d] by F.K.[1] 2 pitchers   13
4 Chamb pots   6

February 19, 1796
contingency expense p.[d] Pasquier & C[o]
   for China p.[r] bill p.[r] order of Mrs. W[2] $50.00

March 28, 1796
contingency exp.[s] p.[d] by F.K.
   for . . . Earthen Cream pans 12/
   1 Set of blue Mugs 22/6 & d[o] of
   Dishes for M[rs] Washington 36/   £7. 6. 4.
       $19.51

April 1, 1796
p.[d] Arch[d.] McCall for China &c p.[r] bill[3] $92.96

June 6, 1796
p.[d] for 2 setts china pint mugs   5.00

November 21, 1796
p.[d] James Gallagher for China p bill   47.89

February 6, 1797
contingency exp p.[d] Pasquier & C.[o] for
   table ornaments & c per bill   58.00

February 13, 1797
contingency exp.[s] p.[d] John Inskeep
   for a sett of china[4]   22.33

March 6, 1797
p.[d] J[s] Gallagher for China & Glass to
   send to Virg[a]   58.70

March 7, 1797
contingency expense, p.[d] Decamps &
   C.[o] for 2 table ornaments & packing[5]   25.00

March 13, 1797
contingency expense, p.[d] R. Lindsay for
   packing China etc.   15.00

1. F.K.: Frederick Kitt, the president's steward at 190 High Street. His accounts were kept in Pennsylvania currency.
2. Pasquier and Company, china merchants, 91 South Second Street, Stafford's 1797 *Philadelphia Directory*.
3. Archibald McCall (1727–1799), merchant, 35 Spruce Street (home), 187 South Second Street. 1793, 1796, and 1797 Philadelphia directories. McCall was prominent in Philadelphia's East India trade. His son's ledger book of 1798–1803 at the Historical Society of Pennsylvania reveals that the firm also did business in Germany and England. McCall was associated with Tench Coxe and Robert Hazlehurst and Company. See also Abraham Ritter, *Philadelphia and Her Merchants* (Philadelphia, 1860), p. 191, and *The Pennsylvania Magazine of History and Biography* 6 (1882): 207.

4. John Inskeep (1757–1834), china merchant, 31 South Second Street, 1796 and 1797 Philadelphia directories. Before opening his china shop in 1794, Inskeep kept a tavern at the Sign of the Jolly Bacchus on Arch Street. In 1800, he was elected mayor of Philadelphia. *The Pennsylvania Magazine of History and Biography* 46 (1922): 360–61 and 28 (1904): 129–35.
5. Decamps and Company, 95 North Third Street, 1796 *Philadelphia Directory*. *Pennsylvania Packet*, June 25, 1796: "Mrs. Decamps from Paris, informs the public, that she has just opened her store, north Third Street, No. 95, where she engraves . . . in the most elegant, fashionable, neat and new style—all sorts of glasses." Decamps later advertised at "the China-store, No. 91, South second-street," *Aurora*, April 4, 1800. She evidently joined or replaced the Pasquier firm at that address.

February or March 1797
LC 110
List of Articles, Public and Private, 1797.
Household furniture

. . . Nothing herein has been said relatively to the Table Linnen, Sheeting, China and Glass-ware which was furnished at the expence of the United States; because they have been worn out, broken, stolen and replaced (at private expence) over and over again. . . .[1]

1. President-elect John Adams reiterated Washington's statement. On February 4, 1797, he wrote to Mrs. Adams, ". . . all the glasses, ornaments, kitchen furniture, the best china, settees, plateaus, &c., all to purchase, all the china, delph or wedgwood, glass and crockery of every sort to purchase. . . ." Charles F. Adams, ed., *Letters of John Adams to His Wife* (Boston: Little and Brown, 1841), vol. 2, p. 235. Adams obviously feared the cost of the precedents set by Washington in furnishings and carriages.

February or March 1797
Washington's Manuscript Account of Furnishings for the Official Residences of the President in New York and Philadelphia. Henry Francis du Pont Winterthur Museum, Joseph Downs Manuscript Collection.

Sundries—bo[t] on account of George Washington
May 27, 1790, Wm Constable & Co
   freight & Charges Table ornaments
   &c[a] from France   £20. 4. 9
June 3, 1790, Paid duties on Table
   Ornaments from France   £17. 1. 4.
June 18, 1793, I. Bringhurst a sett
   of China $211.
February 19, 1796, Pasquier—
   China pr Bill   50.
April 1, 1796, Arch[d] McCall—
   China &c[a]   92.96

Drawn from the Accts
March 8, 1790, C[te] de Moutier—
   Stoves China &c, &c, &c   £665. 16. 6.
June 3, 1791, Porcelaine &c[a]
   Table first cost   2384 livres
June 18, 1793, Jn[o] Bringhurst—
   china— $211.
Feb 19, 1796, Pasquier—China—   50.
April 1, 1796, Arch[d] McCall D[o]   92.96

March 17, 1797
LC 110
Invoice, furnishings sent to Mount Vernon on the sloop Salem *from Philadelphia [enclosed with March 20 letter from Tobias Lear].*

Ninety-seven boxes, fourteen trunks, forty-three Casks; thirteen packages; three hampers . . . [long list of other individual items such as venetian blinds, a sopha, two plate baskets, a carpet, and a bidet.]

August 14, 1797
W 36:9
GW (Mount Vernon) to James McHenry[1] (Philadelphia)

. . . my Table ornaments and the Coolers [are] in your possession . . . the . . . articles I pray you to have carefully packed (the Porcelain in fine Saw dust) and sent to Colo. Biddle. . . .

1. James McHenry was secretary of war under Washington.

August 14, 1797
W 36:10
GW to Clement Biddle (Philadelphia)

. . . When I left Philadelphia, Mr. Lear and Mr. Dandridge who remained, were directed to dispose of my Household furniture (such parts I mean as were not packed for a removal to this place) but from some misapprehension the Ornaments of my dining Table, and some Plated bottle Coolers, were not disposed of as were expected; but left in the care of Mr. McHenry subject to future orders, when they came away.

   I have now to request that you will receive these from him, and if you can, to dispose of them . . . on the best terms you can. it is not probable that any one, unless the Presidt. or any of the foreign Ministers should be so disposed, would take the *whole* of course to *retail* them, would be the most likely means of getting them off.

The articles you will receive, if I mistake not, will consist of two four bottle Coolers. A Platteau in nine pieces.[1] three large groupes with glasses over them, two vases, and twelve small single figures, of Porcelain.

The Invoice of the Platteau I am unable, at present, to come at; but that of the figures is enclosed, . . .

. . . the other things I am certain will fall much below (the original cost) as they have not only been used, but the Porcelain in some of its nicest parts, is injured. Although I have not been able to find the cost of the Platteau I have a memorandum which informs me that they stand me in 486 *Livres in Paris* exclusive of all the subsequent charges of transportation from thence to Havre, freight Insurance duty &ca &ca. . . .

1. Gouverneur Morris had sent two additional *plateaux* for the *surtout* in 1791.

August 23, 1797
W 36:17
GW to Clement Biddle

. . . Your motive for delaying the sale of my Table furniture is not only good as it respects the yellow fever but if you think any advantage would result from the measure it might be delayed until the assembling of Congress in Philadelphia some of the members might incline to become purchasers if the articles are retailed. . . .

January 29, 1798
W 36:146
GW to Clement Biddle

. . . If the Plateaux are not sold, nor a probability of getting nearly what they cost, say currency for Sterling, I request that they may be carefully packed up and sent to me, together with the two smallest of the large groups of Porcelain, and the twelve single images (Arts and Sciences) with which my Table, on Public days, was ornamented. The large group (Apollo instructing the Shepherds) and the two Vases, may be sold for what

ever they will fetch. Great care, by a skilful hand, must be used in packing the Porclain, or all the delicate and finer parts will be broken off. . . .

February 12, 1798
Ledger G[1]
(contra Robert Gordon)

By One Dozen earthen Mugs &
  one d° potts [also fine shoes
  for Frank, etc.][2]   £0. 14. 9.

1. Account book for Washington's farms, including the "Mansion" or Mount Vernon.
2. *Diaries*, vol. 6, p. 282: "February 12, 1798. Went with the family to a Ball in Alexa. . . ."

March 19, 1798
W 36:188
GW to Clement Biddle

. . . By the first regular Packett from Phila—I shall expect to receive the Groceries, the Table Ornaments. and the Encyclopedia. . . .

April 10, 1798
Ledger C, p. 19
(contra Clement Biddle)

for Packing & Postage of China Images $4.00

Metchie J.E. Budka, ed., Under Their Vine and Fig Tree (journal of Julian Ursyn Niemcewicz), vol. 14 in the Collections of the New Jersey Historical Society (Elizabeth, N.J.: Grossman Publishing Company, 1965).

June 9, 1798
Mrs. Washington made me a gift of a china cup with her monogram and the names of the states of the United States. . . .

June 13, 1798
On our return to Mount Vernon [from fishing] we found a notable and unexpected company from Alexandria. The table in the great hall was set out with a Sèvres porcelain service with places for 20. . . .

June 14, 1798
LC 112
Niemcewicz (City of Washington) to GW

. . . With my most grateful acknowledgements to Mistress Washington . . . for the present of a cup marked with her initials, which, when sipping my coffee will daily remind me of Mount Vernon. . . .

June 17, 1798
W 36:294
GW to Clement Biddle

. . . if after trying the Table Ornaments awhile longer, at a reduced price, they will not sell, I must give some further order respecting them. . . .[1]

1 Table Ornaments: the large, central group and two vases.

Ledger G
(contra Robert Gordon)
June 22, 1798

	£	s.	d.
By 1 ½ Dozen Milk pans		16	

August 17, 1798
By 12 Milk pans		12	

September 28, 1798
8 Stone Muggs for Mrs Washington		6	
Earthen flour pots for the Gardener	1	18	6

K. W. G. Vail, ed., "A Dinner at Mount Vernon from the Unpublished Journal of Joshua Brooks (1773–1859)," The New-York Historical Society Quarterly 31 (1947): 80.

February 4, 1799
. . . The sitting parlor, a small back room with the chimney in the corner, contains several views. Over the fireplace is a miniature marble likeness of G. Washington, one of Dr. Franklin and other pieces, three or four of which were landscapes painted by Miss Custis . . . The drawing room . . . is elegantly furnished . . . on the mantle piece marble jars and blue china ones in which were placed some blue and red bachelor's buttons. . . .[1]

1. The Washington and Franklin portraits were the biscuit-porcelain plaques presented by Richard Champion. The blue

china jars were the Worcester vases from Samuel Vaughan. The marble jars may have been the vases from the set of biscuit-porcelain ornaments for the president's *surtout*. The central group and vases had not been sold by June 17, 1798, and their fate is unknown.

1799–1800
Inventory of the Contents of Mount Vernon made after the death of General Washington; manuscript in the Mount Vernon Ladies' Association archives.[1]

IN THE NEW ROOM
2 Side Boards on each of wch is an	
Image & China flower pot[2]	$160.
5 China Jarrs[3]	100.
All the Images[4]	100.

IN THE LITTLE PARLOR
1 Likeness of General Washington in an	
oval frame[5]	4.
1 do. Dr. Franklin	4.
1 do. Lafayette	4.

IN THE DINING ROOM
1 Water Pitcher	.50

IN THE FRONT PARLOUR
5 China flowers pots	5.

IN THE PASSAGE
4 Images over the door[6]	20.

IN THE FIRST ROOM ON THE SECOND FLOOR
Wash bason & Pitcher	1.

IN THE SECOND ROOM
Wash bason & Pitcher	1.

IN THE THIRD ROOM
1 washstand, bason & bottle	4.

IN THE FOURTH ROOM
1 Wash bason & Pitcher	1.50

Glass & China in the China closet up	
Stairs & that in the Cellar	850.

IN M^{RS} W^{NS} OLD ROOM IN THE CLOSET
Wash bason	.50

LUMBER ROOMS
2 Sets Platteaux	100.

IN THE CLOSET UNDER FRANKS DIRECTION[7]
24 China Dishes	15.
2 ″ butter boats	.25
20 ″ deep plates	3.
48 ″ Shallow do	8.
2 ″ Sallad dishes	.50
8 China Pickle Plates	.50
10 ″ Custard Cups	1.
48 Saucers	
25 Cups	3.
1 Tea Pot	.50
1 Egyptian China do	.50
6 China Mugs	1.50
2 do Soup dishes[8]	3.
5 Tart Moulds	.05

IN THE CELLAR
20 Pickle Pots	9.50
8 Soap Jarrs	25.
7 Pickle Pots [Entire line was later	
crossed out]	3.50

UP THE KITCHEN STAIRS
2 Clay Milk pans	.10

1. The inventory manuscript was taken from Fairfax County Courthouse during the Civil War. Eventually it was given to the Mount Vernon Ladies' Association, where it is now in the manuscript collection.
2. Image: the two large Angoulême biscuit groups intended for the ends of the *plateaux*; flower pot: there were "2 flower pots" with Moustier's white-and-gold service. See text p. 126. The vases which had come from Paris with the biscuit figures were supposed to have been sold in Philadelphia with the large central figure group of "Apollo Instructing the Shepherds."
3. 5 China Jarrs: three were the Worcester vases which Vaughan had sent to adorn the mantel in the New Room. See text, p. 97. The other two may have been the jars which Judge Bushrod Washington bought at the sale of Martha Washington's personal property in 1802. Bushrod Washington's grand-nephew, John Augustine Washington III, told Benson Lossing in 1858 ("Mount Vernon as it is," p. 451) that the two covered jars then on the mantel "were tenants of the same places when Washington received his guests in that spacious hall." See also text, p. 163. White "marble" (biscuit-porcelain) jars were seen on the mantel with the Worcester vases in 1799.
4. All the Images: probably the twelve Angoulême single figures, and at least three other sets of biscuit figures. See text, page 118.
5. After the presidency, Washington was again called "General." The "Likenesses" of Washington, Franklin, and Lafayette are thought to have been the mezzotints by C.W. Peale, not the two Bristol porcelain plaques (portraying Washington and Franklin) given to the president in 1791 by Richard Champion and noted in the Little Parlor in 1799 by Joshua Brookes. The plaques may have been removed by the time of the inventory or they may have been included in another entry: "6 others [likenesses] of different paintg . . . $12."
6. Possibly not ceramic.
7. Steward or butler at Mount Vernon.
8. Soup dishes: tureens.

September 22, 1800
Last Will and Testament of Martha Washington. The Mount Vernon Ladies' Association archives, reprinted in Benson J. Lossing, George Washington's Mount Vernon or Mount Vernon and Its Associations *(Alexandria, Va.: The Fairfax Press, 1977), pp. 420–25.*

I give and bequeath to my grandson, George Washington Parke Custis . . . the sett of Cincinnati tea and table China, the bowl that has a ship in it, the fine old China jars which usually stand on the chimney-piece in the new room . . . also, the set of tea china that was given me by Mr. Van Braam, every piece having M.W. on it. . . . I give and bequeath to my grand-daughter, Eleanor Parke Lewis . . . all the blue and white china in common use. . . .

May 24, 1802
Inventory of Property that belonged to Mrs Martha Washington Taken the 24.th of May and Eleventh of July 1802. *G. Freeland Peter Collection, The Mount Vernon Ladies' Association.*[1]

LARGE ROOM
3 China Jarrs	$20.

FRONT PARLOUR
5 China Jarrs	[no value]
2 do Images	4.

DINING ROOM
1 Jugg[2]	1.

STORE ROOM IN THE GARROT
1 Composition Image	1.
2 Earthen Jars	.50
1 Stone pot w^t Raisins	.75

SWEET MEAT CLOSSET
28 blue glass bowls	7.
9 Tumblers	2.
Box empty bottles	2.
6 sweet meat Plates	3.
1 glass Bowl	4.
10 d.^o Bowls	8.
3 do. dishes	6.
1 large Gobblet w.^t Cover	6.
3 doz Jelly Glasses	5.

8 China Bowls	44.
1 Sett green & White China (Tea)[3]	30.
1 sett G.W. Do.[4]	30.
1 sett Common Red & White D.°[5]	8.
3 blue & White flour Potts	3.
1 set Coloured Images[6]	9.
Red./blue & White Flower Potts[7]	
1 Blue & white Jug & Bason	1.50
2 " " Pitchers[8]	1.
3 large waiters	1.
1 China flour bottle[9]	.12
5 blue & White Jarrs[10]	8.
5 Cornicopias[11]	1.25
1 Water Pitcher	.75
1 Tea Kettle	1.
2 Knife Cases w.t Knives & forks	20.

HOUSE KEEPER'S CLOSSET

2 Water pitchers	1.50
2 Earthen Potts with covers	1.
4 Jelly Moulds[12]	.75
Table orniments [*sic*]	3.
1 China Bowl	2.

COMMON CELLAR

2 plate Baskets[13]	2.

SOAP CELLAR

8 Soap Jarrs[14]	16.
12 Stone Pots	10.

SERVANTS HALL

2 Jugs	1.78

LARGE ROOM, NEW APPRAISEMENT

2 Images & glasses[15]	8.00

1. There are two manuscripts, the earlier one a first draft, the later a copy with many deletions. The entries above are from the first draft unless noted. See The Mount Vernon Ladies' Association, *Annual Report*, 1956, p. 23.
2. Listed as "Water Jugg" on July revision.
3. Not identified. See text, p. 171.
4. The Niderviller tea and coffee service given to the Washingtons by Custine. See text, p. 72.
5. Not identified. See text, p. 171.
6. Not identified. The colored figures of 1759 (text, p. 49) were supposedly given to Tobias Lear's niece years before the date of the first inventory of 1802.
7. Crossed off on May 24, 1802, inventory. No value given.
8. Thomas Peter bought "3 Jugs and Bason" for $3 at the estate sale on July 20, 1802.
9. See text, p. 171.
10 The jars appear with "2 Cream potts" valued at .25 on the later list.
11 Cornicopias: wall-pockets or vases for flowers. Probably creamware.
12 Jelly Moulds: creamware molds for gelatin desserts or calves' foot jelly. They were either hollow vessels or wedges, cores, or pyramids to which the transparent jelly adhered. Mrs. Washington's jelly molds seem not to have survived.
13 Plate Baskets: hampers used for transporting and storing china. See text, p. 51.
14. Soap Jars: see text, p. 167.
15. Probably reappraised for the sale on July 20. The Angoulême figure groups came from Paris with glass comes. See text, p. 12. Since only two were appraised in 1802, it seems likely that the central group of "Apollo Instructing the Shepherds" was sold in Philadelphia in 1798. See text, p. 62.

July 20, 1802

Account of Sales of the Personal Estate of Martha Washington (not specially devised) late of Mount Vernon deceased—as rendered to me by Thomas Peter the Executor[1]

2 China Jars[2]	Judge Washington	$41.00
3 Images[3]	ditto	16.00
Bust of Washington	ditto	
" " Paul Jones	ditto	
" " Neckar[4]	ditto	80.00
3 Flower pots	Thos Digges	1.00
1 Water Jug	ditto	1.00
2 Cases Knives and forks[5]	Francois Roger	20.00
3 White Jars	ditto	.25
1 lot stone pots	ditto	.75
1/3 set china[6]	E.P. Law	12.67
1/3 set china	Lawrence Lewis	12.67
3 Soap Jars[7]	ditto	6.00
2 cases knives & forks	G.W.P. Custis	26.00
3 Jugs and Bason[8]	Thomas Peter	3.00
Bowls glass and Waiter	"	33.00
1/3 Set China	"	12.67
4 Cracked Bowls	"	2.00

1. There were two sales after Mrs. Washington's death. The first was among the heirs and the second, also attended by the heirs, was the public sale on July 20, about which one disgruntled buyer noted that "all the furniture worth moving" had been sold earlier. See The Mount Vernon Ladies' Association, *Annual Report*, 1959, pp. 21–27. The above excerpts are from the public sale account.
2. Probably the jars seen by Lossing on the Vaughan mantel in the New Room in 1858. See text, p. 174.
3. Possibly three of the "4 Images over the door" of the Passage appraised at $5 per piece in 1800. See Appendix, p. 220.
4. See text, p. 138.
5. Included because of the remote possibility that these were the china-handle knives and forks ordered in 1762. See text, p. 51. Under the terms of Mrs. Washington's will, George Washington Parke Custis received "all the silver plate of every kind."
6. Probably the white-and-gold Sèvres. See text, p. 174. The relatively low value of $38 for the complete set is curious.
7. See text, p. 167.
8. See Appendix, p. 221.

BIBLIOGRAPHY

Acomb, Evelyn M., ed. *The Revolutionary Journal of Baron von Closen*. Chapel Hill: University of North Carolina Press, 1958.

Adams, Charles Francis, ed. *Letters of John Adams to His Wife*. Boston: Little and Brown, 1841.

Alberts, Robert C. *The Golden Voyage*. Boston: Houghton Mifflin, 1969.

Alciatus, Andreas. *Emblematum Libellus*. Darmstadt: Wissenschaftliche Buchgesellschaft, 1967. Reprint of 1552 ed.

"An Account of a Visit made to Washington at Mount Vernon, by an English Gentleman, in 1785. From the Diary of John Hunter." *The Pennsylvania Magazine of History and Biography* 17 (1893): 76–81.

Armes, Ethel, ed. *Nancy Shippen, Her Journal Book*. New York: Benjamin Blom, 1968.

Armstrong, William. "Some New Washington Relics from the Collection of Mrs. B.W. Kennon." *Century Magazine* 18 (1890): 14–22.

Bailey, Robert. *The Prospect of Philadelphia*. Philadelphia: 1795.

Baker, Abby Gunn. "The China of the Presidents." *Munsey's Magazine* 30 (1903): 321–29.

Baker, William Spohn. *Washington After the Revolution*. Philadelphia: J. B. Lippincott, 1898.

Balch, Thomas, ed. *The Journal of Claude Blanchard, 1780–1783*. Albany, N.Y.: J. Munsell, 1876.

Barber, Edwin Atlee. *Salt-glazed Stoneware*. Philadelphia: Pennsylvania Museum, 1907.

Barnsley, Edward R. "China's Retreat." Paper read before the Bucks County Historical Society, May 6, 1933.

Barrett, Franklin A. *Worcester Porcelain*. London: Faber and Faber, 1966.

Bellaigue, Geoffrey de. "A Diplomatic Gift." *Connoisseur* 195 (1977): 99.

Belote, Theodore T. "Descriptive Catalogue of the Washington Relics in the United States National Museum." *Proceedings of the United States National Museum* 49. Washington, D.C.: U.S. Government Printing Office, 1915.

Berling, K. *Meissen China*. New York: Dover, 1962. Reprint of 1910 ed.

Beurdeley, Michel. *Chinese Trade Porcelain*. Rutland, Vt.: Charles E. Tuttle, 1962.

Bigelow, John, ed. *The Works of Benjamin Franklin*. New York: G.P. Putnam's Sons, 1888.

Birch, Thomas, auctioneer. *An Extraordinary Collection of Washington's Letters, Washington Relics, Revolutionary Documents . . .* Catalogue no. 677. Philadelphia: December 15 and 16, 1891.

————. *Valuable and Extraordinary Collection of the Effects of General George Washington*. Catalogue no. 657. Philadelphia: December 10, 11, and 12, 1890.

Birch, W. *The Country Seats of the United States of North America*. Bristol, Pa.: 1808.

Bixby, W.K. *Inventory of the Contents of Mount Vernon, 1801*. Privately printed from the manuscript in the collection of W.K. Bixby of Saint Louis. Cambridge, Mass.: University Press, 1909.

Blacker, J. F. *The ABC of English Salt-glazed Stoneware*. London: S. Paul and Company, 1922.

Bonsal, Stephen. *When the French Were Here*. New York:

Kennikat Press, 1968.

Bourgeois, Emile, and Lechevallier-Chevignard, Georges. *Le Biscuit de Sèvres*. Paris: Manufacture Nationale de Sèvres, n.d. [ca. 1890].

Boyd, Julian, ed. *The Papers of Thomas Jefferson*. Vol. 18. Princeton: Princeton University Press, 1971.

Brears, Peter C.D. *The English Country Pottery, Its History and Techniques*. Newton Abbot, England: David and Charles, 1971.

Breton, Arthur J., ed. *A Guide to the Manuscript Collection of The New-York Historical Society*. Westport, Conn.: Greenwood Press, 1972.

Brissot de Warville, Jean-Pierre. *New Travels in the United States of America*. Edited by Durand Echeverria. Cambridge, Mass.: Harvard University Press, 1964. Reprint of 1792 ed.

Bristol Porcelain Bicentenary Exhibition. Bristol, England: City Art Gallery, 1970.

Brunet, Marcelle, and Préaud, Tamara. *Sèvres*. Fribourg: Office du Livre, 1978.

Budka, Metchie J.E., ed. *Under Their Vine and Fig Tree: Travels Through America in 1797–1799, 1805* (journal of Julian Ursyn Niemcewicz). Volume 14 in the Collections of the New Jersey Historical Society. Elizabeth, N.J.: Grossman Publishing Company, 1965.

Buhler, Kathryn C. *Mount Vernon Silver*. Mount Vernon, Va.: The Mount Vernon Ladies' Association of the Union, 1957.

Burnett, Edmund Cody. *Letters of Members of the Continental Congress*. Washington, D.C.: Carnegie Institution, 1934.

Camerarius, Joachim. *Symbolarum ac Emblematum Ethico-Politicorum Centuriae Quatuor*. Mainz: Ludwig Bourgeat, 1702.

The Campbell Museum. *Selections from the Campbell Museum Collection*. Camden, N.J.: 1978.

Carpenter, Charles H., Jr. "The Chinese Collection of

A.E. van Braam Houckgeest." *Antiques* 105 (1974): 338–47.

Chastellux, Marquis de. *Travels in North America in the Years 1780, 1781 and 1782*. 2 vols. Edited by Howard D. Rice. Chapel Hill: University of North Carolina Press, 1963. Published for the Institute of Early American History and Culture at Williamsburg, Va.

Chavagnac Comte X. de, and Grollier, Mis de. *Histoire des Manufactures Françaises de Porcelaine*. Paris: A. Picard, 1906.

Chinard, Gilbert, ed. *George Washington As The French Knew Him. A Collection of Texts*. Princeton: Princeton University Press, 1940.

"China's Retreat." *Bucks County Life* 3 (September 1962): 16–17.

Colonial Williamsburg Today. Report of the Colonial Williamsburg Foundation, 1978.

Les Combattants Français de la Guerre Américaine, Listes établies d'après les documents . . . aux Archives Nationales et aux Archives du Ministère de la Guerre. Baltimore: Genealogical Publishing Company, 1969. Reprint of 1905 ed.

Constable, William, papers. *See* New York.

Conway, Moncure Daniel. *Barons of the Potomack and the Rappahannock*. New York: The Grolier Club, 1892.

Cooper, John K.D. "Bristol Hard-Paste Porcelain." *Antiques* 101 (1972): 685–86.

Cushion, John P. *Pottery and Porcelain Tablewares*. New York: William Morrow and Company, 1976.

Custis family papers. *See* Richmond.

Custis, George Washington Parke. *Recollections and Private Memoirs of Washington*. Philadelphia: J.W. Bradley, 1861.

Cutler, William Parker, ed. *Life, Journals, and Correspondence of Rev. Manasseh Cutler, L.L.D. by His Grandchildren*. Cincinnati: R. Clark and Company, 1888.

Dauterman, Carl Christian. *Sèvres*. New York: Walker and Company, 1969.

Davenport, Beatrix Cary, ed. *A Diary of the French Revolution, 1789–1793*. Boston: Houghton Mifflin, 1939.

Davis, Richard Beale. *William Fitzhugh and his Chesapeake World, 1676–1701*. Chapel Hill: University of North Carolina Press, 1963.

Decatur, Stephen, Jr. "A Gift from Washington." *Antiques* 32 (1937): 67.

———. *Private Affairs of George Washington from the Records and Accounts of Tobias Lear*. Boston: Houghton Mifflin, 1933.

Detweiler, Susan Gray. "French Porcelain on Federal Tables." *American Ceramic Circle Bulletin*, no. 3, in press.

Dorman, Charles G. "Captain Dale at Canton." *University Hospital Antiques Show*. Catalogue. Philadelphia: 1972.

Ducret, S. *Keramik und Graphik des 18. Jahrhunderts (Vorlagen für Maler und Modelleure)*. Braunschweig: Klinkhardt und Biermann, 1956.

Dunshee, K.H. *As You Pass By*. New York: Hastings House, n.d.

Earle, Alice Morse. *China Collecting in America*. New York: Empire State Book Company, 1892.

Eberlein, Harold Donaldson. "190 High Street." *Transactions of the American Philosophical Society* 43 (1953): 161–77.

Elliot, Wallace. "Bristol Biscuit Plaques." *The English Ceramic Circle Transactions* 1, no. 1 (1933): 23–29.

Fanelli, Doris D. "Furnishings Plan: Deshler–Morris House, Independence National Historical Park." Mimeographed report. Philadelphia: Independence National Historical Park, 1976.

Farley, John. *The London Art of Cookery and Housekeeper's Complete Assistant*. 3d ed. London: J. Scatcherd and J. Whitaker, 1785.

Feller, John Quentin. "China Trade Porcelain Decorated with the Emblem of the Society of the Cincinnati." *Antiques* 118 (1980): 760–68.

The Final Sale of the Relics of General Washington Owned by Lawrence Washington, Esq., Bushrod C. Washington, Esq., and Thomas B. Washington, Esq. Catalogue. Philadelphia: Thomas Birch's Sons, Auctioneers, 1891.

Fisher, Stanley W. *Worcester Porcelain*. London: Ward Lock and Company, n.d.

"The Fitzhugh Family." *The Virginia Magazine of History and Biography* 8 (January 1900): 91–92.

Fitzpatrick, John C., ed. *The Last Will and Testament of George Washington and Schedule of His Property to Which is Appended the Last Will and Testament of Martha Washington*. Mount Vernon, Va.: The Mount Vernon Ladies' Association, 1960.

———. *The Writings of George Washington from the Original Manuscript Sources 1745–1799*. 37 vols. Washington, D.C.: U. S. Government Printing Office, 1931–1944.

Fleming, John, and Honour, Hugh. *Dictionary of the Decorative Arts*. New York: Harper and Row, 1977.

Ford, Worthington Chauncey, ed. *Inventory of the Contents of Mount Vernon 1810*. Privately printed, 1909.

Franks, David, ed. *The New York Directory*. New York: Shephard Kollock, 1786.

Freeman, Douglas Southall. *George Washington. A Biography*. 6 vols. New York: Charles Scribner's Sons, 1948.

The French Family Cook. London: J. Bell, 1793.

Freneau, Philip. *Poems Written Between the Years 1768 and 1794*. Monmouth, N.J.: printed by the author, 1795.

"From the Collection of Edmund Law Rogers, Esq." *Century Magazine* 18 (May 1890): 10–13.

Gauthier, Serge. *Les Porcelainiers du XVIIIᵉ Siècle Français*. Paris: Hachette, 1964.

Glasse, Hannah. *The Art of Cookery*. 6th ed. London: T. Longman, 1796.

Godden, Geoffrey A. *Caughley and Worcester Porcelain*. New York: Praeger, 1969.

———. *An Illustrated Encyclopedia of British Pottery and Porcelain*. New York: Bonanza Books, 1965.

————. *Oriental Export Market Porcelain and Its Influence on European Wares*. New York: Granada, 1979.

Goldstein, Jonathon. *Philadelphia and the China Trade, 1682–1846*. University Park: The Pennsylvania State University Press, 1978.

Gottesman, Rita Susswein, ed. *The Arts and Crafts in New York*. New York: The New-York Historical Society, 1954.

Gottschalk, Louis, and Bill, Shirley A., eds. *The Letters of Lafayette to Washington, 1777–1799*. Philadelphia: Memoirs of the American Philosophical Society, vol. 115, 1976. Originally published in 1944.

Grimod de la Reynière, Alexandre Balthazar Laurent. *Almanach des Gourmands*. Paris: Libraire Milsson, 1805.

Griswold, Rufus Wilmot. *The Republican Court*. New York: D. Appleton, 1867.

Gruber, Alain-Charles. "Les Décors de Table Éphémères aux XVIIᵉ et XVIIIᵉ Siècles." *Gazette des Beaux-Arts* 83 (May 1974): 285–300.

Guillebon, Régine de Plinval de. *Porcelain of Paris, 1770–1850*. New York: Walker and Company, 1972.

Guttridge, G.H., ed. *The American Correspondence of a Bristol Merchant, 1766–1776, Letters of Richard Champion*. Berkeley: University of California Publications in History, vol. 22, 1934.

Hadfield, Joseph. *An Englishman in America, 1785*. Edited by D.S. Robertson. Toronto: The Hunter–Rose Company, 1933.

Haggar, Reginald, and Adams, Elizabeth. *Mason Porcelain and Ironstone*. London: Faber and Faber, 1977.

Harrison, Eliza Cope, ed. *Philadelphia Merchant: The Diary of Thomas P. Cope, 1800–1851*. South Bend, Ind.: Gateway Editions, 1978.

Hart, Charles Henry, and Biddle, Edward. *Memoirs of the Life and Works of Jean Antoine Houdon*. Philadelphia: Privately printed, 1911.

Haslem, John. *The Old Derby China Factory*. London: George Bell, 1876.

Henderson, Daniel. *Yankee Ships in China Seas*. New York: Hastings House, 1946.

Heuser-Speier, Emil. "Niederweiler, Eine Keramische Kunststätte des 18. Jahrhunderts." *Der Cicerone* 6 (1914): 52–56.

Hillier, Bevis. *Master Potters of the Industrial Revolution, the Turners of Lane End*. New York: Born and Hawes, 1965.

Hindle, Brooke. "How Much Is a Piece of the True Cross Worth?" In *Material Culture and the Study of American Life*, pp. 5–20. New York: W.W. Norton and Company for the Henry Francis du Pont Winterthur Museum, 1978.

Hobson, R.L. *Chinese Pottery and Porcelain*. London: Cassell and Company, 1915.

Hodge, Robert; Allen, Thomas; and Campbell, Samuel. *New York Directory & Register for 1789*. New York: 1789.

Hodnett, Edward. *Francis Barlow, First Master of English Book Illustration*. London: The Scholar Press, 1978.

Hoffman, Henry B. "President Washington's Cherry Street Residence." *The New-York Historical Society Quarterly Bulletin* 23 (July 1939): 90–99.

Honey, William Bowyer. *The Ceramic Art of China and Other Countries of the Far East*. London: Faber and Faber, 1955.

————. "English Saltglazed Stoneware." *The English Ceramic Circle Transactions* 1, no. 1 (1933): 12–22.

Honey, William Bowyer; Rackham, Bernard; and Read, Herbert "Early Derby Porcelain." *Burlington Magazine* 49 (1926): 292–302.

Hood, Graham. "Refurnishing the Governor's Palace at Colonial Williamsburg." *Antiques* 119 (January 1981): 216–23.

Hunt, Leslie B. "The Gilding of European Porcelain." *Connoisseur* 204 (1980): 106–13.

Hutchinson, William. *Treatise on Naval Architecture*. Liverpool: T. Billinge, 1794.

Jackson, Donald, and Twohig, Dorothy, eds. *The Diaries of George Washington*. Charlottesville: University Press of Virginia, 1976–1979.

Jackson, Joseph. "George Washington in Philadelphia." *The Pennsylvania Magazine of History and Biography 56* (1932): 140–52.

Jacquemart, Albert. *History of the Ceramic Art: A Descriptive and Philosophical Study of the Pottery of all Ages and all Nations*. London: Sampson, Low, Marston, Low, and Searle, 1873.

Jenkins, Charles Francis. *Washington in Germantown*. Philadelphia: William J. Campbell, 1905.

Jenyns, Soame. *Later Chinese Porcelains: The Ch'ing Dynasty (1644–1912)*. London: Faber and Faber, 1951.

Jewitt, Llewellynn. *The History of Ceramic Art in Great Britain*. New York: Scribner, Welford, and Armstrong, 1878.

Johnson, Samuel. *A Dictionary of the English Language*. 6th ed. London: Rivington et al., 1785.

Kimball, Marie. *The Martha Washington Cook Book*. New York: Coward–McCann, 1940.

King, George H.S. "Washington's Boyhood Home." *William and Mary Quarterly*, 2d ser., 17 (1933): 265–70.

King, William. *Chelsea Porcelain*. London: Benn Brothers, Ltd., 1922.

Kirkland, Thomas J., and Kennedy, Robert M. *Historic Camden*. Columbia, S.C.: The State Company, 1905.

Klapthor, Margaret Brown. *Official White House China: 1789 to the Present*. Washington, D.C.: Smithsonian Institution Press, 1975.

Kline, Mary Jo. *Gouverneur Morris and the New Nation*. New York: Arno Press, 1978.

Knight, Franklin, publisher. *Monuments of Washington's Patriotism Containing a Fac Simile of His Public Accounts Kept During the Revolutionary War, June 1775–June 1783*. Washington, D.C.: Trustees of Washington's Manual Labour School and Male Orphan Asylum, 1844.

Kouwenhoven, A. *The Columbia Historical Portrait of New York*. New York: Doubleday and Company, 1953.

Lancour, Harold. *American Art Auction Catalogues, 1785–1942*. New York: New York Public Library, 1944.

Lane, Arthur. *English Porcelain Figures of the Eighteenth Century*. London, Faber and Faber, 1961.

Latourette, Kenneth Scott. "Voyages of American Ships to China, 1784–1844." *Transactions of the Connecticut Academy of Arts and Sciences* 28 (1927): 240.

Lawrence, Heather. *Yorkshire Pots and Potters*. Newton Abbot, England: David and Charles, 1974.

Liggett, Barbara. *Archaeology at New Market: Exhibit Catalogue*. Philadelphia: The Athenaeum of Philadelphia, 1978.

Loehr, George R. "A.E. van Braam Houckgeest, the First American at the Court of China." *Princeton University Library Chronicle* 15 (1954): 179–93.

Lossing, Benson J. *George Washington's Mount Vernon or Mount Vernon and Its Associations*. Alexandria, Va.: The Fairfax Press, 1977. Reprint of 1870 ed.

———. "Mount Vernon as it is." *Harper's New Monthly Magazine* 18 (1859): 433–51.

———, ed. *Recollections and Private Memoirs of Washington, By His Adopted Son, George Washington Parke Custis* . . . New York: Derby and Jackson, 1860.

Mackenna, F. Severne. *Chelsea Porcelain, the Gold Anchor Period*. London: F. Lewis, 1952.

———. *Chelsea Porcelain, the Red Anchor Wares*. London: F. Lewis, 1951.

Maclay, Edgar S., ed. *The Journal of William Maclay, 1789–1791*. New York: D. Appleton, 1890.

Mankowitz, Wolf. *Wedgwood*. London: B.T. Batsford, Ltd., 1953.

Meteyard, Eliza. *The Life of Josiah Wedgwood*. London:

Hurst and Blackett, 1865.

———. *The Wedgwood Handbook*. London: George Bell, 1875.

Miller, Helen Hill. *George Mason, Gentleman Revolutionary*. Chapel Hill: University of North Carolina Press, 1975.

Minchinton, Walter E. "Richard Champion, Nicholas Pocock and the Carolina Trade." *South Carolina Historical and Genealogical Magazine* 65 (1964): 87–97.

Mitchell, Stewart, ed. *New Letters of Abigail Adams, 1788–1801*. Boston: Houghton Mifflin, 1947.

Monaghan, Frank, and Lowenthal, Marvin. *This Was New York*. New York: Doubleday, Doran and Company, 1943.

Moreau de Saint-Méry, M.L.E. *An Authentic Account of the Dutch East-India Company to the Court of the Emperor of China in the Years 1794 and 1795 . . . Taken from the Journal of André Everard Van Braam*. London: R. Phillips, 1798.

Morgan, George. *The City of Firsts*. Philadelphia: Historical Publication Society in Philadelphia, 1926.

Morison, Samuel Eliot. *The Oxford History of the American People*. New York: Oxford University Press, 1965.

Morris, Gouverneur. *A Diary of the French Revolution, 1789–1793*. Edited by Beatrix Cary Davenport. Boston: Houghton Mifflin, 1939.

Morristown, N. J. Morristown National Historical Park. Lloyd Smith Collection.

Morse, Hosea Ballou. *The Chronicles of the East India Company Trading to China, 1635–1834*. Cambridge, Mass.: Harvard University Press, 1926.

Mottahedeh, Suzanne Stocking. "Numismatic Sources of Chinese Export Porcelain Decoration." *Connoisseur* 172 (1969): 111–18.

The Mount Vernon Ladies' Association of the Union. *Annual Report*. Published annually, 1936–1980.

———. *Mount Vernon China*. Mount Vernon, Va.: The Mount Vernon Ladies' Association of the Union, 1962.

Mount Vernon, Va. The Mount Vernon Ladies' Association of the Union. Manuscript material including wills, inventories, and invoices.

Mountford, Arnold R. *The Illustrated Guide to Staffordshire Salt-glazed Stoneware*. New York: Praeger, 1971.

———. "Staffordshire Salt-Glazed Stoneware." In *Ceramics in America*. pp. 197–215. Edited by Ian M.G. Quimby. Charlottesville: University Press of Virginia, 1973.

Mudge, Jean McClure. *Chinese Export Porcelain for the American Market*. Newark, Del.: University of Delaware Press, 1962.

Musée de Rennes. *Les Français dans La Guerre d'Indépendance Américaine*. Exhibition catalogue. Rennes: 1976.

Neill, Edward D. *The Fairfaxes of England and America*. Albany; N.Y.: J. Munsell, 1868.

Nelligan, Murray H. *"Old Arlington": The Story of the Lee Mansion National Memorial*. Washington, D.C.: United States Department of the Interior, National Park Service, National Capitol Parks, 1953.

New Webster Encyclopedic Dictionary of the English Language. Chicago: Consolidated Book Publishers, 1970.

New York. The New-York Historical Society. Miscellaneous manuscripts, Constable and Company.

New York. The New York Public Library. William Constable Papers, Constable–Pierrepont Collection.

Noël Hume, Ivor. *A Guide to Artifacts of Colonial America*. New York: Alfred A. Knopf, 1970.

———. *Here Lies Virginia*. New York: Alfred A. Knopf, 1963.

———. *Pottery and Porcelain in Colonial Williamsburg's Archaeological Collections*. Williamsburg: Colonial Williamsburg, 1969.

———. "The What, Who and When of English Creamware Plate Design." *Antiques* 101 (1972): 350–55.

Olivar Daydi, Marçal. *La Porcelana en Europa desde sus orígenes hasta principios del siglo XIX*. Barcelona: Editorial Seix Barral, 1952–1953.

Owen, Hugh. *Two Centuries of Ceramic Art in Bristol.* Gloucester, England, 1873.

Palmer, Arlene. *A Winterthur Guide to Chinese Export Porcelain.* New York: Crown Publishers, 1976.

Peter, Armistead, III. *Tudor Place Designed by Dr. William Thornton and Built Between 1805 and 1816 for Thomas and Martha Peter.* Georgetown, Washington, D.C.: Privately printed, 1969.

Philadelphia. The Historical Society of Pennsylvania. Washington's Household Account Book, 1793–1797.

Phillips, John Goldsmith. *China-Trade Porcelains.* Cambridge, Mass.: Harvard University Press, 1956.

Price, Jacob M. "Who was John Norton? A Note on the Historical Character of Some Eighteenth-Century London–Virginia Firms." *William and Mary Quarterly,* 3d ser., 19 (1962): 400–407.

Price, R. "Some Groups of English Redware of the Mid-Eighteenth Century." *The English Ceramic Circle Transactions* 4, pt. 5 (1959): 1–9.

Prime, Alfred Coxe. *The Arts and Crafts in Philadelphia, Maryland, and South Carolina, 1786–1800.* The Walpole Society, 1932.

Prudhomme, Louis-Marie. *L'Ancienne et du Nouveau Paris.* Paris: Prudhomme, fils, 1806.

Prussing, Eugene E. *The Estate of George Washington, Deceased.* Boston: Little, Brown, and Company, 1927.

Quimby, Ian M.G., ed. *Ceramics in America.* Winterthur Conference Report 1972. Charlottesville: University Press of Virginia, 1973.

Quincy, Josiah, ed. *The Journals of Major Samuel Shaw.* Boston: William Crosby, 1847.

Rackham, Bernard. *Catalogue of the Schreiber Collection.* London: The Victoria and Albert Museum, 1928.

"Randolph and Tucker Letters." *The Virginia Magazine of History and Biography* 43 (1935): 44.

Read, Raphael W., ed. *A Reprint of the Original Catalogue of the Chelsea Porcelain Manufactory, Sold by Auction by Mr. Ford, 29 March 1756.* Salisbury, England: Privately printed, 1880.

Rice, Howard C., Jr. *Thomas Jefferson's Paris.* Princeton: Princeton University Press, 1976.

Rice, Howard C., Jr., and Brown, Anne S.K., eds. *The American Campaigns of Rochambeau's Army.* Princeton and Providence: Princeton University Press and Brown University Press, 1972.

Richmond. Virginia Historical Society. Custis family papers.

Rogers, Edmund Law. "Some New Washington Relics from the Collection of Edmund Law Rogers, Esq." *Century Magazine* 18 (1890): 22–25.

Rosenblatt, Samuel M. "Credit in the Tobacco Consignment Trade." *William and Mary Quarterly,* 3d ser., 19 (1962): 385–86.

Roth, Rodris. "Tea Drinking in 18th-Century America: Its Etiquette and Equipage." Paper 14 in *United States National Museum Bulletin 225.* Washington, D.C.: U.S. Government Printing Office, 1961.

Sandon, Henry. *The Illustrated Guide to Worcester Porcelain, 1751–1793.* London: Herbert Jenkins, 1969.

Savage, George, and Newman, Harold. *An Illustrated Dictionary of Ceramics.* New York: Van Nostrand Reinhold, 1974.

Scheurleer, D.F. Lunsingh. *Chinese Export Porcelain, Chine de Commande.* London: Faber and Faber, 1974.

Schmidt, Robert. *Porcelain as an Art and a Mirror of Fashion.* London: George G. Harrap, 1932.

Schreider, Louis. "Gouverneur Morris: Connoisseur of French Art." *Apollo* 93 (1971): 470–83.

Scoville, Joseph A. [Walter Barrett]. *The Old Merchants of New York City.* New York: Carleton, 1870.

Sellers, Charles Coleman. *Benjamin Franklin in Portraiture.* New Haven: Yale University Press, 1962.

Sèvres. Manufacture Nationale de Sèvres. Registre de vente, vol. 7, p. 15.

Shaw, Simeon. *History of the Staffordshire Potteries*. New York: Praeger, 1970. Reprint of 1829 ed.

Sherrill, Charles Hitchcock. *French Memories of Eighteenth Century America*. New York: Charles Scribner's Sons, 1915.

Sizer, Theodore, ed. *The Autobiography of Colonel John Trumbull*. New Haven: Yale University Press, 1953.

Solon, Louis Marc Emmanuel. *Salt Glaze: The Catalogue of a Small Collection Now Exhibited in the Technical Museum at Hanley*. Hanley, England: Albert and Daniel, 1890.

Stetson, Sarah P. "The Philadelphia Sojourn of Samuel Vaughan." *The Pennsylvania Magazine of History and Biography* 73 (1949): 459–74.

Stokes, I.N. *The Iconography of Manhattan Island*. New York: Robert H. Dodd, 1926.

Tainturier, A. *Recherches sur les Anciennes Manufactures de Porcelaine et de Faience, Alsace et Lorraine*. Strasbourg: 1868.

Tapp, William H. *Jefferyes Hamett O'Neale, 1734–1801, Red Anchor Fable Painter*. London: University of London Press, 1938.

Teller, Barbara Gorely. "Ceramics in Providence, 1750–1800." *Antiques* 94 (1968): 570–77.

Templeman, Eleanor Lee. "The Lee Service of Cincinnati Porcelain." *Antiques* 118 (1980): 758–59.

Thomas, William Sturgis. *Members of the Society of the Cincinnati, Original, Hereditary, and Honorary with a Brief Account of the Society's History and Arms*. New York: T.A. Wright, 1929.

Thomas, W. Stephen. "Major Samuel Shaw and the Cincinnati Porcelain." *Antiques* 27 (1935): 176–79.

Toppin, Aubrey J. "The China Trade and Some London Chinamen." *The English Ceramic Circle Transactions* 3 (1935): 37–56.

Towner, Donald. "The Melbourne Pottery." *The English Ceramic Circle Transactions* 8 (1971): 18–30.

Trubner, Henry, and Rathbun, William Jay. *China's Influence on American Culture in the Eighteenth and Nineteenth Centuries*. Seattle: China Institute in America, 1976.

Truxtun, Thomas. *Remarks, Instructions, and Examples Relating to the Latitude and Longitude; also, the Variation of the Compass. . .* Philadelphia: T. Dobson, 1794.

Vail, R.W.G., ed. "A Dinner at Mount Vernon from the Unpublished Journal of Joshua Brookes (1773–1859)." *The New-York Historical Society Quarterly* 31 (1947): 72–85.

Valentine, David T. *Manual of the Corporation of the City of New York*. New York: 1842–1866.

Verlet, Pierre. *The Eighteenth Century in France*. Rutland, Vt.: Charles E. Tuttle, 1967.

Verplanck, G.C.; Bryant, W.C.; and Sands, R.C., eds. *The Talisman for 1830*. New York: 1830.

Wallace, H.E. "Sketch of John Inskeep." *The Pennsylvania Magazine of History and Biography* 28 (1904): 129–35.

Walton, Peter. *Creamware and Other English Pottery at Temple Newsam House*. Leeds, England: Leeds Art Collections Fund, 1976.

Wansey, Henry, F.A.S. *An Excursion to the United States of North America, in the Summer of 1794*. Salisbury, England: J. Easton, 1798.

Washington, D.C. Library of Congress. Manuscript Division. George Washington Papers.

———. Presidents' Papers Index Series. *Index to the George Washington Papers*. 1964.

Washington's Household Account Book, 1793–1797. *See* Philadelphia.

Watson, Katharine J. "Sugar Sculpture for Grand Ducal Weddings from the Giambologna Workshop." *Connoisseur* 199 (1978): 20–26.

Wayland, John W. *The Washingtons and Their Homes*. Berryville, Va.: Virginia Book Company, 1973. Facsimile reprint of 1944 ed.

Wecter, Dixon. "An Unpublished Letter of George Washington." *The South Carolina Historical and Genealogical Magazine* 39 (1938): 151–56.

Wharton, Anne H. *Martha Washington*. New York: Charles Scribner's Sons, 1897.

———. "Washington's New York Residence." *Lippincott's Monthly Magazine* 43 (1889): 741–45.

Williamson, G.C. *The Book of Famille Rose*. London: Kegan, Paul, Trench, Trubner and Company, 1927.

Woodhouse, Samuel W., Jr. "Martha Washington's China and Mr. Van Braam." *Antiques* 27–28 (1935): 186–88.

———. "The Voyage of the Empress of China." *The Pennsylvania Magazine of History and Biography* 43 (1939): 24–36.

PHOTOGRAPH CREDITS

The author and publisher wish to thank the museums, libraries, and private collectors for permitting the reproduction of works of art and documents in their collections. Photographs have, in many instances, been supplied by the owners or custodians of the works and are acknowledged in the captions. Will Brown, Philadelphia, made the following photographs: frontispiece, title page, 5, 7, 8, 10, 11, 13–17, 22, 24, 25, 29, 31, 32, 34, 38, 39, 48, 49, 52–55, 58–64, 70, 73–75, 77–82, 88, 89, 91–98, 100–107, 109–12, 114–17, 123–25, 127–31, 135, 136, 139–44, 146, 148, 149, 151, 154–56. Photographs supplied by the Mount Vernon Ladies' Association were made by: Dunlop Studios, Washington, D.C., 50; Marler, Alexandria, Va., 97; and Ted Vaughan, Manheim, Pa., 9, 26, 56, 108, 113, 126, 137, 150, 152, 153. E. Laemmel, Archives Municipales, Strasbourg, supplied the photograph for fig. 41; M.A.S., Barcelona, supplied the photograph for fig. 90; and Philip Pocock, New York, supplied the photograph for fig. 67.

ACKNOWLEDGMENTS

The idea for this book emerged from the American Presidential China Index, a survey of the tableware used by presidents from George Washington to the present. Both the survey and the book were sponsored by The Barra Foundation, Inc., whose president, Robert L. McNeil, Jr., has been a constant source of encouragement and guidance.

The Mount Vernon Ladies' Association of the Union has supplied splendid research resources as well as fine hospitality on several occasions. Christine Meadows, the Association's curator and the author of the Prologue and Epilogue, contributed much information and made excellent suggestions which invariably improved the accuracy of the manuscript. She has always been generous with her time and knowledge. The enthusiasm of Mount Vernon's resident director, John A. Castellani, and the Association's Regent, Mrs. John H. Guy, Jr., is also appreciated.

Mrs. Walter G. Peter, Jr., whose information about the Custis, Washington, and Peter families has been invaluable, graciously shared her knowledge and made possible a nearly complete account of surviving examples of the Washingtons' ceramics. Margaret Brown Klapthor, curator of the Division of Political History at the Smithsonian Institution's National Museum of American History and author of *Official White House China: 1789 to the Present*, found time to review the manuscript in spite of her commitment to a large exhibition of Washingtoniana in February 1982. Mrs. Klapthor, whose research and publications have been the foundation for the American Presidential China Index, also facilitated the photographing of the Lewis and Peter collections at the National Museum. Barbara Coffee, assistant curator in the Division of Political History, spent a long day supervising photography in the First Ladies Hall. Photographer Will Brown, editor Louise Heskett, and The Barra Foundation's program officer, Gail Schmidt, have been tolerant and cooperative colleagues in the preparation of the manuscript and illustrations.

The Balch Institute, which owns a complete set of the Library of Congress microfilm edition of the George Washington Papers, has been hospitable on many occasions. Other Philadelphia libraries whose staff members have been helpful include the Historical Society of Pennsylvania, the University of Pennsylvania, Chestnut Hill College, the Athenaeum of Philadelphia, and the Library Company of Philadelphia. Barbara S. Sevy, librarian of the Philadelphia Museum of Art, has been especially kind in answering bibliographic questions. Contributing institutions also include: the Henry Francis du Pont Winterthur Museum and Library, the Virginia Historical Society, the New-York Historical Society, the Virginia State Library, the Maryland Historical Society, the Judicial and Fiscal Branch of the National Archives, the Library of Congress, the Frick Art Reference Library, Yale University, the American Philosophical Society, Pennsylvania Academy of the Fine Arts, the Philadelphia Maritime Museum, Morristown National Historic Park, Independence National Historic Park, and the American Ceramic Circle.

The following people have also contributed time, information, and assistance in various ways, and they deserve recognition beyond the mere listing allowed by limitations of space. My sincere thanks to: John C. Austin, curator of ceramics and glass and assistant director of collections, the Colonial Williamsburg Foundation, Williamsburg, Virginia;

Edward R. Barnsley of Beach Haven, New Jersey; Jerry M. Bloomer, director, the R.W. Norton Art Gallery, Shreveport, Louisiana; Eleanor Boyne, secretary, Division of Political History, Smithsonian Institution; Elizabeth Browning, curator, Valley Forge National Historical Park; David Buten, director, the Buten Museum of Wedgwood, Merion, Pennsylvania; John L. Cotter, associate curator emeritus, American Historical Archeology, University Museum, the University of Pennsylvania; Philip Curtis, curator of ceramics and glass, the Henry Francis du Pont Winterthur Museum, Winterthur, Delaware; Carl Christian Dauterman, curator emeritus of Western European Arts, the Metropolitan Museum of Art, New York; Aileen Dawson, research assistant, Department of Medieval and Later Antiquities, the British Museum, London; Mona Dearborn, keeper, Catalogue of American Portraits, the National Portrait Gallery, Washington, D.C.; Charles G. Dorman, museum curator, Independence National Historical Park; Nancy Emison, assistant curator, the Mount Vernon Ladies' Association of the Union, Mount Vernon, Virginia; H.A. Crosby Forbes, founder-curator, the Museum of the American China Trade, Milton, Massachusetts; Robert L. Giannini III, assistant curator, Independence National Historical Park; Geoffrey A. Godden, author and ceramics expert, London; Régine de Plinval de Guillebon, author and ceramics historian, Paris; Kathryn B. Hiesinger, curator, European Decorative Arts after 1700, Philadelphia Museum of Art; Clare Le Corbeiller, associate curator, European Sculpture and Decorative Arts, the Metropolitan Museum of Art, New York; Jean Gordon Lee, curator, Far Eastern Art, Philadelphia Museum of Art; Stephen Little, curator of Chinese Art, Asian Art Museum of San Francisco; Capt. David A. Long, the Naval Historical Foundation; John V.G. Mallet, keeper, Department of Ceramics, Victoria and Albert Museum, London; Betty C. Monkman, office of the curator of the White House, Washington, D.C.; Arnold R. Mountford, director of museums, City of Stoke-on-Trent; Tamara Préaud, archivist, Manufacture Nationale de Sèvres; Gaye Blake Roberts, curator, the Wedgwood Museum, Barlaston, Stoke-on-Trent; Mr. and Mrs. George Rosborough, Jr., of Saint Louis, Missouri; Henry Sandon, curator, the Dyson Perrins Museum, Worcester; Arlene Palmer Schwind, ceramics expert and consultant, Yarmouth, Maine; Philip C.F. Smith, director, the Philadelphia Maritime Museum; Patricia L. Taylor, head of reference, Virginia State Library, Richmond, Virginia; Wendy Wick, curator of prints, the National Portrait Gallery, Washington, D.C.; and to the many other friends who offered time and information.

Finally, special thanks to my family—Will, Margit, Sara, and John—for their interest, encouragement, and patience.

BRIEF CUSTIS FAMILY GENEALOGY

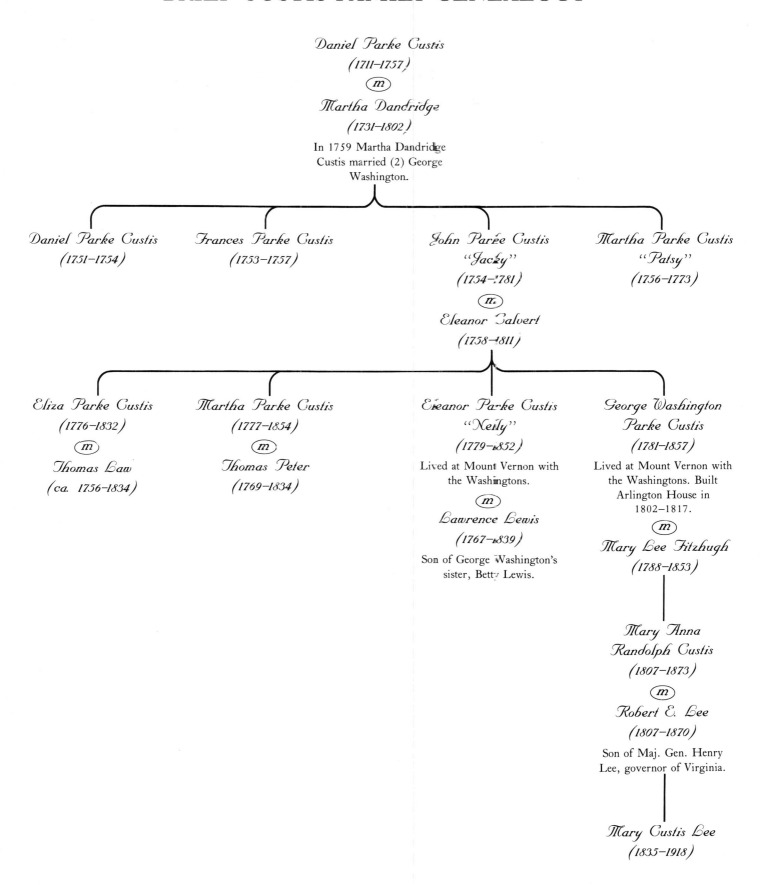

Daniel Parke Custis
(1711–1757)
ⓜ
Martha Dandridge
(1731–1802)

In 1759 Martha Dandridge
Custis married (2) George
Washington.

Daniel Parke Custis
(1751–1754)

Frances Parke Custis
(1753–1757)

John Parke Custis
"Jacky"
(1754–1781)
ⓜ
Eleanor Calvert
(1758–1811)

Martha Parke Custis
"Patsy"
(1756–1773)

Eliza Parke Custis
(1776–1832)
ⓜ
Thomas Law
(ca. 1756–1834)

Martha Parke Custis
(1777–1854)
ⓜ
Thomas Peter
(1769–1834)

Eleanor Parke Custis
"Nelly"
(1779–1852)
Lived at Mount Vernon with
the Washingtons.
ⓜ
Lawrence Lewis
(1767–1839)
Son of George Washington's
sister, Betty Lewis.

George Washington
Parke Custis
(1781–1857)
Lived at Mount Vernon with
the Washingtons. Built
Arlington House in
1802–1817.
ⓜ
Mary Lee Fitzhugh
(1788–1853)

Mary Anna
Randolph Custis
(1807–1873)
ⓜ
Robert E. Lee
(1807–1870)
Son of Maj. Gen. Henry
Lee, governor of Virginia.

Mary Custis Lee
(1835–1918)

BRIEF WASHINGTON FAMILY GENEALOGY

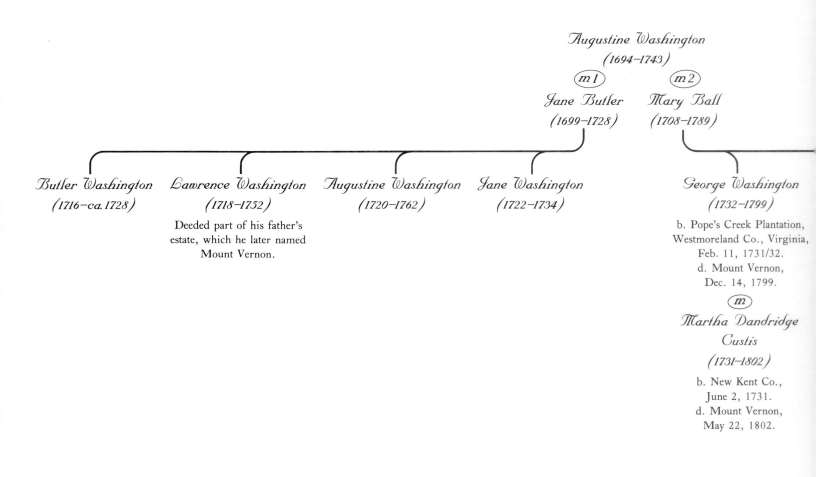

Augustine Washington
(1694–1743)

m 1

Jane Butler
(1699–1728)

m 2

Mary Ball
(1708–1789)

Butler Washington
(1716–ca. 1728)

Lawrence Washington
(1718–1752)

Deeded part of his father's
estate, which he later named
Mount Vernon.

Augustine Washington
(1720–1762)

Jane Washington
(1722–1734)

George Washington
(1732–1799)

b. Pope's Creek Plantation,
Westmoreland Co., Virginia,
Feb. 11, 1731/32.
d. Mount Vernon,
Dec. 14, 1799.

m

Martha Dandridge
Custis
(1731–1802)

b. New Kent Co.,
June 2, 1731.
d. Mount Vernon,
May 22, 1802.

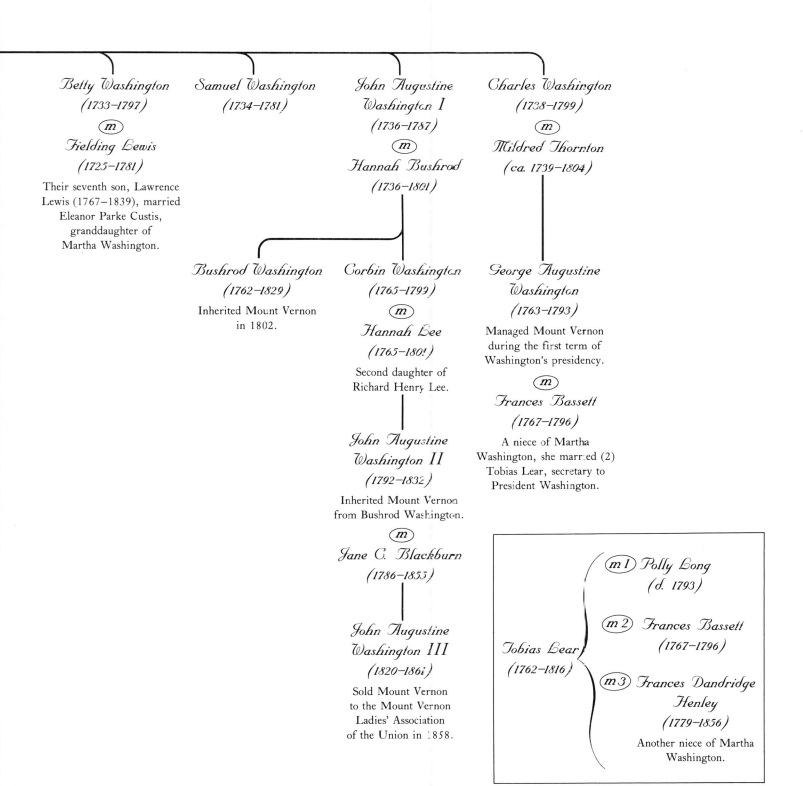

Betty Washington
(1733–1797)
ⓜ
Fielding Lewis
(1725–1781)

Their seventh son, Lawrence
Lewis (1767–1839), married
Eleanor Parke Custis,
granddaughter of
Martha Washington.

Samuel Washington
(1734–1781)

John Augustine
Washington I
(1736–1787)
ⓜ
Hannah Bushrod
(1736–1801)

Charles Washington
(1738–1799)
ⓜ
Mildred Thornton
(ca. 1739–1804)

Bushrod Washington
(1762–1829)

Inherited Mount Vernon
in 1802.

Corbin Washington
(1765–1799)
ⓜ
Hannah Lee
(1765–1801)

Second daughter of
Richard Henry Lee.

John Augustine
Washington II
(1792–1832)

Inherited Mount Vernon
from Bushrod Washington.
ⓜ
Jane C. Blackburn
(1786–1855)

John Augustine
Washington III
(1820–1861)

Sold Mount Vernon
to the Mount Vernon
Ladies' Association
of the Union in 1858.

George Augustine
Washington
(1763–1793)

Managed Mount Vernon
during the first term of
Washington's presidency.
ⓜ
Frances Bassett
(1767–1796)

A niece of Martha
Washington, she married (2)
Tobias Lear, secretary to
President Washington.

Tobias Lear
(1762–1816)

ⓜ1 Polly Long
(d. 1793)

ⓜ2 Frances Bassett
(1767–1796)

ⓜ3 Frances Dandridge
Henley
(1779–1856)

Another niece of Martha
Washington.

INDEX

Numbers in italics refer
to the illustrations.

The text of this book was
set in 10 point Caslon old face no. 2
by U.S. Lithograph, Inc., New York. The display
type was set in 18 point Caslon old face no. 2. The typeface
was designed by William Caslon, an eighteenth-century
English type founder, whose first specimen
sheet appeared in 1734.

The paper for this book is
Top-Coated 157 gram, which was manufactured by the
Kanzaki Paper Company, Ltd., Japan. The book was printed
in four-color offset for the color illustrations and in two-color offset
for the black-and-white illustrations by the Nissha Printing
Company, Ltd., Kyoto, Japan, and was bound by the
Taikansha Seihon Company, Ltd.,
Saitama, Japan.